The Mayor
of Shantytown

The Mayor
of Shantytown

The Life of Father
James Renshaw Cox

RICHARD GAZARIK

McFarland & Company, Inc., Publishers
Jefferson, North Carolina

ISBN (print) 978-1-4766-7339-4 ∞
ISBN (ebook) 4766-3384-8

LIBRARY OF CONGRESS CATALOGUING DATA ARE AVAILABLE

BRITISH LIBRARY CATALOGUING DATA ARE AVAILABLE

Front cover image: Cox's "Army" preparing to move out from
Pittsburgh's Strip District on their way to Washington, D.C., in January
1932 (Dr. and Mrs. Mason, Father James Renshaw Cox Collection, Saint
Patrick–Saint Stanislaus Kostka Parish, Pittsburgh, Pennsylvania)

Printed in the United States of America

*McFarland & Company, Inc., Publishers
Box 611, Jefferson, North Carolina 28640
www.mcfarlandpub.com*

To Fritz,
and Tony the Barber

Table of Contents

Acknowledgments

The historic Strip District is no longer a Pittsburgh neighborhood teeming with job-seeking immigrants, living in crowded tenements, eking out a living working in the mills or factories that once populated the Strip. It now is a hip, crowded place of stores, bars, restaurants, nightclubs, art studios, antique shops, bakeries, ethnic food stores and a fish market. People walk shoulder-to-shoulder on the Strip's narrow streets on weekends and pass by St. Patrick's Church without knowing the history of the small parish and its pot-bellied pastor, who saved thousands from starving during the Great Depression.

St. Patrick's is located near St. Stanislaus Kostka Church, which resembles a Polish cathedral and was built in 1891. By the end of the 20th century, the Strip remained one of Pittsburgh's most unpretentious neighborhoods. As the population of the city declined, so did the number of parishioners attending Mass at the church. St. Patrick's was unable to remain independent. The Catholic Diocese of Pittsburgh merged St. Patrick's with nearby St. Stanislaus Kostka Church and St. Elizabeth's in 1993 to become St. Patrick's–St. Stanislaus Kostka.

Father James Renshaw Cox's church remains, with its outdoor garden in honor of the Grotto at Lourdes along with statues of the Blessed Virgin and Saints Bernadette, Ann Joseph, Patrick, Anthony and Blessed Kateri Tekawitha, Lady of the Mohawks. The garden is spot for solitude and reflection amidst the bustling, noisy Strip.

I picked up a copy of Kenneth J. Heineman's *A Catholic New Deal: Religion and Reform in Depression Pittsburgh*, published in 1999, which served as a roadmap for piecing together the life of Father James Renshaw Cox. Heineman's book stoked my interest in Cox and led to a search for more information about the priest who became a national figure in the 1930s before falling into disgrace. I can remember my father telling my

St. Patrick's Church as it is today. A weekly mass is celebrated each Thursday (author's photograph).

mother whenever she cooked a meal that she had made enough food to feed "Cox's Army."

I grew up in western Pennsylvania. My grandparents and parents survived the Great Depression and their stories about life in those difficult times drew my interest because of their tales of family hardship. My research into the effects of the Great Depression made me fully understand the difficulties my family faced in surviving the hardships. My paternal grandparents had nine children, plus two boys that they raised after their parents died from the flu. Neither my father nor his brothers or sisters ever finished high school and were forced to find work to survive. Thanks to the Civilian Conservation Corps, my father was able to find work and make it on his own.

This book could not have been written without the assistance of the staff at St. Stanislaus-Kostka Church in Pittsburgh's Strip District, who allowed me to read news clippings and scan photographs from scrapbooks and photo albums of Cox's life that were donated to the church by Cox's family. Darris Jeffcoat, who oversees the records on Father Cox, deserves special thanks for allowing me access to the church's records.

The staff at the Archives Service Center at the University of Pittsburgh went out of their way to provide me other documents, photographs and recordings of sermons from the James R. Cox Papers at the Archives of Industrial Society during my repeated visits to the center.

The H. John Heinz History Center, which is located in the Strip District, contains additional information about Cox from the personal papers of the late Allegheny County Judge Henry Ellenbogen, who accompanied Cox on his historic march to Washington, D.C., in 1932, and who remained a lifelong friend.

The first stop in any research about Pittsburgh history is The Carnegie in Pittsburgh. The staff at the Pennsylvania Room are always helping in digging up old clips and articles about historic events.

Finally, my wife, Lucy, serves as a sounding board and editor for my ideas and drafts, along with David Lester, a friend and colleague from my newspaper days. An expert on all things related to the Benedictines, David spent considerable time reviewing the manuscript and catching numerous errors. Without their support and encouragement, this book never would have been published.

Preface:
"Plump Little Priest"

In a hot, stuffy room on the third floor of the rectory of Saint Patrick–Saint Stanislaus Kostka Catholic Church in Pittsburgh's Strip District, the life of Father James Renshaw Cox is documented in musty, deteriorating scrapbooks and photo albums detailing the life of this Catholic priest who was the voice of the hungry, unemployed and desperate during the Great Depression. Photographs of his march lie strewn across a table along with newspaper clippings that yellow with age and are so brittle that they break at the slightest touch and fall to the floor like confetti.

The paper trail contained in the church documents are an incomplete account of this "plump little priest" who made history in January 1932 by leading his starvation army of 25,000 unemployed men on a hunger march to the nation's capital, hoping to stir President

Portrait of Father James Renshaw Cox, ca. 1930 (James R. Cox Papers, 1923–1950, AIS. 1969.05, Archives & Special Collections, University of Pittsburgh Library System).

Herbert Hoover to legislative action to end the suffering. Cox hoped to convince Hoover by his action that government intervention was the only way to lift the nation out of the Great Depression.[1]

Cox was headline news during the 1930s and 1940s for his charitable works, but his life was reduced to a historical footnote after he ran for president of the United States in 1932 and narrowly escaped conviction for mail fraud in 1938, an episode that left him in disgrace. The poor and homeless viewed him as a saint while critics saw a man with an insatiable ego and little common sense. He became a media celebrity before there were media celebrities by using radio to propel himself to fame. He professed to be a patriot who believed in democratic ideals but was fascinated by fascism and dictators.

Cox wanted Hoover to spend the nation out of the economic morass with a $5 billion public works jobs program, unemployment insurance, help for farmers and higher taxes on the wealthy. He also wanted to counter an earlier Communist Party demonstration in December 1931 and demonstrate to the public, and government officials, that he and his followers were patriotic Americans not aligned with radicals or Communists.

The 1930s generated several ideas for solving the nation's economic problems. Writer Upton Sinclair had EPIC—End Poverty in California. Sinclair's program would have created public works projects, tax reform and a guaranteed pension for the elderly.

Louisiana Gov. Huey Long, who had his "Share Our Wealth," wanted to cap fortunes at $50 million, restructure the tax system and distribute the added benefits through government and public works jobs. He also wanted to limit annual incomes to $1 million and cap inheritances to $5 million. Every citizen would receive a guaranteed income of $2,000 under Long's plan.

The Communist Party emerged during the Great Depression as the voice of Americans disenchanted with capitalism. The party staged hunger marches and formed Unemployed Councils to push for government aid.

The anti–Semitic radio firebrand Father Charles Coughlin wanted monetary reform and government nationalization of industry and railroads. Then there was Dr. Francis Townsend with his "Townsend Old Age Revolving Plan," which was a precursor for Social Security.

Cox confronted Herbert Hoover at the White House that winter, challenging the president at a face-to-face meeting demanding the government do more to help his desperate countrymen.

After the meeting, Cox went on national radio, telling the American public he hoped the president "will rise to the occasion and recommend to Congress enactment of the measures we have proposed."[2]

If Cox thought the demonstration would spur immediate changes in Hoover's economic policies, he was sadly disappointed. The president believed his economic plan of reducing government spending would right the nation's financial ship, but Cox saw things differently. Unless there was immediate and massive aid, Cox warned there would be revolution in the streets.

Back in Pittsburgh, families were disintegrating. Fathers abandoned their families when they could no longer support them.[3] People were evicted from their homes when they couldn't pay their rent or mortgage. Exhausted men, devoid of hope, rummaged through garbage searching for food and walking the streets looking for jobs that no longer existed. Men slept on the streets and learned the art of begging.[4]

The economic foundation of Pittsburgh was built on coal and steel. The Depression devastated both industries, causing an impact on manufacturing that led to widespread unemployment. Workers who lost their jobs turned to Cox and other Catholic priests in the Diocese of Pittsburgh who served as a safety net by providing food and clothing. These parish priests also were instrumental in swaying their parishioners, mainly blue-collar Democrats, into electing FDR and supporting New Deal legislation.

Cox cared deeply about the poor, but critics charged that his empathy was fueled by an insatiable ego fed by Pittsburgh newspapers who loved Cox because he made good copy and constantly sought his opinion on world and local events. Cox claimed to be a patriotic American, though he once expressed admiration for Hitler and Mussolini.

Photographs of people standing in bread lines are embedded in the American memory. The homeless and hungry began appearing outside St. Patrick's Church in 1930 as the depression began strangling Pittsburgh. Without hesitation, Cox began feeding everyone who showed up at his door. He served 2.3 million meals during the worst years of the Great Depression, saving thousands from starvation.

A journal that Cox kept between 1930 and 1934 indicated he also distributed 500,000 food baskets and gave homeless men 2,000 haircuts and 40,000 shaves. He also distributed 21,000 gallons of milk, 2,100 tons of coal, and 5,000 pieces of clothing to the poor. Each article of clothing he handed out was carefully noted in his journal.[5] Homeless men built a block-long shantytown next to St. Patrick's, and Cox created his own currency the men could use to barter for clothes and necessities at his church.[6]

The public couldn't get enough of Cox. Newspapers eagerly reported

Homeless, hungry men sometimes lined up for blocks outside St. Patrick's Church waiting for food, ca. 1932 (James R. Cox Papers, 1923–1950, AIS.1969.05, Archives & Special Collections, University of Pittsburgh Library System).

everything he did. The *Pittsburgh Press* published his daily schedule to show how hard he worked. Cox slept in until noon each day because he didn't go to sleep until after midnight. Then he had breakfast and spent several afternoon hours meeting with between 75 and 100 people. He wrote letters and made his pastoral calls, visited the shantytown and worked on his relief activities until he had dinner at 5:30 p.m. with his mother. He held services in the evening and then had speaking engagements around Pittsburgh.[7]

Cox also was a shameless politician who tried to build a political party to propel him to the presidency by using desperate World War veterans who stormed Washington in 1932, demanding immediate payment of a bonus for their wartime service so they could feed their hungry families. He had no chance of winning the presidency, but the issues brought to the fore by his failed candidacy forced the Democrats and Republicans in the 1932 election to confront the economic problems facing the country and made the economy a campaign issue. Cox lived long enough to see

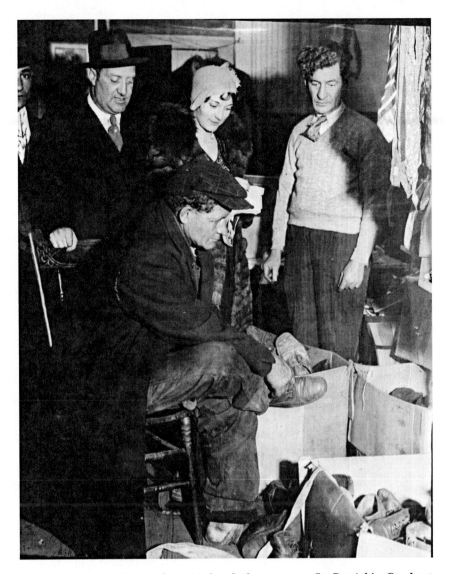

A homeless man tries on shoes in the clothes room at St. Patrick's. Cox kept meticulous records of every article of clothing he distributed to the poor in his Clothes Room Journal, ca. 1930 (Dr. and Mrs. Mason, Father James Renshaw Cox Collection, Saint Patrick–Saint Stanislaus Kostka Parish, Pittsburgh, Pennsylvania).

some of his political goals realized. FDR instituted pensions, unemployment insurance, public works projects, relief for farmers, and shorter work days and work weeks. Even so, Cox later soured on Roosevelt and switched his party registration to Republican.[8]

Cox was a man of many contradictions whose ego sometimes clouded his common sense. After returning from Washington in January 1932, Cox formed the Jobless Party to run for president that year, pledging to represent Main Street rather than Wall Street. Party members wore blue work shirts like the fascist paramilitary groups such as the Brown, Black, Silver and Khaki shirt movement of the 1930s. The Blue Shirts adopted an extended-arm salute used by the Nazis, leading critics to label Cox a fascist.[9]

Cox once praised Hitler as "a greater man than Napoleon" and commended Hitler "for killing his enemies instead of being killed by them." He once endorsed the assassination of Engelbert Dolfuss, the chancellor of Austria by Austrian Nazis in 1934. In the next breath, he said there "is no room in America for Nazism or fascism."[10]

The decade saw a growth in fascist paramilitary groups such as the Black Shirts, Brown Shirts, Khaki Shirts and Silver Shirts that led his critics to claim that Cox was himself a fascist. Photographs of Cox depict him standing before supporters extending his arm in a Hitler-like salute. During one of his trips to Italy in 1935, he attended fascist rallies. He visited Italy and Germany with the intention of visiting Adolf Hitler and Benito Mussolini to get their views on how to run the United States after he was elected president.[11] He denied that he ever intended to seek their advice, but admitted to meeting with an emissary of Hitler on a trip to Germany.

He agreed to assume the leadership of the fascist Khaki Shirts under certain conditions.[12] "I prefer to put up a united front as a political organization but if you continue the Khaki Shirts in the semi-military manner, as I understand they now exist, I am willing to take over leadership of that group," Cox said.[13]

The coarse tone of his rhetoric made him even sound like a fascist. Cox opposed capitalism and thought the U.S. Supreme Court was "a bunch of petrified fossils."[14] He objected to the growth of chain stores, wanted tighter regulation of banks, and demanded that Congress impose higher taxes on the wealthy. He wanted the Army and Navy to stage a coup and install Franklin Roosevelt as dictator: "President Roosevelt is the man for the job. He is honest, fearless and just, and a man with ideas."[15] He continued: "This all sounds like Fascism but it's more than Fascism: it's the only way to bring sense out of chaos. Government is bankrupt. There is too much waste. Perhaps the waste of public funds is necessary to insure [sic] re-election under a party system. Under a dictatorship, no."[16]

Cox called for abolishing Congress, calling it nothing but a "rubber stamp." He said the job of governor could be handled by a clerk and criticized

Cox before he embarked on a trip to Missouri to attend the Jobless Party Convention outside St. Louis, 1932 (James R. Cox Papers, 1923–1950, AIS.1969.05, Archives & Special Collections, University of Pittsburgh Library System).

state governments as "puerile" and "unnecessary."[17] The operation of state legislatures would be better left, he said, to the military, because lawmakers were beholden to the politically influential and wealthy. Citizens would be better represented by picking someone at random off the street and making him a senator or congressman. "The people can expect no relief from such men because most of them owe their jobs to money influences at home," he said.[18]

Cox used the pulpit to preach against vice and graft, but he relied heavily on gambling and rigged lotteries to raise money to finance his charitable work. His reputation was ruined after his 1937 indictment for rigging a lottery, even though the trial ended in a hung jury. Testimony revealed that Cox had links to bookies and operated a nightclub outside Pittsburgh that served as a base for his fundraising and gambling enterprises.

In 1938, he denounced the hugely popular Rev. Charles Coughlin of Detroit, an anti–Semitic priest, who had gone from being a New Deal supporter to an ardent opponent of FDR. Coughlin used his radio program to blame the Jews for the world's economic plight and defend Adolf Hitler's persecution of Jews. Cox publicly rebuked Coughlin as "a Hitler hatchet man" who defiled the church's teachings by his anti–Semitic rhetoric. The criticism of Coughlin touched off a dispute within the church that led to a demand from the Papal Nuncio to the United States for Bishop Hugh Boyle of Pittsburgh, Cox's religious superior, to reprimand Cox for his criticism of Coughlin.

Cox was viewed skeptically by his critics, who accused him of "bouncing into headlines with one publicity-breeding stint after another."[19] He had a chimney in a man's home dismantled and trucked to St. Patrick's so visitors could view for a quarter what he claimed was the image of Jesus Christ outlined in soot.[20] The *Bulletin Index*, a *Time Magazine*–style publication in Pittsburgh, asked "Sincere or Charlatan? Who is he, what is he and why?"[21]

The Rev. John Ray Ewers, pastor of the East End Christian Church in Pittsburgh, said Cox had the ability to promote himself as well as his charitable causes, but Cox's bishop, Hugh C. Boyle, said: "He is a splendid priest and well-liked by all who know him; I have no reason to interfere with his activities among the unemployed."[22]

Father Cox had a strong sense of injustice, but some admirers never knew whether he was sincere or a charlatan feeding his own ego. Cox was viewed by the unemployed and homeless as their savior, a voice for people who had no voice during the brutal early years of the Great Depression. Cox was a shepherd "who had the smell of his sheep upon him," said another priest.[23]

He became the first American priest to celebrate Mass in the air in the zeppelin *Hindenburg* while returning to the U.S. from Germany.[24] On another flight, he was lost for four hours when the pilot of the plane he was riding in lost his bearings on a trip to Harrisburg. Cox found himself staring down into the water of the Atlantic Ocean. Cox was accompanied by his lifelong friend and confidante, attorney Henry Ellenbogen, who was elected to Congress and later became a judge.

"I think we're lost," Cox said. "I know we are," Ellenbogen replied.[25] The pilot landed in Maryland, got his bearings, and flew safely to Harrisburg after buying 30 gallons of gas. "It was a wonderful experience," Cox said.[26]

In 1927, amid a barrage of newspaper publicity, Cox announced plans to fly from the U.S. to Rome in a plane piloted by Myrtle Brown of Omaha, Nebraska, the sister-in-law of famed aircraft designer Giuseppe Bellanca.[27]

The $33,000 cost of the trip didn't faze Cox, who was confident he could raise the money: "I am sure that I have friends who will aid in backing the flight," he said. "I see nothing unusual in the fact that a priest should make such a flight the same as another man."[28]

The flight never took off because Brown, who was neither a pilot nor a navigator, didn't know how to fly.[29]

Introduction:
Cox's Army

Homeless men living in the shantytown next to St. Patrick's Church in Pittsburgh's Strip District warmed themselves around bonfires on the night of January 4, 1932, waiting for dawn so they could begin the 331-mile march to Washington, D.C. A few men shivering in the cold night air shared a jar of hot peppers that made them forget about the cold.[1] Father James Cox canvassed his friends among the Jewish merchants in the Strip for food donations so the men would have something to eat along the way.[2]

As the darkness turned into a gray dawn, 45,000 people stood four-deep on the sidewalks surrounding the church, shaking in the frigid cold, waiting for their general to emerge from the rectory, take command, and lead "Cox's Army" to Washington. Cox loved military discipline, so he formed the men into companies led by "captains" and "lieutenants." Men with grimy faces were ordered to wash before leaving. Men with beards or stubble were ordered to shave. American flags were unfurled. Men jumped to attention and bands began playing the National Anthem.[3] More than 2,000 cars and trucks blocked the streets as thousands of unemployed men flooded the sidewalks, ready to follow Cox on the arduous trek.[4]

The marchers ranged in age from 17 to 70. There are no accurate figures on the exact number of men who accompanied Cox to Washington because marchers dropped out from exhaustion or joined the caravan along the route. Published accounts estimated there were anywhere from 10,000 to 25,000.[5] It was difficult to determine exactly the size of this ragtag army that slowly snaked its way through the central Pennsylvania mountains in the middle of winter. Cox used 25,000 in his account of the march written for a Pittsburgh newspaper.[6]

11

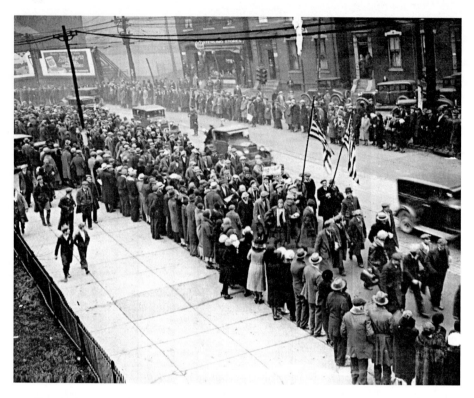

Bystanders wait outside St. Patrick's Church in the early morning hours for Cox to begin the march on Washington. Thousands surrounded the church to watch Cox's Army parade through the city, 1932 (Dr. and Mrs. Mason, Father James Renshaw Cox Collection, Saint Patrick–Saint Stanislaus Kostka Parish, Pittsburgh, Pennsylvania).

Cox's mission was to persuade President Herbert Hoover to allocate $5 billion for public works projects to create jobs for the jobless during the Great Depression. Thirty-eight years earlier, Jacob Coxey, an Ohio businessman and erstwhile politician, arrived in the nation's capital from Massillon, Ohio, at the head of 500 men to persuade President Grover Cleveland to institute a road-building program that would put people back to work.

Coxey was a successful businessman and well-known horse breeder, but he was also a failed politician who ran unsuccessfully for president, governor of Ohio, Congress and the U.S. Senate before winning election as mayor of Massillon.

Coxey and Cox were generals of armies that never fought a war. They marched unemployed men through the streets of Washington, D.C., during hard economic times in different eras, protesting the lack of jobs and begging for help from U.S. presidents who turned a deaf ear to their pleas. People often mistake "Coxey's Army" and "Cox's Army" as one and the same, but the two men were very different individuals despite their common goal of improving the lot of the jobless.

Coxey staged the first significant protest march when he paraded 500 men on foot, horseback and wagon along Pennsylvania Avenue in 1894, demanding the government institute a massive road-building program to put the unemployed to work during the Panic of 1893, a depression that wracked the nation for four years.

Coxey's protest generated concern among government officials that the march would inspire future demonstrations. Two months after President Grover Cleveland took office, the panic struck. During the winter of 1893–94, unemployment hit 18 percent. A rush to buy gold in 1893 led to he failure of hundreds of banks and the collapse of several major railroads. Coxey's Army was one of 40 "industrial armies" on the march to Washington. Most of the contingents dissolved before they reached Washington, and his expectation that at least one million men would mass in Washington in support never materialized. Coxey never got to present his petition for jobs on the Capitol steps because he was arrested for trespassing.

Coxey named his army the "Commonweal of Christ," marching 400 miles in 35 days from Massillon, Ohio, to Washington, D.C. Thousands of bystanders came out to watch Coxey's Army demand the federal government spend $500 million to build roads to end unemployment. He hoped his march would awaken the public to his cause and increase public pressure on Congress to embrace his ideas for economic recovery. He proposed financing the public works project with $500 million in Treasury notes that would require the government to spend $20 million a month building highways. Workers would be paid $1.50 a day for an eight-hour workday.

Cox's invasion of Washington in 1932 was the first mass political protest ever staged in the nation's capital in American history and set a precedent for future demonstrations, according to historians. Marching on Washington was an almost unheard-of practice to Americans in the late 19th and early 20th centuries. Until then, protests were small and attracted little attention. In 1877, a small protest in support of Samuel Tilden's claim to the presidency fizzled. The following year, a small protest was held against Chinese immigration. In 1892, veterans of the Grand Army of the Republican paraded down Pennsylvania Avenue. In 1915, 5,000 women, led by Alice Paul, demonstrated on the eve of Woodrow Wilson's inauguration for the right to vote, making women "a highly visible force in national politics," according to Lucy Barber's *Marching on Washington.*

Cox was inspired to stage his march for the same reasons as Coxey. The Great Depression had left millions out of work and starving, but the Hoover administration was slow respond to the crisis. Cox steered his "Jobless Army" across Pennsylvania on foot and vehicle. After the body arrived in the capital, Cox marched the men in military-like precision down Pennsylvania Avenue to the Capitol before meeting briefly with President Hoover, who sympathized with their cause but made no promises for aid. When Cox announced his plan to march on Washington, Coxey wired Cox, wishing him success: "My heart and spirit will accompany you and my hope is that you will have 500,000 join you in Washington."

Since Coxey and Cox made their historic journeys, millions of people have trekked to the capital to protest war, support civil rights, oppose the draft, and call for an end to the nuclear arms race, forever changing the relationship between the American people and their elected officials.

The idea of a march on Washington had originated a decade earlier when a severe recession slowed the nation's economy. A group of 310 unemployed men told Cox, "We are going to Washington and we want you to lead us."[7] A petition read: "We earnestly and seriously petition you, Mr. President, to consult Rev. James Renshaw Cox, chaplain of Mercy Hospital, for a simple remedy for the distressed unemployment situation through the nation."[8] The economic downturn after the war only lasted seven months, but it was followed by a more severe decline starting in 1920. The American economy had been chugging along during the war, but peace brought a decline in exports and a surplus of American-manufactured products, which resulted in layoffs of workers.

Unemployed men, many of them veterans, were desperate to feed their families, but Cox talked the men out of making the journey. "I'm sure you would not benefit by going to Washington; it would be folly ... just have a little patience. Things are righting themselves now and in the meantime, we will not see you or your families go hungry."[9]

1

"A Town Big
with Its Work"

When James Renshaw Cox was born on March 7, 1886, in the Lawrenceville section of Pittsburgh, the sky above the city was covered by a cloud of smoke so thick that it blocked the sun.[1] Nearly four dozen steel mills operating within a 40-mile radius of the city filled the atmosphere with sulfur dioxide and carbon monoxide, making "Pittsburgh ... a smoky, dismal city at best," wrote a visitor.[2]

His birth came as Pittsburgh was flexing its manufacturing muscle that would make the city a major industrial center. Nearly every street and building in the United States contained something that was produced by the city's steel or industrial manufacturing plants.[3] Pittsburgh produced 26 percent of all steel rails in the nation by 1900. As Pittsburgh moved into the 20th century, its mills led the nation in the production of structural steel.[4] By 1900, the number of mills in the Pittsburgh region increased to 94 as employment in the steel industry rose from 5,500 to more than 45,000.[5]

It was coal, however, that made the region rich. "Coal is the rock upon which Pittsburgh is built—without its vast yield of coal of the Pittsburgh district, the city would still be a town of provincial proportions."[6] More than 900 mines and 30,000 beehive-shaped coke ovens were operating throughout the region, producing coke for steel mills as long lines of coal-carrying barges churned their way slowly down the Allegheny, Ohio and Monongahela Rivers.[7] One observer wrote that "the lines of coke ovens seen from car windows have become huge scythes, saw-edged with fire. The iron-sheeted mills are crested in flame. Great fans of light and shadow wig-wag above furnaces and converters. Here is a town, big with its work."[8]

15

Pittsburgh became an urban laboratory as engineers and scientists developed new technology and production methods.[9] George Westinghouse founded Westinghouse Electric Company the same year Cox was born. As an experiment, Westinghouse set up a series of dynamos in a Lawrenceville building and sent an electrical charge four miles to downtown Pittsburgh that lit 400 lamps.[10] Westinghouse became the largest electrical manufacturing plant in the world.[11]

Pittsburgh was becoming a modern city. The Electric Light and Power Company was formed and used the light bulb invented by Thomas Edison to illuminate homes. An electric railway system crisscrossed the city, carrying passengers from the downtown business district to distant sections of the city within 15 minutes.[12] In 1890, the city began installing water meters. By the beginning of the 20th century, thirty percent of the homes in the city had telephones.[13] Dirt streets were paved. Electrical lines were installed, providing light for homes.[14]

The Pittsburgh Chamber of Commerce boasted that the top five banks in the city had $210 million in capital, $5 million more than the banks of England, Scotland, Ireland, Germany and Russia combined. Pittsburgh's railroad system made the city a distribution point for its products around the nation and the world, heralded the Chamber.[15]

Lawrenceville was founded along the Allegheny River in 1814 by William B. Foster, the father of composer Stephen Foster. The elder Foster described the residents as a "sober class of people."[16] The composer was born in a white cottage on lot number nine on July 4, 1826. A bank foreclosed on the cottage two months before Foster was born, but his family continued living there, paying rent to the bank. The town was named after Capt. James Lawrence, who commanded, "Don't give up the ship" after being mortally wounded during the War of 1812.

The Irish made up 20 percent of Pittsburgh's population working in the city's mills, foundries, and machine shops, as well as boatmen and dock hands.[17] Cox's ancestors likely came over in the first wave of Irish immigrant families in the early 19th century. His father, James, was born in Pittsburgh in 1856.[18] His mother, Julia Mason Cox, was born in Pittsburgh's South Side in 1867, the daughter of Thomas and Maria Mallon Mason. She was 11 years younger than Cox's father when they married in 1885. They had two sons, James and Earl, and a daughter, Gertrude. His paternal grandfather, Capt. John Cox, born in Ireland, piloted the tugboat, *Pathfinder*, on the Monongahela River.

Although Cox was the son of a Methodist father and a Catholic mother, religion was never an issue within his family. "I have an old aunt who lives in our convent and attends Calvary Methodist Church.... I have no more ardent supporters than my Protestant relatives," he said.[19]

Cox's childhood, as he recalled, was an idyllic time when people sang and played the piano on summer evenings. To Cox, home was the foundation of the American family. He was devoted to his mother and remained close to her until her death in 1932, shortly after he made his historic march on Washington.

His mother regaled reporters about her son's childhood when he ran for president. "He wasn't a bad boy, and I guess he wasn't a sissy boy, either. He was, I guess, just about what you would call a regular sort of boy, full of mischief at times but a pretty good boy at that," said his mother.[20] Cox also was a tease. He liked to sleep in the nude, which upset his brother. "'Mom!' Earl would call to me after they had got into bed. 'Jimmy ain't got his night clothes on. Come in here and make him put them on.'"[21]

Cox attended public school until his mother enrolled him at St. Mary's Catholic School, which was built before the Civil War and run by the Sisters of Mercy.[22] When his mother took Cox and his brother to enroll, the parish priest took one look at the scruffy-looking brothers and thought they were orphans. Cox came home from school one day and announced he wanted to be a priest.[23]

"The calling followed him right along during the years he was selling newspapers on Pittsburgh streets, during the time he was working for a taxi cab company, during the times he was working for the express company and when he was working in the post office," said Julia Cox.[24] Cox helped serve soup to the unemployed during the Bankers' Panic in 1907, which crippled the New York Stock Exchange and led to a shortage of hard currency.[25]

The Depression of 1920–21 hit the nation fourteen months after the end of World War I. Discharged veterans were unable to find work and businesses began to fail. Father Cox wrote to President Warren G. Harding for help, asking the government to create public works projects to put the jobless veterans to work. He gathered food and clothes to help families and became a one-man employment agency, appealing to local steel companies and other businesses to hire veterans."[26] Said his mother: "He's always been interested in the jobless. I guess it goes back for a long time, back 30 or 40 years ago when his father was out of work much of the time and I took in sewing to support the children. I didn't take in washing or ironing but I would have had it been necessary."[27] She added, "I have seen him give out as many as 200 overcoats in one day. Everything we receive we give away and Father Cox gives away most of his salary."[28]

Cox kept a boyhood diary, although the leather-bound book isn't a complete account of his childhood years. Cox studied Greek, Latin, and Spanish, elocution, history and math. His mother gave him a gun as a gift and Cox and his brother fired the weapon near their home: "This morning, mother gave me a revolver."[29] Later Cox writes: "Earl shoot [*sic*] night before on 46th Street."[30] Pittsburgh was a heavily ethnic town and Cox referred to his Italian neighbors as "guineas," which reflected the attitude one ethnic group had toward the other.[31]

Politics in Pittsburgh during Cox's childhood was controlled by Christopher Magee and William Flinn, who created a classic big-city political machine that allowed them to personally benefit from the region's growth. Their political hold on Pittsburgh evolved because city government could not handle Pittsburgh's rapid expansion. Flinn's construction firm, Booth & Flinn, won millions of dollars' worth of projects through rigged contracts, bribes, payoffs and backroom deals. Flinn controlled the awarding of contracts with an iron grip because Magee's cousin, Edward M. Bigelow, was director of public works. Bigelow steered contracts to Booth and Flynn, and outmaneuvered competitors even though the company's bids were always higher.[32]

Booth & Flinn paved streets using contractually required paving stones that only Flinn could provide from a quarry that he owned. The firm built streets and roads, installed water and sewer systems, and laid underground utility lines for telephones and natural gas. Flinn enriched himself even more through his political clout after he was elected to the Pennsylvania General Assembly. Thirteen days after taking office as a state senator, Flinn introduced a series of measures calling for the paving of streets, alleys and sewers in Pittsburgh. Using front men to introduce his bills so his name wouldn't appear on any of the measures, Flinn steered $16 million in business deals to his firm in a 24-year period for public projects at the expense of taxpayers, making him a multimillionaire.[33] He also used public monies to pave a road leading from the city to his farm outside Pittsburgh.[34]

Magee owned two trolley firms and served as a director of five others. His companies built rail lines across the city on financial terms that he dictated. Streetcars led to the creation of new neighborhoods such as Oakland, Squirrel Hill and Shadyside. The East End of the city drew the wealthy, and by 1900, more than half of Pittsburgh's richest denizens lived there.[35] Magee and Flinn sold slot machine concessions and the rights to operate speakeasies and houses of prostitution that were managed by their ward bosses. Magee and Flinn even sold furniture to the madams who operated the houses.[36]

It cost more to live in Pittsburgh than any other American city at the time. Pittsburgh had more millionaires per capita than anywhere else in the country. In the U.S., there were millionaires, multimillionaires and Pittsburgh millionaires.[37] Among the 86 millionaires in the city were Andrew Carnegie, Henry Clay Frick, Andrew Mellon, George Oliver, William Thaw, Henry Phipps, Jr., and members of the steel-making Jones and Laughlin families.[38] In the decade between 1895 and 1905, thirteen buildings were constructed standing 25 stories tall. By 1900, property values increased by $80 million.[39]

Cox, as an infant, is held by his mother, Julia, 1897 (Dr. and Mrs. Mason, Father James Renshaw Cox Collection, Saint Patrick–Saint Stanislaus Kostka Parish, Pittsburgh, Pennsylvania).

Prosperity came at a price. Amid the wealth, another Pittsburgh existed. The expansion of the steel industry created economic and social problems. As the city prospered, the workingman's position weakened in the last half of the 19th century. Wages declined, work days grew longer, and the cost of living rose. A short walk from downtown led to neighborhoods where workers and their families squeezed into one-room tenements. Half of Pittsburgh's 3,364 tenement houses were built to house one family, but more than 1,300 were living in 505 rooms. Out of 239 families, 51 lived in one room. Another 157 families were found to live with an average of three persons to a room. There was no indoor plumbing, so residents had to carry buckets of water from spigots on the streets up flights of stairs.[40]

Pittsburgh was "two cities, one old and congested with a high mortality, and the other new and spacious with a very low death rate," noted an official of the city's Health Department.[41] Streets in poor neighborhoods went unpaved and were covered by raw sewage. Housing conditions were unsanitary. Outdoor privies were often full and foul smelling. A thousand people a year were dying from typhoid fever because of dirty drinking water.

Towns surrounding Pittsburgh dumped their sewage into the rivers where the city drew its water. At one point, Pittsburgh had the highest death rate from typhoid in the nation because people were drinking contaminated water. Foreign-born children died at twice the rate of American children. Attempts to purify the water system were met with political opposition.[42]

Tenement roofs leaked, soaking a family's living space.[43] Alleys were strewn with trash. Children were "grimy and pale faced."[44] Workers labored 12 hours a day, seven days a week in the mines and mills, destroying families.[45] An estimated 6,000 children were under the care of welfare organizations because their parents were too poor to care for them.[46] Some families were so hard-pressed to survive that they placed their children in orphanages.[47]

Writer H.L. Mencken remarked in 1910 that Pittsburgh was a place of "distressing extremes of wealth and poverty."[48] Mencken was no fan of Pittsburgh and frequently wrote critically about the appearance of the city, whose landscape was littered with the detritus of industrial production and rivers that became depositories for slag and sludge. To Mencken, Pittsburgh was a giant "ash pile."[49] "It is a town of enormous enterprise, of prodigious prosperity, of fabulous income. On the one hand its desperate energy makes millionaires, but on the other hand it also makes a wretched and degraded proletariat."[50]

Prostitution flourished under the protection of police.[51] By the start of the 20th century, there were at least 1,000 prostitutes working in 334 houses of prostitution.[52] The growth of industry and corporate influence were intertwined.

Politics. business and banking were dominated by the Scotch-Irish Presbyterians. The Mellon family, led by Andrew Mellon and his nephew, William Larimer Mellon, who founded Gulf Oil, would control Pittsburgh until the election of Franklin Delano Roosevelt in 1932.

While merchants saw a city teeming with wealth, others saw a city where wealth and squalor existed side by side, where smoke, grime and garbage were scattered in the working-class neighborhoods. "It looked like hell, literally," wrote Lincoln Steffens.[53]

Reformers had a difficult time raising alarms about the social and environmental problems facing Pittsburgh and instituting changes. It was Catholic priests who led the vanguard for reform. Priests, relying on the papal encyclicals *Rerum Novarum* and *Quadragesima Anno* as their textbooks, educated their blue-collar parishioners about the rights of workers and the dangers of capitalism.

2

Seminary Years

Westmoreland County Miners are on strike again
Against the masters' tyranny
We are fighting might and main
We don't go down the coal mine
Where we never see the sun;
Unless we get fair wages
For the labor to be done
—"Westmoreland Miners' Strike" by James Coles[1]

Cox graduated from high school and enrolled at Holy Ghost College, a Catholic school founded in 1878 by a group of missionaries known as the Spiritans. It began with an enrollment of 40 students and six professors who held classes above a bakery. Initially known as the Pittsburgh Catholic College of the Holy Ghost, it later became Duquesne University. The school was founded initially to educate priests and the children of the city's Catholic immigrants.[2]

Cox worked during the summers to earn money to stay in school. He worked in a steel mill, as a taxi cab dispatcher, for the post office, and as department store clerk. In his letters to his mother, Cox acknowledged the sacrifice she made to ensure that her son could remain in college. When Julia Cox gave her son money to buy a new suit, he wrote how much he appreciated her effort because he realized his family didn't have much money to spare. "It fits me like the paper on the wall," he wrote. "I hate to take so much from you; you will never get that much in return for the sacrifices you are making."[3]

Cox was plagued by poor eyesight and worried the ailment would prevent him from entering the seminary after he graduated from Holy Ghost. But he experienced what he claimed was a miracle after rubbing holy water from the Shrine of Our Lady of Lourdes in France in his eyes. "All hope for a cure was abandoned by everybody but I knew Our Lady would help me," Cox said. "For years, the best doctors at Mercy Hospital in Pittsburgh had attended me. It was necessary to have my right eye bandaged and to wear smoked glasses."[4]

The shrine of Our Lady of Lourdes, located at the foothills of the Pyrenees, is the place where an apparition of the Blessed Mother appeared eighteen times to 14-year-old Bernadette Soubirous in 1858. Soubirous reported hearing a gust of wind and then seeing a vision of the Blessed Virgin Mary in the dark, cold grotto. The virgin ordered Bernadette to drink from a small spring that reportedly has cured a variety of ailments from paralysis to blindness.

"The miracle happened," said his jubilant mother. "Jimmy's eyes were cured of the affliction that we feared would result in blindness." Cox believed so strongly in the mystical power of the consecrated water that he developed a formula to stay healthy. He added two drops into his water glass or sprinkled the fluid on his food. He even claimed the recipe worked for non–Catholics. Cox imported holy water from Lourdes by the barrel, along with medals and rosaries that he sold to his parishioners.[5]

Lourdes became a major part of Cox's spiritual life. He led 20 pilgrimages over 28 years to the shrine except during World War II. In 1947, he flew for the first time to Lourdes with 31 pilgrims. At Lourdes, priests bless the sick and infirm as people carried on litters, walking on crutches, riding in wheelchairs or crawling on their knees struggling to reach the shrine, hoping for a cure from the miraculous waters. A procession of priests walks past them as they chant together, "Lord, make me see! Lord, make me walk! Lord, make me talk!"[6]

The pilgrimages at Lourdes featured torchlight processions in the evenings with people holding lighted candles singing "Ave Maria." Stations of the Cross were held on a hillside overlooking the shrine.[7]

Cox's devotion to the Blessed Virgin was so strong that he commissioned a film, *Bernadette of Lourdes*, produced in Pittsburgh using local actors. The film was shot in Lourdes and in areas near Pittsburgh and was written by Margaret Gallagher, a graduate of Carnegie Tech. After he became pastor of St. Patrick's, Cox held novenas to Our Lady of Lourdes every Sunday as children dressed in white marched with the Blessed Sacrament. When a new St. Patrick's was built after a devastating fire in 1935, Cox commissioned a replica of the Lourdes shrine constructed outside his church, although no one ever reported experiencing any miracles.

Cox entered St. Vincent Seminary near Latrobe in 1908 when he was 22. Latrobe was a mining and railroad center 40 miles southeast of

Pittsburgh. St. Vincent was founded in 1846 by Boniface Wimmer, a Bavarian monk, who established a monastery for the Benedictines in the virgin forests of Westmoreland County at the foothills of the Chestnut Ridge. St. Benedict of Nursia, who was born in 480 and is considered the founder of monasticism, wrote rules for monasteries known as the Rules of St. Benedict. The Benedictines' motto is *ora et labora,* "pray and work." The Rules separate a brother or monk's life into periods of prayer, work and spiritual reading.

Benedict believed monastery life should be based on a passionate faith that teaches monks should "prefer nothing to Christ. You must become [priests] only to be united to Jesus Christ more closely, to follow Him more faithfully, to do more for Him and, if necessary to suffer and endure more for Him." The monks stressed hospitality and moderation in all aspects of life.

Cox rode the train from Pittsburgh to Beatty Station a mile from the campus. St. Vincent was a small campus then with brick buildings trimmed in sandstone. It had seven baseball fields, five tennis and eight handball courts. Tuition was $125 for a five-month session.[8]

Cox studied theology, sacred scriptures, modern languages, canon law, moral theology and sacred liturgy, according to a listing of courses during the 1909–1910 term. He lived a Spartan existence at St. Vincent. The rooms were cold, the food was unappetizing, and the portions were small. The nuns managed to sneak Cox extra helpings and fellow seminarians shared food sent from home. "I've been eating all kinds of fine food from other fellows," he wrote.

George Cardinal Mundelein, the Archbishop of Chicago, attended St. Vincent and remembered the quality of the food years later. At a dinner in Chicago, everybody except Mundelein became sick after eating. "After my time at St. Vincent's, no food can poison me," he said.

Seminarians followed a monastic lifestyle at St. Vincent. They awoke at 5 a.m. every day and attended mass at 6 a.m. Then there were meals, classes and time for recreation before the day ended at 5:30. Walking along the grounds, the seminarians and monks smelled the freshly baked bread made from flour ground at the Gristmill, or the vinegary smell of cabbage coming from the "Sauerkraut Tower," a 90-foot-high water tower that the monks used to store cabbage in because of its cool interior.

While Cox was a seminarian, 10,000 coal miners staged a violent and lengthy strike in the Westmoreland coal field that resulted in 20 deaths. Once the strike began, 26 families were evicted from their homes and forced to live in tent camps on surrounding hillsides near the mines, which were protected by deputy sheriffs, private detectives, the Coal and Iron Police and the Pennsylvania State Police.

In 1866, the state legislature enacted a law allowing corporations to establish private police forces. Companies received a state commission for a dollar to hire officers who were armed and had the same legal powers as regular police officers. The Coal and Iron Police were especially brutal because their ranks comprised gunmen, thugs, drunkards and ex-convicts who carried rifles and pistols and truncheons used to crack the heads of striking miners or anybody else who got in their way.[9]

The priests and seminarians at St. Vincent knew all too well how the miners were suffering because the priests in the churches based in the coal patches came from the seminary. Cox witnessed the oppressive measures that coal operators unleashed on miners to quell a strike that began in 1910, threatening them into submission by evictions and arrests. The anger he felt at the time remained with him throughout his life and later led him to lobby lawmakers to abolish the Coal and Iron Police, who ruled the western Pennsylvania coalfields under the protection of the law. The violent scenes he witnessed of daily life in the coal camps surrounding St. Vincent were seared into his memory and resurfaced in 1927 during another bitter coal strike that led him to aid relief efforts.

The coal fields of southwestern Pennsylvania were dotted with company towns known as "coal patches," from the German *pacht*, which means to rent.[10] St. Vincent was surrounded by villages with names like Dorothy, Marguerite, Pleasant Unity, St. Vincent Shaft, Whitney, Baggaley, Calumet, United and Standard Shaft. Coal operators were wealthy and politically powerful men who acted like barons, ruling over miners and their families as if they were serfs in these hardscrabble villages. While the mine owners dwelt in baronial-style homes built with the profits from the coal industry, their employees lived in company-owned row houses.

"Always one feels the same thrill of anger against men, who, lounging in palatial homes or in well-furnished offices and comfortable clubs, look on calmly at the desolation and despair they have caused," wrote Gertrude Gordon, a reporter for the *Pittsburgh Press* who covered the human side of the strike.[11]

In March 1910, more than 16,000 miners went on strike against the 30 coal companies operating in the Irwin coal field in Westmoreland County. The walkout became known as the "Slovak strike" or "Hunky strike" because most of the miners were Slovak immigrants, although they later were joined by Irish, German and English miners. Coal operators viewed the Slovak miners as "an ignorant lot of Slavs anyway, and don't know what they want."[12] Miners were recruited from eastern and central Europe, brought to America, transported to Pennsylvania, and taken immediately under guard from the trains to the mines.[13]

"They work here from 10 to 13 hours for less wage than union miners who works only eight hours a day. If you complain to the boss that you have a bad job, the bosses say, 'Go hunky if you don't like it here,'" miner Andrej Buday wrote in *Jednota*, a Slovak Catholic newspaper.[14]

The United Mine Workers of America tried unsuccessfully from 1890 to 1910 to organize miners in the Westmoreland and Irwin coal fields but suffered defeat after defeat by the coal operators who had the financial and political muscle to beat back any attempts to unionize the miners. Cox also would have been exposed to union leadership, which he first supported and then turned against. Frank Morrison, secretary of the American Federation of Labor, and Francis Feehan, president District 5 of the Mine Workers of America, inspected the mining camps.[15] By the time the strike ended in July 1911, 20 people had been killed—ten in the Latrobe area—and the union had suffered another setback.

Feehan testified before a U.S. House committee that even though 18 deputies were convicted of murder, they were only sentenced from three to six months in jail. "Some of men killed were shot by deputies who followed them to their homes and shot them to death on their own property."[16]

The union accused coal operators of keeping foreign-born replacement workers in peonage. At some pits, miners were locked in stockades to prevent them from leaving because many of them had fled the region or quit working in sympathy with the strikers.[17] Attorney William McNair, who later would be elected mayor of Pittsburgh, complained to judicial authorities that miners were not allowed to leave the stockade and were being fed through openings in the enclosure. Although the local district attorney refused to investigate the allegations, 300 men were released the next day.

Mining coal was a hard way to make a living, but it was often the only job immigrants could find. Miners in the Westmoreland field earned an average of $2.30 a day. The men went on strike demanding the same wages that miners in the Pittsburgh coal field earned. Miners in Westmoreland were paid 58 cents for a carload of coal, compared to 67 cents for Pittsburgh miners. Pittsburgh miners also were paid for "dead time" spent removing slate or water from the mines before digging coal. Miners starting their shift often had to drain the water that accumulated in the shafts before they could start digging. Otherwise they would have to stand in cold water a foot deep in the cold mine shafts for their entire shift.[18]

Miners' wages declined 15 percent between 1908 and 1911 while the cost of living increased by forty percent. The strikers wanted an eight-hour work day instead of the punishing 12-hour shifts they were forced to work. One miner complained that he worked so many long days underground that he hadn't seen daylight in nearly two weeks. Coal company officials maintained a pretense that the strike had failed, claiming scores of miners had returned to the pits. "I will wager you that you cannot find more than 200 or 300 men out of the mines," said a coal company official.[19]

When the strike started, the coal operators evicted miners and their families from company homes, so the men built wooden barracks to live in, surviving on one dollar a week in strike benefits. Families had no fuel, food or clothing. Families survived by picking berries and mushrooms in the woods. Rain leaked through the roofs and cold air seeped through the cracks in the walls. Other strikers moved their families into tent cities erected on surrounding hillsides on small plots that held 400 people but could only comfortably accommodate 100. When it rained, the water washed away the tents, but the strikers rebuilt them.[20]

The strike caught the attention of former President Theodore Roosevelt, who arrived in Pittsburgh during the strike. "There is a frightful amount of suffering among the miners," he said. "They are living in tents, inadequately sheltered, inadequately clothed and inadequately fed."[21]

Ministers in Pittsburgh sent a railroad car filled with clothing to Latrobe for the families. The Catholic Diocese of Pittsburgh, worried that hundreds would die of hunger and cold, sent aid to these villages to ease the suffering. Babies were born in fields. When 18 pregnant women were due to have babies in the camps, social workers discovered not one woman had a nightgown or blanket for the newborns.[22]

In Latrobe, 120 babies out of 263 born during the dispute died from exposure during the strike because there were no blankets to keep them warm.[23] During the winter, children went barefoot. One writer described the living and working conditions in the Westmoreland field as "Pennsylvania's Russia" and the mine owners as the "Romonoffs [sic] of Pennsylvania's Russia." He sarcastically observed:

> The miner is a particularly unappreciative creature.... He was allowed to work twelve hours a day to go into the ground at dawn and come out at dusk, thus avoiding the annoyance of sunlight; he was given a nice large car to fill, with no extra financial investments to worry over. The company store and the house rent relieved him of any cash that his pay envelope was supposed to hold. In fact, he usually found that his pay envelope contained polite little statements that he was under obligations to the company. He wondered why he had come to America.[24]

Anne Morgan, daughter of financier J. Pierpont Morgan, came to the Westmoreland coal field, along with social worker Jane Addams of Hull House in Chicago, to see conditions firsthand. Morgan was appalled by what she found. She reported that babies were born in tents, children were dying because of a lack of food, and many went barefoot because they didn't have shoes.[25]

During the strike, coal operators brought in scabs to mine coal so the wives of striking miners stood outside the portals calling them names, harassing them and singing union songs, claiming they were only "serenading" the men with pots, bells and utensils.[26]

Sheriff's deputies arrested the women and took them to jail in Greensburg to face charges of disorderly conduct. Mother Jones, the elderly labor activist, arrived and urged the women to bring their babies with them. A judge gave the women the option of paying a $30 each or serving 30 days in jail. Since the mothers had no one to watch their children, the babies were locked up also. Jones told the women to sing around the clock in shifts to prevent anyone else from sleeping. "Just you all sing and sing," said Jones.[27]

The constant singing and wailing of infants unnerved the sheriff's wife, who lived in a house next to the jail, as well as residents of nearby boarding houses. After five sleepless nights, the sheriff persuaded a judge to release the women.[28]

Violence stalked the mining camps. When a contingent of deputies marched through a coal patch and recklessly fired a volley of gunshots at laughing miners, the miners retaliated by throwing stones at them. Several men were killed. Although the deputies were convicted of manslaughter, they were only sentenced to three months in jail. The pregnant wife of a miner was forcibly evicted from a company home, suffered a miscarriage and later died.[29]

Miners also were dying in the mines through unsafe working conditions. In Westmoreland County, there were 60 fatal mining accidents in 1909. Two years later, the death toll increased to 81.

"Strikers are shot at from ambush along lonely roads; so frequently do these attacks take place that they no longer draw forth any comment," wrote a columnist for *Colliers*. "In the picket lines, the strikers must walk meekly and silently if they do not want the hickory club of a deputy sheriff brought down on their heads."[30]

A superintendent of a Latrobe area mine shot and killed striker Mike Chekan, leaving his wife to raise five children. After he died, his widow was evicted from her home. Deputies removed her furniture from their company-owned home and deposited her possessions along the side of the road. The superintendent said he had shot Chekan in self-defense to stop Chekan from attacking a state trooper with a pick.[31] He was exonerated even though the miner's wife testified that her husband was chased into a bar and killed as he was pleading for his life.[32]

Six other miners were shot and killed by deputy sheriffs. Coal company operators placed spotlights on the top of coal tipples which swept the landscape around mines looking for signs of trouble from the strikers as mounted state troopers patrolled company property.[33]

Some Catholic priests supported the miners. They allowed families evicted from company housing to store their furniture in church basements and signed petitions asking the governor of Pennsylvania to force the coal companies to negotiate with the union. Some priests even lived among the miners during the strike.

Coal operators pressured the Archabbot at St. Vincent to recall one of the parish priests because he was such a staunch union supporter.[34] A priest was arrested for trespassing because he was walking along coal company property on his way to perform his pastoral duties.[35] A few priests refused to enter the camps to conduct baptisms or funerals "until the money was in hand," forcing Bishop Regis Canevin of Pittsburgh to order them to perform their priestly duties. Until then, parents baptized their own children and performed burial services over the dead.[36] By the time the strike ended in failure for the United Mine Workers on July 1, 1911, 15,000 striking miners had stopped production at 65 mines.

Cox never forgot the miners and the way they were forced to live. When the Jacksonville Agreement expired in 1927, 45,000 miners walked out of the pits in southwestern Pennsylvania, closing 200 mines. The agreement set the basic wage scale for miners but was broken by the Pittsburgh Coal Company and its owner, Richard Beatty Mellon. Other mine owners followed suit, leading to the walkout.

The strike pitted the United Mine Workers against coal operators who refused to negotiate or submit to arbitration and had the wealth and resources to withstand a long strike. Miners complained about working 12-hour days, paying high prices at company-run stores, and being forced to vote for candidates supported by the mine owners.

Miners and their families were evicted by the coal companies and forced to live in wooden barracks after legal appeals by the union failed to halt the evictions. The winter of 1927 was brutal, with temperatures hovering between eight and 10 degrees above zero. Conditions in the coal camps were deplorable, forcing families evicted from company-owned homes to seek shelter in drafty and leaking wooden shelters hastily built by the union to house strikers and their families. People were wearing rags instead of clothes. The cold spread illness through the barracks as the Coal and Iron Police evicted the sick from their beds.

Cox used his radio program to urge donations for the strikers and to defend the demands of the miners and condemn coal operators. Mine owners wanted to reduce wages while the union fought to keep wages gained in earlier contracts.

He collected 12,000 pairs of shoes along with food and clothing that was distributed to various coal camps. He also took up collections at his church to buy milk for the children of the miners' families. The Central Labor Council in Pittsburgh adopted a resolution praising Cox for his plea for aid and for denouncing "from his pulpit and over the radio, the action of those who nefariously wish to hold labor in subjugation and pay starvation wages...."[37]

The council proclaimed Cox was "one fearless reverend who was doing his utmost to help relieve the sufferings of the poor unfortunates." Cox used his radio program to rally support for the striking miners. "I certainly give the Rev. J.R. Cox praise for having the nerve to ask for aid for the locked-out miners over the radio," said one coal miner.

Cox attacked politicians for allowing civil rights violations to continue. "The people must and will be heard," he said. There are rumblings everywhere which promises a real upset in Pennsylvania politics unless the Republican leaders treat the people as human beings."

Pennsylvania authorities used the Sedition Act, which empowered the steel and coal companies to keep order and prevent workers from organizing. County sheriffs banned meetings and public gatherings and limited freedom of speech to prevent workers from holding union organizing meetings.

Cox later lobbied legislators to abolish the Coal and Iron Police, calling the Republican-proposed reforms "half measures. "I am disappointed and dissatisfied. We will continue the fight against the Coal and Iron Police. There is no compromise."

The state legislature had passed a bill in 1865 allowing railroads, steel mills and coal operators to create their own police forces to protect their properties, but the policemen exceeded their authority and became the sole dispensers of justice in the region's coal patches and mill towns.

Cox was part of a coalition of civic, labor and religious leaders who banded together after the brutal 1929 murder of miner John Barcoski to lobby for the abolition of the Coal and Iron Police. Barcoski was beaten to death by three officers employed by Richard Beatty Mellon's Pittsburgh Coal Company. The killing angered Cox, who said the authority bestowed on the quasi-police agency was a "tyranny by the wealthy industrial people."

The coal lobby worked to prevent passage of any reform legislation. Cox called the effort the "greatest insult" to Pennsylvania citizens. "It gives a reason for the people to believe that democracy is a mockery. It makes some believe that the dictatorships like those of Mussolini, Rivera and King Boris are, after all, decent systems by comparison to ours," Cox said.

After Gifford Pinchot succeeded Gov. John Fisher in 1931, Pinchot introduced his own bill to ban the police without consulting labor. Cox criticized Pinchot for breaking his promise to coal miners, calling the governor's measure "a miserable subterfuge."[38] Later that year, Pinchot revoked the commissions of every Coal and Iron Police officer in Pennsylvania.

"The people of western Pennsylvania are positively against the Coal and Iron Police," railed Cox. He said American businesses and corporations should not be "granted special privileges...."[39]

3

"Hell Was Not
Made for Us"

Father James Renshaw Cox was one of 58 seminarians ordained in 1911 by Pittsburgh Bishop Regis Canevin.[1] Cox left the seminary's isolated, bucolic atmosphere and returned to Pittsburgh, where he was appointed assistant pastor of Epiphany Church in the lower end of the city's Hill District. Epiphany, built in 1903, was the largest Catholic church in Pittsburgh.

Epiphany was a majestic-looking edifice built in Romanesque style with Byzantine detail and filled with religious symbolism. A ruby-colored light in the sanctuary cast a purple shadow along the aisle. A mural depicted Christ with his hands held upward toward to heaven, blessing the earth. A painting of the four evangelists was symbolized by a man for Matthew; a lion for Mark; a calf for Luke; and an eagle for John. A dove, representing the Holy Spirit, was surrounded by angels bearing a scroll with the inscription: *Sanctus, sanctus, sanctus. Dominus Deus Sabaoth Pleni Sunt caeli et terra gloria tua.*[2]

Pastor Lawrence O'Connell appointed Cox director of the Pittsburgh Lyceum, located across the street from the church. O'Connell opened the Lyceum in 1903 to serve young Catholic men and also opened a shelter for homeless women. The Lyceum had a swimming pool, a dance floor, a running track and a 4000-book library. One of Cox's other duties was to take a turn celebrating Sunday Mass at 2:30 a.m. for printers at Pittsburgh's newspapers whose shift ended at 2 a.m. O'Connell was a stickler for decorum. Cuss and you found yourself banned from the Lyceum for life. Boxer Billy Conn was eating an orange one day and dropped the peels on the floor. O'Connell delivered a stern lecture and made Conn picked up every piece.

31

Group photo of Cox (front row, center, hands on knees) with members of St. Patrick's Church, 1929 (Dr. and Mrs. Mason, Father James Renshaw Cox Collection, Saint Patrick–Saint Stanislaus Kostka Parish, Pittsburgh, Pennsylvania).

The Lyceum was an athletic club where Cox staged boxing matches, plays, dances and musicals. Conn, along with boxer Harry Greb, trained at the Lyceum. The money raised from these events was used to fund a free night school where immigrants could learn English and prepare for their citizenship tests, and high school dropouts could finish their education.[3] When Greb, a champion in the middle and lightweight divisions, couldn't find a place to train, Cox allowed him to use the Lyceum, and was inspired by Greb's work ethic in his Sunday sermons after Greb died in 1926.[4] "I said to myself I will devote the same amount of time to my spiritual work," said Cox.[5]

Since most homes in the neighborhood didn't have bathrooms, residents could take a bath or shower at the Lyceum for $5 a year. It served as a social, cultural and recreational center sponsoring basketball and football teams, swimming classes, tennis and handball, and boxing tournaments that featured appearances by notable boxers of the day. Pittsburgh newspapers noticed the impact Cox was having on his parish. "Father Cox, being a young man himself and greatly interested in athletics, has instilled the old sports into the hearts of young members," said the *Pittsburgh Press*.[6]

The Hill District had an international flavor when Cox arrived at Epiphany. The Irish immigrated there after the Civil War, followed by the Germans. In the 1880s, Italians and Slavs came as part of a mass migration from southern and eastern Europe to work in the mines and mills. Then Russian and Polish Jews arrived, along with Syrians and Lebanese.[7] A visitor could tell which neighborhood he was in by the aroma of food. The smell of gefilte fish, borsch and marinated herring filled the nostrils in Jewish neighborhoods. The smell of corned beef and stew permeated the Irish section. One could smell the aroma of sauces and the veal, chicken and various pastas in Italian neighborhoods. Around the corner from the church, Italian groceries hung garlic and dried cod, which sold for three cents a pound.[8]

For Cox, being a priest meant never passing up an opportunity to tell people they were important to God. "All of these conditions [of being a priest] were opportunities to tell people they were important, their daily lives were heroic and holy, and God had great love for them."[9] Cox developed an even deeper personal and spiritual connection to people after he left to become pastor of St. Patrick's Church in the Strip District. He believed ordinary individuals were filled with holiness. He saw goodness in the everyday lives of the men and women who came to St. Patrick's for religious services: "The men and women who compose the great mass of society, they have no great ambitions and aspirations for themselves. They only ask that they have sufficient food, clothing and shelter for themselves and their offspring. When you come down, for instance, from the altar rail after

Father Cox in a reflective moment, ca. 1932 (Dr. and Mrs. Mason, Father James Renshaw Cox Collection, Saint Patrick–Saint Stanislaus Kostka Parish, Pittsburgh, Pennsylvania).

a worthy reception of Holy Communion, for all practical purposes you are a saint. You know, hell was really not made for us."[10]

Cox always found time to listen to people and their problems. He invited people to stop in at his unlocked church any time of the day or night because Cox, or one of his assistants, would be there to listen to them. "Anything which causes pain or trouble to the least of God's little ones is never silly or trivial to me," he said.[11] A profile of Cox in a Pittsburgh newspaper talked of his empathy for people. "No matter what their station in life, from merchant prince to peanut vendor, thousands sought out Father Cox when they were in trouble and he gave ear to them."[12] He considered ordinary people to be saints.[13]

Cox served as a priest during a period when Catholicism was at its height and attendance at religious rituals were a way of life in the coal patches and mill towns throughout western Pennsylvania. Between 90,000 and 100,000 worshipers jammed Forbes Field in 1930 for Eucharistic Day. People knelt in the darkness holding lighted candles that resembled fireflies on a summer's night.[14] Another 10,000 participants knelt in Pittsburgh streets as a procession of priests carried the Holy Eucharist to Forbes Field.[15]

The period also was an era when the labor movement was beginning to take hold, and parish priests used two powerful papal encyclicals to urge workers to form unions and demand better wages and working conditions. In *Rerum Novarum, On Capital and Labor*, Pope Leo XIII stressed the right of workers to earn a livable wage and form unions.

> Once the passion for revolutionary change was aroused—a passion long disturbing governments—it was bound to follow sooner or later that eagerness for change would pass from the political sphere over into the related field of economics. In fact, new developments in industry, new techniques striking out on new paths, changed relations of employer and employee, abounding wealth among a very small number and destitution among the masses, increased self-reliance on the part of workers as well as a closer bond of union with one another, and, in addition to all this, a decline in morals have caused conflict to break forth.[16]

Leo wrote that workers went on strike because of the hard work, long days and low pay. "Labor which is too long and too hard and the firm belief that the pay is inadequate not infrequently gives workers cause to strike and become voluntarily idle," he wrote.[17]

The message in *Quadragesimo Anno, After Forty Years*, by Pope Pius XI was more radical. Pius wanted major changes in the economic system. He warned of the dangers posed to human freedom by unchecked capitalism and communism. He advocated a relationship between labor and management which broadened the church's concern for the poor. There could be no compromises with capitalism and communism, he wrote, and the church had a duty to concern itself with these issues. "The function of the rulers of the State is to watch over the community and its parts; but in protecting private individuals in these rights, chief consideration ought to be given to the weak and the poor," wrote Pius.[18]

Pittsburgh was a city of immigrants at the beginning of the 20th century. Many of the workers who filled the pews of Catholic churches each Sunday were foreign born and had brought their religious practices with them from Europe. Workers lacked a formal education and were unskilled, so organized labor wouldn't allow them to join unions.[19] The Catholic Church slowly began shifting its focus from vice and sin to the welfare of workers by preparing the next generation of priests for a different type of ministry. The Catholic Church's long-standing belief was that Catholics should use charity to care for the poor, and were urged by the church to accept their lot in life. The church didn't always believe in social equality, but slowly changed its view amid Vatican fears that disaffected Catholic workers might be attracted to socialism.[20]

The encyclicals became the church's blueprint for reforming the nation's social order and improving working-class lives. Pius feared the quickening pace of industrialization would mean less freedom for workers because of the rampant spread of capitalism. Pope Leo also warned of the dangers of unrestrained capitalism and the need to lessen the burden of the working man and the right to form labor unions. He tried to find a middle ground between socialism and liberalism by emphasizing the need for trade unions so workers could bargain for a living wage and alleviate the brutal working conditions they faced.

Pius called for sweeping reforms to correct the social obstacles Catholics faced both socially and economically. Priests in the 1920s supported unions as the only way for workers to achieve some form of bargaining power with employers. "A small number of very rich men have been able to lay upon teeming masses of the laboring poor a yoke that is little better than slavery,"[21] wrote Leo. Pius argued that businessmen needed a social conscience. Their employees had a right to a fair, livable wage since the production and profits of business and industry were created by labor.[22] Workers owed employers an honest day's work. "This is human and Christian in contrast to the purely commercial and pagan ethics of industry," wrote American bishops.[23]

Monsignor John Augustine Ryan, a noted theologian and writer, said without the intervention of the Catholic Church, "no practical solution will be found...."[24] The encyclicals declared the workers have a right to organize unions, work an eight-hour day and receive a living wage. It was the "ordained mission" of the church, wrote Ryan, "to teach men not only what to believe but how to live."[25]

Monsignor Ryan published a list of reforms that included a minimum wage, an 8-hour day, an end to child labor, and unemployment insurance. He called for public ownership of utilities, control of monopolies and an income tax. He said Leo's encyclical was a "description of industrial evils, a condemnation of the spurious remedies proposed by Socialism."[26]

Ryan wrote that "the claim to a living wage is a right. The right is personal, not merely social: that is to say it belongs to the individual as an individual and not as a member of society. It is a laborer's personal prerogative, not his share of social goods; and its primary end is the welfare of the Laborer, not that of society. In brief, the right to a Living Wage is individual, natural and absolute."[27]

Ryan believed the only way to solve the economic and social problems facing workers was by church intervention. "The business of the state, then, is to protect men in the enjoyment of their opportunities that are essential to a right and reasonable life."[28] He rejected the arguments of businessmen that the church had no right to interfere in their affairs. "It has everything to do with business, insofar as business involves questions of right and wrong, of justice and injustice."[29]

Diocesan priests in Pittsburgh embraced the encyclicals. The Rev. Raymond Dietz, along with the Rev. Charles Owen Rice, the Rev. Carl Hensler and Monsignor George Barry O'Toole, were in the forefront of social reformers who were critical for public acceptance of the New Deal.[30] They used the Mass as a way to educate workers about the ideas contained in the encyclicals and, along with labor and political leaders Philip Murray and David Lawrence, moved immigrant groups from the edge of American politics to the center in the 1930s and into the Democratic Party.[31]

Many priests in western Pennsylvania came from humble, working-class backgrounds, and their parishioners were blue-collar immigrants who were at the mercy of the Scotch-Irish Presbyterians who dominated Pittsburgh business, industry and banking.[32] The Catholic clergy knew best the economic and spiritual needs of their parishioners. It was working-class Catholics who suffered the most from the Depression. The brightest of their children were forced to cut short their educations and find work to support their families.

Bishops, like Hugh Boyle of Pittsburgh, spoke for workers in the early years of the 20th century, but it was priests like Cox who were advocates for workers as the Depression placed a stranglehold on the nation's economy. Parish priests were supported by their bishops, such as Boyle, who helped write "Our Bishops Speak," a condemnation of greed, and said the nation's economic problems were caused by an "orgy of speculation."[33] "Unless capital purges itself of its sins and unless labor does the same, something terrible will happen to our social order," said Boyle.[34]

4.

"Metropolis of Corruption"

Cox enlisted in the U.S. Army during World War I, was commissioned a chaplain and assigned to a field hospital in Angers, France, that was staffed by doctors and nurses from Pittsburgh. The government asked university medical schools across the country to form hospital units to serve overseas. The University of Pittsburgh created Pittsburgh Base Hospital 27, consisting of 48 doctors, 7 dentists and 105 nurses.

When Cox told his pastor, Father Lawrence O'Connell, he had joined the Army, O'Connell was stunned. "Jimmy, I thought you were only fooling when you said you were going. You can't go. Please don't go," pleaded O'Connell.[1] O'Connell walked away with tears streaming down his face.[2] The diocesan newspaper praised Cox for enlisting, calling him a "man of sterling qualities of mind and heart."[3]

Being a military chaplain usually was a patronage job arranged through the influence of a congressman or senator until 1913. During the war, morale among chaplains was poor, and they were viewed as 'handymen."[4] "Ministering to the spiritual needs of the men was utterly disorganized if the word disorganized can be applied to the almost non-existent," wrote another chaplain.[5]

Base Hospital 27 was sent to Allentown, Pennsylvania, for training before shipping overseas.[6] The detachment traveled to New Jersey, then boarded the SS *Lapland* bound for England. The ship arrived in Southampton after a 13-day journey over heavy seas.[7] During the crossing, Cox became very seasick but maintained good humor about it. "Oh, boy. I vomited a barrel. When the boat rolled, some of the fellows belched forth their disgust and stomach," he wrote in a letter home.[8]

The weather was so rough that Cox was knocked ten feet off the altar while he celebrated Mass, and the chalice containing the body and blood of Christ slid sideways from the ship's motion.[9] He had to wear his life belt every day and participated in daily lifeboat drills.[10] Cox tended to his pastoral duties during the crossing, baptizing "two of our young soldier boys," hearing 400 confessions, and serving Holy Communion to 800. Cox loved being a soldier: "The uniform of a soldier had always made a thrilling impression upon me even as a child. I remember how I insisted that my mother and father buy one of those old-fashioned soldier uniforms at Christmas time, and I paraded all over Butler St., with a high hat, breast plate and sword and I was the happiest boy in the world."[11]

The unit arrived in Angers, a town of 60,000 with narrow streets and stone buildings which sits at the entrance to the Loire Valley. The Americans took over the Petite Seminaire de Mongazon d'Angers and transformed the seminary into a 4,800-bed hospital to treat the wounded during the battles at St. Mihiel and the Argonne Forest, who were suffering from concussions, gunshot wounds and infections. Some of the more seriously wounded were hospitalized for as long as 135 days.[12] In addition to ministering to the sick and wounded, Cox led the hospital band.[13]

The hospital was surrounded by a garden, and its blooming flowers in springtime made Cox think of home. "Easter is early this year," he wrote. "Our garden has all kinds of flowers ... wonderful and makes it look like Easter."[14] His letters reflected his deep love for his mother. "The only thing I miss is you," he wrote in 1918.[15] Cox addressed his letters to his "dear, dear momma" but signed them formally, "Your loving son, James R. Cox." Julia Cox chastised him for his lack of letters. "Well, it's not my fault because I have written to you faithfully and the letters must have gone to the bottom of the ocean or you would have certainly received them by this time," he wrote.[16] Cox wrote his brother Earl that he had been too busy to write every family member, so he told his brother to share his letters with the other relatives. "This letter will have to satisfy each of you so why write 3 letters when one will suffice."[17]

Cox worked tirelessly as a chaplain, visiting wounded soldiers and administering the sacraments. He talked of men being gassed by the Germans and of stunned soldiers returning from the front suffering from shell shock.[18] He mentioned a soldier who hadn't been to confession or received Holy Communion for five years but "came back" at Cox's urging.[19] One day, Julia Cox received a letter from a French woman who had met Cox. The woman praised Cox for "working without rest,"[20] and added, "Although I am a stranger to you, my letter will be, I think welcome, since it will bring you news of your dear son, Father James Cox. He is a loyal and frank character, responds to our tastes, sharing the same religious conviction, this also, for us, is a new time. Believe me, madam, all my consideration and my sympathies is with your son.[21]

Cox made pastoral rounds at 20 military camps and three hospitals where he said he heard 3,000 confessions during his stay in France and offered Holy Communion to 90 soldiers each morning. He comforted men who had been gassed by the Germans or were suffering from shell shock from artillery bombardments. He said victims of poison gas attacks were brought into the hospital "a mass of bleeding flesh, burned from head to toe."[22]

Pittsburgh veterans who served with Cox in France saw that he was a man of great compassion. "Many a nerve-wracking sleepless night Father Cox put in tending to the wants of badly wounded soldiers and writing home to the parents to offer words of encouragement," wrote a former veteran.[23] A Jewish soldier from Pittsburgh was recuperating at Base Hospital 27 after losing a leg in combat. "There was no rabbi at the hospital so Father Cox repeated a prayer from the Old Testament," said the man.[24] Cox told the soldier, "God doesn't consider creeds. It's what's in your heart."[25] As the war neared an end, Cox allayed his mother's fears about the danger: "Don't worry about me; I am just fine. The war will end soon. We are not near the firing but hundreds of miles behind in a fine hospital. Your boy is safe. Every day I will write even if it is only a short letter to let you know I am well and happy. Don't you think from the way the Germans are hurrying to Berlin that the Kaiser will soon ask and beg for peace?"[26]

Cox wrote that he had survived two bombing raids and artillery barrages. "This is the only real war I have known so far," he said, noting that the air raids "were extremely thrilling and dangerous."[27] One day, Cox was returning to the hospital with an officer and two nurses when he fell and injured his knee. The injury would plague him for the rest of his life and made Cox a bitter man after the government cut his pension benefits since there was no record of his injury or treatment by doctors.[28] His mother embellished her son's injury when she was interviewed by reporters in 1932 after he decided to run for president: "He was shot in the right knee and was decorated twice but for what reason I cannot recall."[29]

Cox returned to the United States on November 24, 1919. After he was discharged, he returned to Pittsburgh. Four years later, on September 6, 1923, he was named pastor of St. Patrick's in the Strip District. Cox was surprised by his appointment as the youngest pastor of the oldest Catholic church in the city because "most priests do not get a city parish until they have served 18 years or more."[30]

The church was in the heart of the neighborhood surrounded by smoke from the nearby rail yards and industries along the Allegheny River. The Strip was more of a "federation of small nations" than one political body. In a city dominated by Scotch-Irish Presbyterians, the hatred toward Catholics was extreme. Preachers stood outside St. Patrick's on Sunday mornings stirring up street demonstrations and haranguing Catholics as they left Mass.[31] Cox threw himself into his work by renovating St. Patrick's. Buildings were painted. The rectory and convent were renovated. The altars were enameled and lengthened and new fire escapes were installed.[32]

St. Patrick's had a long history in Pittsburgh. The first St. Patrick's was built in 1808 to serve 20 Catholic families. Its pastor was the Rev. Charles McGuire, who had faced death by the guillotine in Paris during the Reign of Terror during the French Revolution, only to be spared at the last minute.[33] The church was a small frame structure near a canal leading from the Allegheny River. River men could steer their boats to unload cargo on the front lawn of St. Patrick's.[34] It was largely a parish for German Catholics until 1840, when English-speaking Catholics took over. The German congregants then built their own church. In 1854, the church was destroyed by fire. Four years later, a new church was dedicated. That church was torn down when the Pennsylvania Railroad purchased the property to expand its rail lines. Another St. Patrick's was built, but it later was destroyed by a fire.[35]

St. Patrick's membership was no more than 15 families, but more than half a million people came to worship at the Strip District church in a single year after a radio station began broadcasting his sermons. The diocese had to assign Cox four assistants to help with the pastoral work because of the number of people who attended Mass and other services.[36] Cox transformed the sub-basement of the church into catacombs where he held religious services, complete with skulls and sarcophagi.[37]

The Strip District was known as the "hog trough"[38] of Pittsburgh. A visitor could taste the Strip in every breath and feel it on everything he touched. "Part of what he sees, part of what he hears, part of what he smells, part of what he tastes, part of what he touches, stamp indelibly upon his mind and heart this impression," wrote a minister.[39] The neighborhood was two miles long and three-tenths of a mile wide. It was filled with factories, manufacturing plants and saloons. At one time in its history, the Strip had 78 saloons, 10 clubs, plus speakeasies owned by city politicians. "No one need go alcoholistically thirsty in the strip," wrote a clergyman.[40] Cox said, "Husbands and fathers drink, carouse while their wives labor to support needy children."[41]

Cox celebrates Mass in the catacombs beneath St. Patrick's Church, 1931 (James R. Cox Papers, 1923–1950, AIS.1969.05, Archives & Special Collections, University of Pittsburgh Library System).

Cox became pastor of St. Patrick's Catholic Church when Pittsburgh's city hall was controlled by an unholy alliance of bankers, politicians, businessmen and racketeers. Mobsters paid politicians and the police to protect the bootleggers, prostitution and gambling that were entrenched in Pittsburgh. A national magazine called Pittsburgh the "metropolis of corruption."[42]

Walter Liggett, a crusading journalist and editor of *Plain Talk* magazine, said Pittsburgh was the most corrupt city in the nation. He blamed the city's industrial leaders for the corruption and singled out U.S. Treasury Secretary Andrew Mellon as their leader.[43] Wrote Liggett: "The overlords of Pittsburgh have never wanted well-paid, self-respecting, independent workers. Instead they deliberately imported foreigners, exploited them ruthlessly and virtually maintained feudalism. The result is a festering sore that is a stench in the nostril of the nation."[44]

Across the street from St. Patrick's was a house of prostitution operating with the full knowledge of police who were paid to protect it. From his pulpit, Cox attacked the police for looking the other way. Cox went to the district attorney to demand action. "I am willing to go before the grand jury at any time and tell what I know," he warned. "You might as well call nobody as to the police to enter a complaint. I had to almost coax them to remove a disorderly house across the street from the church."[45]

He attacked bootleggers for turning the Strip into an oasis of liquor. "Drunkenness is rampant. The district is polluted."[46] Ward bosses and city councilmen sold gambling and liquor concessions to the highest bidder. The police became a collection agency for political payoffs. Speakeasies were immune from raids if they made payoffs to police and politicians. Pittsburgh was a city awash in booze and "wet enough for rubber boots," and western Pennsylvania was "the wettest spot in the United States."[47] In a three-year period in the 1930s, there were 105 unsolved murders and 15 unsolved bombings in Pittsburgh.[48]

Street brawls between rival political groups characterized election campaigns.[49] Elections were tainted. Near the home of Andrew Mellon, ward bosses created ghost voters with phony addresses. In 1931, election officials purged 16,000 names from for the rolls because the individuals didn't exist. Dozens of voters in one ward all were named "Frank Smith." Ward bosses produced tax receipts to make people eligible to vote.[50] In one Strip District precinct, 567 votes were cast even though there were only 466 registered voters. "Night riders" stole ballot boxes and changed votes for Democratic candidates to Republican. An investigation resulted in the indictment of 68 politicians for vote fraud, including several entire election boards.

There were demands from civic groups for reform. Mellon and his cousin, William Larimer Mellon, controlled county politics through the Republican Party. Mellon was so strongly tied to special business interests that the American Civil Liberties Union battled Andrew Mellon after Gov. John Fisher refused to reform the brutal Coal and Iron Police, who served as hired guns protecting the interests of the coal and steel industrialists.

Mellon became the symbol of corruption in Pennsylvania. A magazine cartoon depicted a winged Mellon afloat in a red, smoky sky high above the belching steel mills while beneath him lay dilapidated shacks and silk-hatted bankers making payoffs to corrupt politicians.

5

Celebrity Priest

Cox inherited a radio program from his predecessor, Father Thomas Coakley, when he became pastor at St. Patrick's. Coakley is considered the first Catholic priest in the nation to broadcast services over the radio, starting on November 28, 1921, after radio station KDKA installed a microphone in the pulpit.[1]

Eleven months earlier, on January 2, KDKA in Pittsburgh broadcast the first religious service from the Calvary Episcopal Church as two station engineers, one Jewish and the other Irish Catholic, donned robes and mingled with the church choir to monitor the broadcast during the service.[2] The station later began broadcasting sermons by ministers of other denominations on a rotating basis.

Recordings of many of Cox's sermons no longer exist, but artist Victor Paul drew a series of 48 pen and ink drawings to illustrate some of Cox's early sermons that were published in book form as *Illustrated Lectures.* Each three-panel cartoon presented a synopsis of one of Cox's sermons. One read: "Many a mill-hand would be an important engineer—had he the opportunity to pursue higher education." Another: "Love and happiness is found in homes when both husband and wife use diplomacy in their relationship with one another, with in-laws and neighbors."[3]

Religious broadcasting was new and commercial radio was just beginning to develop. Until the 1920s, charismatic evangelists, like Dwight Moody, Amy Semple McPherson and Billy Sunday, had used the force of their personalities to reach the masses. Preachers like Cox realized the potential of radio to spread the gospel. "Through radio we can take the church to the people who can't get out of their homes or live in areas where there are no churches and wouldn't get to hear mass if it wasn't for us," he said.[4] Parishioners like Veronica Burton, who lived next to St. Patrick's Church and was confined to her bed for 35 years and unable to attend Mass. Cox had a hole cut into the wall of the church so she could see and hear Mass from her residence.[5]

By 1930, radio stations in the city produced various religious programs featuring sermons, music and religious services in addition to sporting events and entertainment programs. Ads for the sale of radios began appearing in newspapers as reporters started to cover the radio industry.[6]

Cox used the medium to scold public officials and police. He went on the air to attack Police Superintendent Peter Walsh, one of the most corrupt cops in the city, for allowing vice to the spread throughout Pittsburgh.[7] He became the voice of morality in what he viewed as a corrupt, sin-ridden city. He also used radio to express his political opinions and help elect and defeat candidates for public office.[8]

His radio sermons reached more than just Catholic listeners. When Al Zimmerman was a boy, his family sat around the radio listen to Cox preach. "When he came on the radio, we all would sit down and listen even though we were Lutherans."[9]

After Pittsburgh Mayor William McNair appointed Cox as a city tax assessor, Cox went on the air to urge that McNair be appointed "dictator of Pittsburgh," only to see McNair resign after 34 months in office after turning city government into a three-ring circus.[10]

He used radio to endorse the corrupt Charles Kline's successor, John Herron, for mayor. Cox was hosting an event to raise money for his relief fund when he turned the occasion into a campaign rally for Herron. "I don't want to turn this into a political event but I want to say that Mayor John Herron is the greatest and best mayor we've ever had."[11] Cox had ulterior motives in endorsing Herron. Earlier in the day, Cox had appealed to Herron to have city council's help in alleviating a $60,000 debt in Cox's relief fund.[12] Cox used radio to accuse officials of a nearby municipality of political corruption charging that 1,700 voted in an election for the town's political machine when there were only 900 registered voters. Officials denied the charges, saying Cox couldn't count.[13]

Cox supported FDR for president and endorsed the New Deal, but by 1935 he was disillusioned with Roosevelt. He went on the radio to announce he was defecting to the GOP and urged his listeners to vote Republican in the next election. He claimed the Democratic Party platform was "founded on the insecure pillars of economic heresies. I was for Roosevelt but the travesties which the New Dealers insist on calling good government convinced me that my support of the Democratic Party would be in contradiction with my views on social welfare."[14]

During Gifford Pinchot's campaign for governor, Cox told listeners he was offered a bribe to abandon Pinchot and support Pinchot's opponent, John Hemphill. Cox said he had three witnesses to the alleged bribery and Hemphill's supporters challenged Cox to identify them. It would be the first time a bribe ever was offered in front of witnesses, said Hemphill supporters.[15] Cox attacked vice and the city's corrupt police force. He decried the lack of morality in the Strip District and used radio to publicize his campaign.

People were in awe of the sound of radio in the 1920s. They were transfixed by the sound coming from the box because radio was immediate. It allowed listeners to learn quickly what was happening in the United States and the world. The price of a radio dropped from $139 in 1929 to $47 by 1932. By late 1933, 60 percent of American households had radios.[16] Even with money tight, radio was a form of free entertainment and a distraction from daily hardships. In 1930, radio sales continued to increase rapidly during the Great Depression as the number of radio stations also grew from 618 to 847 between 1929 and 1939.[17]

Radio broadcasters became celebrities. "Jimmy Cox, as we priests affectionately called him, was made for radio with his pleasant, flexible voice and his ease without scripts for him or within strict time limits, to fit the occasion," said Monsignor Charles Owen Rice. "There were few voices for social justice but he was one."[18] A Pittsburgh newspaper survey named Cox the most popular radio personality in the city. He received 16,664 votes, 10,000 more than the runner-up.[19]

His sermons sometimes were too frank, and not all of them were broadcast because of his candor. WJAS once cut him off in mid-broadcast when Cox began to criticize John D. Rockefeller.[20] After World War II, WJAS censored Cox again when he planned to deliver a sermon on birth control to protest what he called "birth control propaganda."

Cox favored large Catholic families and urged his parishioners to follow the rhythm method known as Knaus-Ogino developed by Drs. Herman Knaus and Kyusaku Ogino. The rhythm method, dictated by the Catholic Church, was the only birth control Cox believed in. "No sensible couple will use contraception when they know birth control can be controlled more surely in a natural way. Let the truth be told so nature's laws can be used instead of ignorantly abused."[21] In a 1945 broadcast, Cox preached that if married couples practiced birth control, there wouldn't be enough men to serve in the military during war. The whole purpose of marriage, he said, was to procreate. He said the government was trying to frighten the poor in having fewer children.[22] "Without the sons of the poor, there wouldn't be 11 million men defending democracy. With the eyes of a baby, you can see the eyes of God. Why should we try to be wiser than God? I say to you follow God's natural system."[23]

The church had preached since AD 300 that any form of birth control was a sin. In 1930, Pope Piux XI's encyclical, *Casti Connubii*, "On Christian Marriage," allowed married couples to practice the rhythm method of birth control.

On one tape, marked "Do Not Broadcast," Cox condemned birth control as "race suicide."[24] He opposed birth control since 1929, when he began holding "baby day" at St. Patrick's, where he blessed 500 babies.[25] He complained that "10 million future American fathers" were being given birth control information.[26] Although the sermon never was broadcast, Cox promised the sermon be delivered at Sunday mass "fully, freely and frankly" warning parishioners "there will be nothing left to their imagination."[27]

During World War II, condoms were distributed to servicemen. Pope Pius XI in 1930 had prohibited any form of birth control except the rhythm method. The National Catholic Welfare Council linked a manpower shortage to birth control and cited that as the reason why more family men had been inducted into the military during the war. Cox worried that by the end of the century, the country might be left without enough manpower to defend the nation.[28]

"We'll be cited in future history as a great race that became extinct because of illegitimate birth control," Cox said.[29] "Better to go to war than to not have existed at all."[30]

Cox said a womb is a "beautiful home made by God" and "we say no contraceptives should ever be used for prevention of children. It's our business to teach the right methods."[31] "There is no joy in night clubs," he said, "but there is joy in having children."[32]

Cox referred to sexual intercourse as "the thing" and many Catholic families followed Catholic teaching by raising large families. The church viewed procreation as tantamount. Since the time of St. Augustine, recreational sex was considered a sin. Intercourse was not for pleasure but to create children.[33] An increase in the American standard of living, the church said, couldn't be achieved without a significance population growth.[34] Cox conceded his sermon was too frank and perhaps shouldn't be broadcast.[35]

Radio spurred public religious devotion, which made Cox popular. Other Pittsburgh priests, notably Charles Owen Rice, who had a radio program on another Pittsburgh station, were active in public affairs and preached a social gospel to blue-collar workers. They were liberal when it came to economics and politics and were crucial to public acceptance of FDR's New Deal programs.[36]

Cox began his broadcasts by telling listeners, "I feel that you love God or you would not have tuned in on the radio this morning."[37] He used radio to spread the gospel and to preach the acceptance of Jews and urged people, regardless of their faith, to pray.

His Sunday sermons were Monday's news. He criticized the executions of Sacco and Vanzetti in Massachusetts for the murders of a payroll clerk and guard and second-guessed the judge, prosecutors and conflicting testimony that resulted in their guilt. He also blamed Gov. Alvan T. Fuller for his refusal to grant the condemned men clemency, saying their deaths played into the hands of communists. "Gov. Fuller had chance to show greatness but he went along with the group and gave martyrs to the Reds."[38]

He lectured his listeners on romance, courtship, marriage, divorce, and the decline in morals. Too many young women, he said, were searching for wealthy, older men to provide "beautiful and expensive apparel." Young men, he added, sought riches. "They desire wealth because they suppose it brings pleasure. What is the result? Girls go wrong, fill our disreputable houses, then wither and die or commit suicide. Our boys become bandits, are caught in the meshes of law, are imprisoned, disgraced and all opportunity for a respectable career is wrecked."[39]

One mother, a widow with a 24-year-old daughter, wrote Cox expressing concern that her daughter was staying out all night. She explained how she forced her daughter to listen to Cox's radio sermons. "We both listen to your broadcasts before going to work at 8:30 and I would like her to hear what you have to say without knowing that I wrote you. Please do not mention my name," wrote the woman.[40]

He assailed women who dressed as "flappers" and men posing as "sheiks" who modeled themselves after actor Rudolph Valentino. Cox warned that women who drank alcohol would end up with husbands who were "bottle mates" rather than "love mates."[41]

Neither will women and men attracted by the fumes of alcohol be husbands and wives. They may be found in wedlock by the law or church but they are not man and wife. They are merely bottle mates. Alcohol fumes do not spread an aroma of love around them. A hug, a kiss, a drink, and marriage remove a woman's inherent qualities and leave no thrill for the man, and when beauty and thrill is gone, life is not worth living.[42]

Cox compared the morals of Atlantic City to ancient Rome and deplored the Miss America pageants in Atlantic City. "Rome in the worst days of the empire was an example of modesty by comparison with the present day Atlantic City," he said.[43] Atlantic City was "a thousand times worse than ancient Rome,"[44] and Cox predicted "bathing contests will be held in the absolute nude by 1935."[45] He was critical of the pageant's promoters when beauty contestants began wearing one-piece bathing suits. Cox said it may be necessary to recall missionaries from Africa "to teach our people how to wear coverings for their body."

During Lent, Cox held a series of lectures on marriage in which he addressed courtship, morals and divorce. Each lecture attracted as many as 5,000 people.[46] He said young men used to court women by the soft light of a fireplace but now wanted to gaze upon a woman in the full light. "They want full light so they can see everything that the girls show," he said.[47] Cox said women used to buy 20 yards of silk to make a dress but now only need three yards, "and that's too much material."[48]

Cox used radio to complain about Sunday Blue Laws that banned movies, concerts and sports on the sabbath, calling them "silly meddling to prevent legitimate pleasures on the day of rest. What is rest and relaxation? Wouldn't it be restful and easy and enjoyable for our boys and girls and young men to enjoy in harmless contests after they have attended religious services?"[49]

Cox railed against divorce, saying married couples looked for any reason to end a marriage. He wanted the courts to abolish divorce. "Divorce nowadays may be obtained because of a disagreement over a necktie or an argument over the batting average of a favorite baseball player," he said.[50]

Cox endorsed dancing, but in the next breath criticized young people for dancing the "Black Bottom," a dance popular in the 1920s. Quoting Ecclesiastes 3:1–4, Cox preached there is "a time to weep and a time to laugh: a time to mourn, and a time to dance."

> Dancing, as the text indicates, is permitted by God, who desires to be served with joy, gladness and cheer. If the Lord does not condemn it, neither do we. But we must not in our pleasures go beyond the bounds of decency, for then our pleasures become sinful. We do not urge a return to the stately minuet whom, like the horse and buggy, has seen its day. Nor even do we advise the two-step, schottische or the waltz, which belong to an age that is gone forever. But neither do we approve the extreme in dancing as represented in the latest fad called the "Black Bottom." It is a horrible, degrading performance for civilized people. The Black Bottom originated in darkest Africa—a combination of whirling dervish, jumping-jack and spinning wheel—whose contortions could not be performed without a little gin to convulse the body. It is positively immoral.[51]

On romance: "Courtships which should not last longer than a year are now prolonged indefinitely and are interspersed with cabarets, trips to road houses, jazz and auto petting parties in every city and park," he said.[52] Cox hated jazz. "Modern jazz from beginning to end may be summed up as jazz, jazz, jazz, a perfect example of discord in a discordant age."[53]

He once used a skeleton during a sermon to explain the moral difference between men and women. Women, he said, "determined the morality of a people and whatever the women were, so was the nation."[54] Holding a female skull in the pulpit, Cox told his congregation that the brain of a flapper "is mostly by a silly little head that she sins...."[55]

Cox once wrote a movie review for a Pittsburgh newspaper. When *Laughing Sinners* opened in 1931, Cox urged readers to see the movie even though his review read like a Sunday sermon. "[God] extends a helping hand to all unfortunates who have strayed from the straight and narrow and will not only welcome them back, but will love them more than those who have always been just."[56] Then he added: "See it—it will be better than a thousand sermons on the subject of obedience to the commandments of God."[57]

On other issues, Cox could be progressive. In 1915, while he was an assistant at St. Epiphany Church, Cox urged women be allowed to vote.[58] When city police began cracking down on prostitutes, Cox rose to their defense, criticizing fellow clergymen who were demanding the "scarlet women" be arrested and sent to jail for two months.[59] "The blood of Christ was shed for scarlet women and for their redemption. They must not be won as Mary Magdalene was won, and it cannot be done by raids and prison cells."[60] He asked, "If Pittsburgh is such a cesspool of vice, if the city is loaded with scarlet women, where are the scarlet men who have made the women what they are?" He said if men who patronized prostitutes were arrested for soliciting them, there would be no prostitution.

Pittsburgh streets were crowded in the afternoons and evenings as prostitutes loitered outside movie theaters.[61] They also patronized dance halls and lured dancing partners to a back room for women in the sex trade.

> Girls lured into the scarlet world by the emissaries of Satan never return to their former surroundings because no Christ-like hand is extended to them but instead those who helped to put them where they are league themselves with money and politics and voice their demands that the fallen women be jailed. In the name of God and common decency let us do something to prevent their inroads upon our womanhood.[62]

When actress Lana Turner married her fourth husband, Cox led a boycott of her films, referring to Hollywood as a "Sodom. If the law doesn't take care of it, there will be another earthquake."[63]

Cox railed against chain stores, calling them "un–American" and "community wreckers," while praising local merchants as "community builders." Sometimes his talk was all bluster, such as when he claimed to have enlisted a well-known U.S. Senator from the western part of the country to help him in his campaign against chain stores.[64] He said the senator came from a state "where real he-men live, real men who wear ten-gallon hats and if necessary will carry a gun to keep things right" and "tell the effete East what they ought to do in the way of curbing monopolies."[65]

6

Labor Priest

Cox and other Pittsburgh priests used the papal encyclicals to teach their blue-collar parishioners the need to organize. Cox, along with the Rev. Carl Hensler and the Rev. Charles Owen Rice, was in the forefront of the effort to educate workers. Cox and John Brophy, a key figure in the United Mine Workers and later the Congress of Industrial Organizations, introduced Catholic workers to the Bishops Program of Social Reconstruction and the papal encyclical, *Rerum Novarum*, "Conditions of Labor." They also established a workers' school.

Cox earned a reputation as Pittsburgh's foremost "labor priest" for his support of coal miners and cab drivers during violent strikes, but relinquished the title for failing to support the Steel Workers Organizing Committee in 1937 and employees of Heinz Foods when they went on strike the same year. "I am, always will be a union man, one who believes in unionism,"[1] said Cox. That was a lie. His support for the labor movement was lukewarm despite his belief in papal encyclicals urging more rights and better working conditions for workers.

There were other priests more devoted to the rights of workers than Cox. Charles Owen Rice, Adalbert Kazincy, Casimir Orelmanski, Carl Hensler and Barry O'Toole wholeheartedly supported union organizing efforts, and some even joined striking workers on picket lines. Cox backed Pittsburgh firemen when they wanted shorter working days and cab drivers who staged a year-long strike in 1930. In both instances, Cox was outspoken in his support, using his radio program and newspaper interviews to press union demands.[2] "In a democracy, human rights comes before property rights," he said.[3]

Taxi cab drivers voted to strike against the Yellow and Green cab companies in January 1930, beginning a violent labor dispute that lasted four months. Cox became their advocate. *Time Magazine* reported that "like wolves, small packs of strikers ran about the streets of the East Liberty business district, threw bricks, stones, milk bottles at every passing cab." Cox acted as a mediator since he had worked as a dispatcher for a cab company during the summers while he was a student at Holy Ghost College.[4]After the strike began, drivers tied up downtown Pittsburgh traffic for 12 hours, forcing police to arrest them on various charges ranging from illegal parking to obstructing traffic.[5]

City streets became battlefields. A mob of angry drivers pulled a scab driver from a vehicle and began beating him. Police fired tear gas into the midst of the strikers and rescued the man.[6] A passenger in another vehicle was blinded when a brick was thrown through the windshield. Police officers riding motorcycles rode up and down the sidewalks to keep other drivers at bay.[7] Riders getting off streetcars joined in the battle.[8] Police and deputy sheriffs guarded cabs driven by scabs. Mobs surrounded cabs, preventing the passengers from fleeing. Drivers and guards were beaten. The companies hired strikebreakers to break the union.[9] A female passenger hailed a cab driven by a scab at the Pennsylvania Railroad Station. When she reached her destination, she fled the cab as 100 men surrounded the vehicle and beat the driver and a deputy sheriff assigned to guard him.[10]

The American Federation of Labor tried to convince the cabbies to negotiate, but they wouldn't budge, despite the company's offer of a 37.5 percent commission on fares. The drivers initially agreed to the proposal before reversing themselves and increasing their demand to 40 percent.

Privately, Cox urged the drivers to stick to their demands while publicly saying he would back them whatever decision they made.[11] "Boys, I'm with you to the finish. Every labor organization in the city is with you and you are bound to win. If you even think of going back to work before this fight is over it will be the biggest mistake ever made by organized labor" he said.[12]

Cab company owners asked Mayor Charles Kline to intervene, so Kline, accompanied by Father Cox, held a secret meeting at the Moose Temple with a federal mediator. When three constables tried to enter the closed-door session with arrest warrants for several drivers, more than 50 angry drivers chased the constables down the street.[13]

Cox allowed the strikers to use the basement of his church as their strike headquarters. One night, as Cox was discussing strategy with the drivers, three bombs exploded in quick succession, filling the room with thick blue smoke.[14] John Stackhouse, secretary of Union Local 433, said, "The drivers had to get out as quickly as they could. Some chairs were broken in the rush and disorder in the streets followed."[15] Men spilled out of the church in panic just as a cab passed by. The cab was driven by a non-union driver, so striking drivers stoned the cab, causing the driver to lose control and crash into a utility pole.[16]

E.S. Higgins, vice-president of one of the cab companies, was invited to attend a meeting at St. Patrick's under the guise of discussing a settlement, but the meeting as an ambush, with Cox subjecting Higgins to a barrage of insults. Higgins was forced to hold his temper as Cox lambasted him for his treatment of the cabbies. "You should have heard what he listened to," one observer said. "It was like a prize fighter in the ring taking punishment and not hitting back."[17]

At another meeting held at a Methodist church, Cox continued his verbal attack. "There is too much talk of the company, too much talk of the upper crust and not enough talk of the underdog," he said. "We should not interest ourselves solely in the wealthy and believe they are always right just because they sign the checks."[18]

Cox accused cab company officials of deliberately setting fire to their own vehicles so they could blame the damage on the cabbies to turn public opinion against the drivers. "How could strikers or strike sympathizers steal taxicabs out from under the noses of their drivers and guards and police, run them over a hillside and set fire to them? It's absurd," said Cox.[19] "We challenged him to prove this statement," said a company official. "Untruths, misstatements and exaggerations are doing more to delay the settlement of the cab strike than anything else."[20]

After the speech before the Methodist assembly, the company was outraged and accused Cox of lies and exaggerations that only served to prolong the dispute. "Rumors always may be expected in such a situation but it certainly is not to be expected that the ministry would continue the prolongation of controversy and violence by reckless, unfounded utterances," said a cab company executive.

Cox was challenged to prove that officials of the cab company set their own vehicles ablaze. The executive said Cox was offered the "true facts" about the pay dispute, but Cox "has insistently made public his prejudicial opinions without taking the trouble to learn whether or not they are supported by the facts."[21]

The feud between Cox and company management became personal. Cab company officials blamed Cox for prolonging the dispute with his pro-union rhetoric. They accused the priest of spreading rumors via his radio program. The Federal Radio Commission, acting on complaints, ordered Cox to stop the broadcasts. WJAS took Cox off the air, which led him to accuse the cab companies of being behind the decision. A company official responded: "If the priest means to imply that the company was responsible for the Federal Radio Commission refusing him use of the radio station WJAS because of his talks on the strike, he is wrong for we have no knowledge of who instigated the complaint, or made objection. The news came as a surprise to us. We cannot be held responsible if a government agency sees fit to regulate broadcasting according to its own judgment."[22]

The strike finally ended in May, and Cox rode in the first cab through downtown streets followed by a caravan of taxis honking their horns. The company agreed to recognize the union as the drivers' bargaining agent, and to increase commissions to 37.5 percent, but continued to have an open shop. Cox said his former job as a cab dispatcher gave him an insight into the business. "I was a strict boss," he said, "but I insisted that the men be treated square, as human beings. That's why the taxi drivers asked me to represent them during the 1930 strike. I knew a lot of them, and knew about the taxi business. A lot of people wondered why I butted into something I was ignorant of. That answers them."[23]

Cox began to distance himself from the labor movement in the late 1930s when the Steel Workers Organizing Committee began organizing workers in the major steel companies, triggering a series of strikes. He antagonized labor organizers, calling them "labor racketeers who were bringing us closer to the brink of revolution and civil war."[24] He labeled their behavior as "unjust and repugnant."[25] He went on radio to denounce union officials and fellow priests Orlemanski (who had marched to Washington with him), Rice, Hensler and O'Toole. Rice, Hensler and O'Toole had formed the Catholic Radical Alliance and the Association of Catholic Trade Unionists, which were active role in educating workers on the papal encyclicals that Cox once had embraced. In a radio sermon, he lashed out at labor's leaders:

> What do labor leaders to with the money they collect? Whoever obtained an accounting from the American Federation of Labor or from the Congress of Industrial Organizations of the huge sums they are draining from the labor man?[26] This form of dictatorship has to be stopped. Organized labor represents only fifteen percent of the citizens of the country. The great middle class that represents more than 80 percent has not yet spoken. But they will speak definitely and soon.[27] The pendulum of injustice has swung from the five percent of the unjust old privileged class who ruled before the Depression, to the fifteen percent represented in the 1937 mushroom labor ranks of today. Labor racketeerism in America today is mobocracy led by fanatics directed and controlled by aliens.[28]

He singled out John L. Lewis, the president of the United Mine Workers of America and a founder of the Congress of Industrial Organizations, telling his radio listeners, "I think the solution lies in curbing the influence of labor unions."[29]

Father Rice, Cox's former protégé, used his radio program to respond to his former mentor. "What if labor does get the upper hand? I would welcome that day. I am tired of having my country mismanaged by the captains of industry," Rice said. "I pray to God that it is a story that will end soon, and I regret the day that a religious representative has seen fit to add to the flood of hatred and misrepresentation."[30]

Rice continued his attack on Cox in the diocesan newspaper, *The Pittsburgh Catholic:* "If snobbery and propaganda succeed in keeping the white-collar people hostile or suspicious of labor in this country, the result will be class war. Labor wants to cooperate with management and wants to join forces with the middle class. If the advances of labor are repulsed, then will be the twin dangers of Communism and Fascism be realities."[31]

Anita Brophy, the wife of John Brophy, an organizer for the United Mine Workers of America and later an official with the AFL-CIO, repudiated Cox for claiming to be a "friend of labor" when he was labor's foe:

> It is just such speeches as yours on Sunday that lead many people to think the church is on the side of the capitalist and against the workers. Even though we have the encyclicals tell us that labor has the right to organize, far too large a number of the clergy pay lip service to those great documents and say in effect, "don't organize," or at least advise labor not to do anything with an organization. If the position you took on Sunday were to be taken generally by the Catholic clergy in America for any great length of time, the mass of workers will surely be alienated ... for social justice too long deferred breeds revolution.[32]

In 1932, Cox became embroiled in a dispute with William Green, president of the American Federation of Labor. Cox took umbrage when Green refused to appear on the same speaker's platform as Cox during a labor-sponsored event. Green charged Cox was using the movement to further his political ambitions. "Our mass meeting must be free from politics," Green said.[33] Cox countered by accusing Green of being a "tool of Wall Street.[34] "My quarrel is not with labor—I have always been a friend of workers—but with William Green as an individual. He knows I want to support labor and he is trying to prevent labor from supporting me. Just now the drawing card at any rally is Father Cox. This may not always be true but while it is true, I do not see why I should share the limelight with him."[35]

Labor officials tried to reconcile the two men. Pat Fagan, president of the Central Pittsburgh Labor Council, defended Green, saying he wanted to end the feud. "There is no reason why a union member should not join Father Cox's party if one is formed," Fagan said. "Any union member is free to support Father Cox, a third party or any purely political party he wishes to support."[36]

Cox claimed not to have any political aspiration, saying, "I'm not seeking political office. If a third party is formed and I am asked to lead it, I will but I don't want to. I am happy here, helping people and fighting the battle for the jobless. The only title I want is 'Shepherd of the Jobless,' which has been given to me by the people I have helped."[37] At the same time Cox denied his political ambitions, he formed the Jobless Party to use as a base to launch his bid for president.[38] "The Blue Shirt—the shirt of the worker—will be our only symbol," he said.[39]

Father Rice replaced Cox as the city's "labor priest." As Cox saw Rice steal the limelight, he chafed at having to share the mantle of "labor priest" with his former protégé. Rice was a backer of the CIO, which Cox believed was under Communist influence. Rice admired Cox, who was ordained 23 years before him, and served as a pallbearer at the funeral of Cox's mother in 1932.

Cox and Rice were newsmakers. Both came from Irish backgrounds and from families headed by Protestant fathers. Each man suffered from vision problems as children. Both priests attended St. Mary's School, Duquesne University and St. Vincent Seminary. Both were staunch anti–Communists and opponents of capitalism.[40] "We are opposed to capitalism just as we are opposed to the concentration of Russian Bolshevism," Rice said.[41]

Both were committed to feeding the hungry. Cox opened a soup kitchen at St. Patrick's, distributing more than two million meals. Rice fed 600 meals each day to the homeless at St. Joseph's House of Hospitality, which he founded. Both priests used radio to preach and teach. Rice was critical of fellow Catholics "who act, not like followers of Christ but like followers of the devil in their dealings with, and attitude toward, the problem of social justice, toward the workers and the poor."

They are children not of the Church but of the unjust economic and social system that has warped their minds and their conduct. There are many other Catholics who impede the advance of the truth by their blundering. They rant and rave against the menace of Communism, against its Godlessness, with never a word about the menace and Godlessness of finance capitalism. They let hatred of Communism, which is proper, blind them into breaking Christ's law against hatred of persons. The Communists are ... much like the finance capitalists. Neither can see beyond his nose. They both rule out God—the finance capitalist when he says business is business, I'm not running a charitable concern, what do I care if they are not getting enough wages, let them go elsewhere if they don't like it. The best system in the world will

Father Cox blesses the body of his mother during her funeral, shortly after the 1932 march to Washington. When Julia Mason Cox died, four Masses were celebrated simultaneously outside and within the church (Dr. and Mrs. Mason, Father James Renshaw Cox Collection, Saint Patrick–Saint Stanislaus Kostka Parish, Pittsburgh, Pennsylvania).

go on the rocks if individualism and materialism are the ruling ideas. Individualism is, simply, the doctrine of every man for himself. Materialism is the doctrine that we are just animals; that there is no other life but this one, no other values but those we find on earth. These ideas have been in the saddle in modern life and they are what have made such a mess out of civilization. They rule the present system; they rule business today, and they will rule in the Communist or fascist super-state, and don't fool yourself.[42]

Rice's support of workers in the 1937 strike against H.J. Heinz Co. severed once and for all the relationship between Rice and Cox. More than 2,000 Heinz workers wanted to form a union affiliated with the American Federation of Labor, while the company pressed workers to join a company-run union. The stage was set for a showdown between the Canning & Pickling Workers union and the Heinz Employees Association.

Cox owed a debt to Henry Heinz, who had stocked Cox's soup kitchen during the early years of the Depression. After Cox witnessed his fellow priests join workers on the picket line, he grew incensed and denounced Rice, Hensler and O'Toole over the radio. "I simply went over and joined the picketers," Rice recalled. "We were denounced from the pulpits and in the papers, by a few of the clergy.[43] [Cox] was frankly grateful [toward Heinz]. We were denounced by him. He said there were Communists involved in organizing Heinz. Indeed, there were."[44]

Critics of Cox and Rice charged that they weakened the political clout of workers by forcing out communist-trained organizers from the labor movement at a time when they were most needed.[45] Out of the 200 organizers hired by the Steel Workers Organizing Committee, 60 were communists. Communists also held 40 percent of the leadership posts in CIO-affiliated unions.[46] Rabid anti-communist rhetoric was a way Catholics could prove their loyalty to the church and the United States.[47]

7

"God Help Us All"

Mellon pulled the whistle/Hoover rang the bell/Wall Street gave the signal/And the country went to Hell.—Democratic Party campaign ditty

Herbert Hoover became the 31st president of the United States on March 4, 1929, as heavy rain pelted more than 100,000 people standing on the east portico of the Capitol and along the inaugural parade route.[1] The crowd was so tightly packed together to hear this orphaned son of Quakers announce that the nation's future "was bright with hope" that it was impossible for anyone in the crowd to seek shelter from the stinging raindrops.[2]

Rain splattered Hoover's face as he spoke while delivering the first inaugural address to be recorded by newsreel cameras.[3] Hoover wore a mourning coat, striped pants and a black topcoat. He walked to the podium holding a family Bible turned to Proverbs 29:18: "Where there is no vision, the people perish; but he that keepeth the law, happy is he."

Hoover was soaked by the time he finished reading the 3,801-word speech, in which he never once mentioned the economy. Instead, he focused on the National Prohibition Act, commonly known as the Volstead Act, which banned liquor sales in the United States. Hoover proclaimed disobedience to that law was the biggest danger facing the country. Pittsburgh newspapers lauded Hoover's address.

Editorial writers were as oblivious as Hoover to the impending danger lurking on Wall Street.[4] Papers noted the country enjoyed "unprecedented prosperity" and faced a future "with firm assurances" as to the fundamental soundness of business and industry.[5] "His business experience alone will be of inestimable help in the solution of the many problems that await his consideration," wrote one writer.[6]

Hoover had pledged during his campaign to keep the industrial juggernaut running that was driving the nation's economy. People had no reason to disbelieve him. The nation was producing automobiles, refrigerators, toasters and other consumer products. Wages were increasing. The unemployment rate was a mere three percent. The stock market was booming because of investor confidence in Hoover. On September 3, 1929, the Dow Jones hit a record high of 381 points. Hoover retained Andrew Mellon from the Coolidge administration as treasury secretary. Mellon reported a budget surplus of $185 million and the national debt under $17 billion.[7]

Businessmen also saw no reason for concern. The Retail Grocers Association of Pittsburgh displayed tons of food at the Motor Square Gardens in 1929, including a full-size cow sculpted out of butter. Sugar, soft drinks, sausages and bacon also were on display.[8] Thousands of people flooded the Pittsburgh Auto Show to view the newest automobiles.[9]

Economists pointed out that people's vices and leisure activities had not diminished because Americans still were smoking, drinking soda, eating candy, playing golf and tennis, and watching baseball games. They continued to attend movies as much as they did in the fall of 1927.[10] Businessmen and bankers pointed to another hopeful sign. The skies above Pittsburgh were dark with soot from steel mills, which meant that the mines and mills were operating at full capacity. Actress Jean Harlow stopped in Pittsburgh on her way to California in December 1931 and complained to a reporter that her platinum blonde hair was turning gray because of the ash.[11]

There were ominous signs on the economic horizon. Two years before the stock market crash, Wall Street was breaking trading records with 567,990,875 shares traded. That record was soon broken with 920,550,032 shares traded. The problem facing investors, however, was that their trades were only earning one to two percent interest, while the cost of loans to borrow the money to buy stocks ran between eight and 12 percent.[12]

By early 1929, investors were growing uneasy because of unchecked speculation. Stock prices began to fall. The Smoot-Hawley tariff, which was enacted the following year, hurt American exports by raising tariffs on imports.[13] Treasury Secretary Mellon's advice to Hoover was to "purge the rottenness from the economy" so shaky businesses would flounder while the stable ones would survive and allow wages to fall to natural levels, but Hoover wanted wages to remain high.[14] The unemployment rate began to slowly creep up to five percent by October. Between the end of 1928 and 1930, the amount of money in circulation decreased by four percent, triggering inflation.[15]

Pittsburgh was awash in bright light on October 23, 1929, as hundreds of thousands of people turned out for a celebration in honor of Thomas Edison. Floodlights bathed Pittsburgh in brightness, creating a "gala mood" in the city, but darkness was about to envelop the region.[16] The stock market plunged the next day in a wave of frantic selling that left Wall Street a "battered hulk" in what became known as "Black Thursday."[17] More than 13 million shares of stock were traded. Five days later on "Black Tuesday," The Dow plummeted from 261 to 230. Banks called in loans. In one day, $30 billion in stock value disappeared. "The crash was an honest acknowledgment of the breakdown of capitalism—and the cause of the Depression," wrote Amity Shlaes.[18]

The market calmed itself the next day, but the relief was short-lived. Panic continued to spread throughout Wall Street as trading became a matter of survival of the fittest.[19] On October 29, the market plunged again, with sales setting an all-time record. "The bubble has been broken. Millionaires were sent home paupers," wrote a business writer.[20] The market began a roller coaster ride into 1930. Stock prices rose and fell, and traders made huge profits one day and lost it all the next.[21]

Mellon called the collapse of the market "a bad quarter of an hour"[22] and saw no reason for panic. He predicted prosperity would continue into 1930. "I see nothing in the situation that is either menacing or warrants pessimism. I have every confidence that there will be a revival of activity in the spring, and that during the coming year, 1930 the country will make steady progress," he said while vacationing in the Bahamas.[23]

Hoover, who, as Secretary of Commerce, had saved nine million people from starvation in Europe after World War I, and had mobilized efforts to help people rebuild after massive flooding along the Mississippi River in 1927, stared the Great Depression straight in the face without recognizing the economic disaster that was about to befall the United States.

In Pittsburgh, Father Cox saw paychecks suddenly stop. People still working saw their hours and wages reduced. Children were hungry and suffering from malnutrition. Families disintegrated, divorces increased, and marriages and births declined. By 1930, lines of homeless, hungry men began appearing daily at St. Patrick's rectory.

"If you turn one [person] away, Mary, I'll strangle you," Cox jokingly told his housekeeper.[24] A friend, Albert "Buck" Crouse, a washed-up boxer, had a suggestion. "We'll have to start a soup kitchen, Father."[25] "But there isn't any money," Cox replied.[26] "The Lord will provide. He always has," Crouse said.[27] Crouse and Cox had been close friends since Cox's day managing the Pittsburgh Lyceum.

As a boxer, Crouse was a powerful puncher who once broke an opponent's ribs on one side with a one-two combination. He floored 40 opponents and was so sturdy that he fought three matches in three days. Crouse had been a rising star in the national boxing arena by the time he was 21. He fought matches as far away as Australia and Panama, where he was sentenced to 30 days on a chain gang for slugging a police officer.

By early 1932, Cox was feeding 3,500 people a day.[28] Soup lines at his church sometimes ran from the Strip District all the way across the Sixteenth Street Bridge over the Allegheny River into the city's North Side. Critics charged Cox was turning Pittsburgh into a "mecca for bums," but he simply ignored the criticism.[29] By April, Cox was feeding 100,000 people a month and distributing 1,000 food baskets each day.[30] On Christmas Day 1930, Cox chose a dozen homeless men, bought them suits, gave them shaves and haircuts, and treated them to a lavish Christmas dinner at the rectory.[31]

Cox was frustrated by the federal government's lack of intervention to halt the financial slide and the suffering it caused. The Depression was reaching crisis proportions in Pittsburgh and Allegheny County by early 1930. By February 1931, 5,000 were on relief. A year later, the numbers increased to 45,000 and kept climbing.[32] Pennsylvania was hard pressed to raise the money it needed to provide milk for 600,000 children who were undernourished.[33] Hunger was so severe that rural counties surrounding Pittsburgh exchanged surplus fruits and vegetables for canned goods provided by relief officials. In Washington County, just south of Pittsburgh, hundreds were starving. Farmers slaughtered sheep and divided the meat among hungry families of coal miners who were out of work because of the lack of demand for coal.[34]

Western Pennsylvania's winters added to the suffering. The first winter of the Depression was brutal. Temperatures fell into the low 20s and bitter winds made it seem colder. Relief agencies begged the public for winter clothes. A man burned to death on a pile of hot coals while sleeping near a fire to keep warm.[35] A man was found frozen to death in a shack along the Ohio River after his coal fire extinguished. Police found an unconscious woman with her arms and legs frozen stiff. She later died.[36]

In the winter of 1930–1931, Treasury Secretary Mellon and other Pittsburgh business executives created the "Pittsburgh Plan" to provide relief. Each corporation donated an amount equal to a day's payroll, generating $2 million to create jobs by funding public works projects.[37] The Depression struck the city hard by the second winter, and corporations reneged on their pledges of support by no longer funding the plan. The wealthy seemed apathetic to the needs of the poor who were surviving on a meager $12 a week in aid. "It became evident that either Pittsburgh's rich would have to support Pittsburgh's poor directly or as in all the past, the poor would have to share each other's misfortunes," wrote Harvey O'Connor, a journalist and activist, in *Mellon's Millions, the Biography of a Fortune: The Life and Times of Andrew W. Mellon.*[38]

The Helping Hand Association provided one million meals for the hungry during the Great Depression, but another 160,000 people faced starvation. Pittsburgh and Allegheny County relief agencies, unable to meet the demand for aid, were running out of funds. More than 12,000 children in the city's elementary and high schools were underweight.[39]

The directors of the Allegheny County Welfare Fund, in conjunction with the editors of Pittsburgh's three newspapers, the *Pittsburgh Press*, *Pittsburgh Post-Gazette* and *Pittsburgh Sun-Telegraph*, produced fictitious newspaper headlines reading, "What If You Should Read This Tomorrow" and sent to them Pittsburgh's wealthy industrialists. The scare tactic failed to move them and the fundraising effort floundered.

Pittsburgh clergymen blamed capitalism for the demise of the economy and urged voters to defeat any politician who failed to provide relief.[40] Cox warned of looming disaster in a telegram to Hoover. "We are facing the worst winter in the history of the world. This is a nation of big business and big farming. When either one breaks down, we are lost," read the telegram.[41]

The Catholic Church filled the void created by the inability of the state and federal governments to respond to the crisis. Bishop Hugh C. Boyle of the Catholic Diocese of Pittsburgh supported Cox and other priests in their efforts. Boyle had grown up around the steel industry in Johnstown in Cambria County and had been a parish priest in Homestead where Carnegie Steel was based, so he knew the plight of workers, many of whom where his former parishioners.[42] Boyle warned Pittsburgh's business and industrial elite that allowing people to starve endangered the whole of society. "The men in industry who have accumulated fortunes now owe an obligation to society which they should fulfill. I wonder if anyone thinks these men are going to stand by and see their wives and children starve. The Pennsylvania Board may run out of funds this fall and may be unable to immediately get more. If this happens, the federal government will have to put the money or, well, God help us all."[43]

Boyle helped write a paper issued by the American bishops, "On the Present Crisis," which condemned the economic domination of one class over another. It decried the concentration of wealth in the hands of a few and the power that wealth gave them. "The desire of money is the root of all evil. This power becomes particularly irresistible when exercised by those who, because they hold and control money, are able also to govern credit and determine its allotment, and for that reason supply, so to speak, the lifeblood of an entire economic body and grasping, as it were, in their hands the very soul of production, so that no one dare breathe against their will."[44]

The Catholic Church took the lead to prevent starvation. Father Ercole Dominicis was pastor of a suburban Pittsburgh church that operated a soup kitchen. As the Depression worsened, he fed more than 4,000 in a week and 75,000 in two months.[45] Catholic Charities of Pittsburgh cared for 7,000 families in 1932 and distributed $35,000 worth of shoes.[46] The Diocese of Pittsburgh mobilized more than 400 churches to help raise $6 million needed to fund welfare programs and held drives to provide clothing for the poor.[47] More bread lines began appearing around Pittsburgh as volunteers ladled hot soup and handed out bread to hungry people.[48] The volunteers who operated the soup kitchens were running out of money and couldn't afford to buy the ingredients to make soup.[49]

Parish priests, like Cox, "represent the last bulwark against riot and disorder among the unemployed," wrote journalist Lorena Hickok during a trip to Pittsburgh.[50] Hickok worked for FDR aide Harry Hopkins, traveling the nation and assessing the depth of the Great Depression. Hopkins began his career as a social worker but was tapped by Roosevelt to head New Deal programs that included the Federal Emergency Relief Association, the Civil Works Administration and the Works Progress Administration.

Hopkins became the "chief apostle of the New Deal."[51] Hickok visited Pittsburgh and the surrounding towns in southwestern Pennsylvania where the coal and steel industries suffered the most. Hickok felt, as Cox did, the worsening Depression would make the Communist Party more attractive to the jobless. "I still feel, as I felt a week ago, that vast numbers of the unemployed are right on the edge, so to speak—that it wouldn't take much to make Communists out of them."[52]

Parents were desperate and resorted to violence because they could not feed their families. In southwestern Pennsylvania, mobs of unemployed in one community laid siege to a relief office. Several dozen mothers cornered a local relief official and began choking him while demanding food for their starving children. Cox believed Hoover and Mellon's economic policy was undermining the very fabric of the nation. He was critical of the wealthy. "There should be no rich privileged class," Cox said.

"There are starving thousands who need the money the millionaires spend each year to go to the Riviera for a fling...."[53] He continued, "America is not for the few, of the few or by the few."[54]

Cox believed the only way he could persuade the president to provide aid was to march to the capital and tell Hoover himself. "These men and women, having exhausted their meager resources, with strength wasted, their bodies ravished by slow starvation, their spirits broken by despair, now lack shelter, are exposed to the cold, the rain and the snow and stand hungry in breadlines—mute symbols of an economic system out of joint."

People desperately wanted to believe that the economy would improve. The *Pittsburgh Post-Gazette* published eight stories in a single edition predicting better times in 1931.[55] When U.S. Secretary of Labor James Davis spoke at a Labor Day event outside Pittsburgh a month before the market crash, he predicted more leisure time for workers. Davis never realized how right he was until people began losing their jobs. "We do have a little unemployment in America. Even in the best of times there is unemployment. But there is one thing about America and Americans, it is our habit to go out to the root of things. Right now, we are launched on a movement by which the federal government and states are planning the stabilization of employment."[56]

An editorial writer commenting on Davis's speech wrote that "it was a most refreshing address after some of the doleful pictures that have been drawn of the future."[57] Little did they realize that the worst was yet to come.

8

The Mayor of Shantytown

"Come to me all of you that labor and are heavy laden, and I will refresh you."—Matthew 11:28

April Fools' Day 1931 was no laughing matter for Pittsburgh residents. A spring storm played a joke on western Pennsylvania, dumping six inches of heavy, wet snow on the city, surprising shoppers whose thoughts were on Easter. Victor Wavinski had been walking the streets in the city's Hill District neighborhood that day, scrounging food in garbage cans until he staggered and collapsed in an alley. Two police officers approached an unconscious Wavinski, thinking he was drunk. An ambulance arrived and took him to the hospital, where he was pronounced dead of starvation and exposure.[1]

A few blocks away in a boarding house where he had lived, detectives found an unopened government check for $457. Wavinski was unaware the check had arrived. He had been walking the streets trying to borrow money from friends so he could buy something to eat.[2] Wavinski was a naturalized citizen born in Mazowieckie, Poland, who served in the U.S. Army during World War I. His body lay unclaimed in the county morgue awaiting burial when a friend, Joseph Lagoon, identified him.[3] Wavinski and Lagoon had served together in the Army. His death attracted little attention because newspapers were reporting on the thousands of people who were paying their respects to famed Notre Dame Football coach Knute Rockne, who was killed March 31 in a plane crash in Kansas.[4]

In Pittsburgh, it was the worst of times. The Depression had a death grip on Pittsburgh commerce. Layoffs filled the streets with unemployed men. By 1932, 80,000 Pittsburgh residents were out of work. People were being evicted from their homes and apartments. Labor groups and the

Communist Party were marching on city hall and at the state capital in Harrisburg, demanding action from lawmakers.

Makeshift shantytowns began appearing on the city's urban landscape. "Monument Hills" and "Chicken Hill" on the city's North Side were unsanitary and unruly encampments that would be eventually set ablaze by authorities. Homeless men also built a campsite beneath the B & O Railroad Station, washing their clothes in the hot water that came from a waste pipe beneath a bridge.[5] City officials were reluctant to demolish the shanties, knowing their occupants had no place else to live.[6]

In the Strip District, Cox allowed the homeless to erect a shantytown on a vacant lot next to the church.[7] The men elected Cox "mayor of shantytown" and jokingly referred to the camp as "St. Patricksville."[8] Homeless men preferred its rugged living conditions, and Cox's simple hospitality, to the overcrowded conditions at the few city-run shelters.

The shantytown consisted built 89 tightly-packed shacks the length of a city block. The 240 occupants built the hovels from discarded lumber,

Cox allowed homeless men to build a block-long shantytown next to St. Patrick's Church. The men scavenged scrap lumber from a nearby railroad yard to build the shanties, 1932 (James R. Cox Papers, 1923–1950, AIS.1969.05, Archives & Special Collections, University of Pittsburgh Library System).

tar paper and burlap they scavenged from a nearby railroad yard. The men used broken glass as mirrors to shave and tin cans as cooking pots and to heat lukewarm coffee as they sat around small fires to keep warm in the winter. Cox issued his own scrip as currency. The paper, which had Cox's picture on it, could be redeemed at the church for food and clothing.[9] The City of Pittsburgh piped water to the site and built a bathhouse for the men. At night, the shantytown was illuminated by candles, lanterns and bonfires.[10] Cox was proud of the way the men maintained their dignity in the face of poverty:

> These men in shantytowns aren't bums because bums don't build cities. The houses these men live in are the result of their own labors. The shanties are home in truth to these fellows. The Depression hasn't caused a single one of them to lose hope for his country, its flag and its institutions. Remember, there is always a silver lining behind the darkest cloud and it will not be long until that silver lining will show. In this colony there will be but one religion and that will be the law and order. Vacant hours are the devil's hours and we are going to keep you busy at some useful and gainful occupation.[11]

The men loved Cox. "He doesn't give us much but what we get is clean and good," said one resident.[12] "I'll take care of you fellows," Cox promised. "My idea is to keep these men from losing heart. I want them to keep their heads up though their luck may be down. And I want them in shape to fight life's battles so that their bad times now won't shatter their hearts and embitter their souls."[13] Cox also placed 300 cots in the basement of the church so other homeless could bunk there.[14]

City officials called these encampments "human pig-sties" because they lacked proper sanitation.[15] Squatters took refuge in abandoned homes when their owners defaulted on their mortgages. A minister on the city's south side, who operated a soup kitchen, was accused of turning the city into a "mecca for bums." To cut down on panhandling, police chased beggars off city streets and out of city parks.[16]

Cox saw troubling economic signs looming on Pittsburgh's horizon as early as 1928. On New Year's Day, Cox fed a turkey dinner, complete with ice cream, fruit and candy, to 1,000 needy children seated at long tables in the basement of St. Patrick's Church. The children cheered and applauded Cox as he walked down the aisles.[17]

The stock market crash in 1929 hadn't shattered the faith of Pittsburgh's business leaders in the economy even though there were warning signs as early as 1927 that money was in short supply. Sales of new cars dropped and fewer homes were being built. Industrial wages were declining and unemployment slowly began to increase from 3.3 percent in 1927 to 4.2 percent the following year.[18]

Homeless men enjoy a meal at St. Patrick's. Cox never turned anyone away, serving more than 2.2 million meals during the worst years of the Great Depression and saving hundreds of thousands from starvation, ca. 1930 (James R. Cox Papers, 1923–1950, AIS.1969.05, Archives & Special Collections, University of Pittsburgh Library System).

The nation's leading businessmen advised Herbert Hoover that the economy was "so far normal"[19] and they saw no need for measures to stimulate it. Steel makers reported orders for their product "were beyond expectations"[20] and praised Hoover for his efforts to stabilize the economy. Economists predicted 1930 would be a boom year for industrial production and reported the market crash did no serious damage to the county's economic system. The country still was producing goods and millionaires.[21]

Father Cox sent a truck loaded with meat and vegetables to feed 250 hoboes in December 1930. The men were living in an encampment in the Banksville section of Pittsburgh, surviving on food from a nearby garbage dump.[22] Dozens of homeless men lived in cardboard shacks along the banks of the Allegheny River. Others dug holes into the hillside and were

Children of needy families living in the Strip District enjoy a turkey dinner, compliments of Father Cox, ca. 1930 (James R. Cox Papers, 1923–1950, AIS. 1969.05, Archives & Special Collections, University of Pittsburgh Library System).

known as "cavemen." Some men kept a five-dollar bill stuffed in their shoes to avoid being arrested for vagrancy.[23]

The ever-growing lines of hungry men caused other soup kitchens to open throughout Pittsburgh. At one kitchen, men lined up for a hunk of bread and a bowl of soup made from cabbage, lettuce, vegetables and fish. Every few minutes a man would emerge from the kitchen and shout: "Come on, men, and get another piece of bread. There is plenty for all."[24]

Officials at social service agencies in Pittsburgh and Allegheny County resented the emergence of food lines. "Pittsburgh does not need a bread line. It has not needed bread lines and will not need one. Pittsburgh can meet the problem of the homeless man more constructively," said Frank Phillips, chairman of the Hoover Relief Committee in Pittsburgh.[25] Phillips told Hoover that Allegheny County could care for its own without help from the federal government at the same time county officials were desperately trying to raise $500,000 for the county welfare fund. Cox sent

A truckload of bread is delivered to St. Patrick's Church during the Great Depression, ca. 1930 (James R. Cox Papers, 1923–1950, AIS.1969.05, Archives & Special Collections, University of Pittsburgh Library System).

Hoover a telegram criticizing Phillips and warning that the welfare agencies in Pittsburgh "are overrun with demands" for help.[26] "Phillips probably doesn't know there is a Depression, that more than 150,000 need jobs here," Cox said.[27]

Pittsburgh's business and industrial leaders said the year was going to be a year of "readjustment" and expressed continued confidence in the economy even as industrial wages began to fall by 23 percent.[28] U.S. Steel reduced its workers' wages by 60 percent and Westinghouse, the region's largest electrical manufacturer, slashed pay by 32 percent.[29]

Relief in Pennsylvania was overseen by county Poor Boards. Officials distributed vouchers for food, rent, clothing or coal. The directors of these agencies often were hostile toward the needy and blamed the unemployed for their own predicament. No one expected the Depression to last as long as it did, so there was no long-range planning to counter its effects.[30]

Pennsylvania Gov. Gifford Pinchot, a Republican at odds with his own party, called for a special session of the General Assembly in Harris-

Men line up for a meal at St. Patrick's, ca. 1930 (James R. Cox Papers, 1923–1950, AIS.1969.05, Archives & Special Collections, University of Pittsburgh Library System).

burg to enact legislation to allow the state to borrow money for relief efforts and to tax cigarettes and gasoline.[31] Republican leaders in the legislature rejected his request, saying the Depression would not be long and relief efforts could be handled locally.[32] A Republican congressman from western Pennsylvania called on President Hoover to call a special session of Congress to address the problem of unemployment, but Hoover refused, saying current measures were adequate.[33] "A special session of Congress should have been called three months ago," said U.S. Rep. Samuel A. Kendall of Meyersdale, Pennsylvania. "If it had I think there would have been a different story to tell."[34]

Coal and steel, the region's lifeblood, was bleeding to death. Miners were working for starvation wages because of a decline in the demand for coal by utility companies and mills. The steel industry began cutting production, putting thousands of men out of work.[35] Miners were working between 142 and 220 days a year and their annual income was not enough to care for their families.[36] By 1933, the average hourly wage for miners dropped to less than $2.50 a day.[37]

Starving miners staged a demonstration on the city's north side, trickling in from coal patches throughout Allegheny County. More than 7,500 miners and their families marched in 92-degree heat in a mile-long parade to protest the low wages they were existing on.[38]

Catholics and Protestants prayed for relief. More than 500 members of the Christ Reformed Church of Pittsburgh held a 36-hour prayer marathon, asking for divine help to stem the crisis.[39]

Pope Pius XI urged Catholics worldwide to pray for an end to the suffering. Father Cox scheduled a series of devotions. Services were held at every Catholic Church in the city and throughout the diocese. Cox led prayers for thousands gathered at St. Patrick's as parishioners held lighted candles and appealed to the Blessed Virgin for relief.[40]

Prayer didn't seem to be helping. Louise Williams was the mother of a three-year-old son who tried to sell the boy for $500 because she was too ill from hunger to properly care for him. The woman told police she had only two choices: sell her son to someone who could provide for him, or watch him slowly die of starvation.[41]

Two brothers went digging for coal to help their mother heat their home. As one of the boys was loading coal into a basket, his feet became entrenched in the shifting earth. His brother and a friend tried to dig him out, scraping feverishly with their hands just as the hillside collapsed, burying the youngster alive. Five teenagers were asphyxiated when they were overcome by carbon dioxide while scrounging for coal 1,000 feet below the surface in an abandoned coal mine in the city.[42] In an 18-month period, seven children were killed digging coal from pits on the city's south side.[43]

To stay warm during the winter, men reopened closed coal mines and chiseled out as much "bootleg" coal as they could before winter arrived. There were 500 men working 24 hours a day in shifts at an abandoned mine outside Pittsburgh. Each man was allotted 300 bushels of coal for his family.[44] At another shuttered pit, miners kept three tons of coal if they put in four days of work. The men dug 40 tons, enough to provide heat for 180 families.[45] Some families who couldn't get coal stole it from passing coal trains. Children climbed atop coal cars when a train stopped for water and pitched chunks to waiting family members who scrambled to pick up the precious fuel.[46]

A desperate father stole a loaf of bread to feed his children, then killed himself so that his life insurance policy would provide money for his family. After his death, his wife discovered his policy had lapsed.[47] Mike McLaughlin jumped into the Monongahela River because his children didn't have any shoes.[48] Edmund Davis, 69, the organist at St. Patrick's Church, died in poverty because he gave away everything he owned to the poor.[49] A father abandoned his wife and nine children after he lost his job as a carpenter.[50] A young unemployed father of a six-year-old daughter was shot and killed during a burglary after police found him in a grocery store and he tried to flee with six dollars' worth of food in a burlap bag.[51]

Artist John Kane, who rose from painting houses to be a recognized artist, died in poverty. "I'm tired of painting over canvases I've used before and I'm about out of paint," Kane said. "People can do without painting but they must have money. I want a job."[52] A middle-aged gunman held up a store on the city's north side, demanding bread. "Give me a loaf of bread," said the robber. "Now give me another one."[53]

People who were being evicted had their furniture sold for defaulting on their rent. Their utilities were shut off. When three siblings from a Catholic school went home for lunch, they found their house locked, the furniture missing and their parents gone. A landlord had them evicted for failing to pay the rent and sold the furniture.[54]

As business declined, so did charitable contributions, leaving the poor, homeless and hungry without a safety net. In the coal regions of southwestern Pennsylvania, children were starving. They ate dandelions and mustard sprigs. Miners spread lard over two pieces of bread and made "water sandwiches."[55] Families took turns eating. When a nun at one school asked a child if she was ill, the child replied, "No, Sister, it was not my turn to eat."[56]

Residents of Pittsburgh and Allegheny County faced mass starvation. Charitable organizations exhausted their money.[57] More than forty-two percent of the children in Pittsburgh suffered from malnutrition.[58] Prior to 1929, the malnutrition rate in the city was ten percent.[59]

Richard Beatty Mellon and Howard Heinz created the Helping Hand Association of Pittsburgh along with the Pittsburgh Plan to Stabilize Employment. The Helping Hand Association delivered 2.3 million meals in 1932 and placed 500,000 men in shelters. The Pittsburgh Plan, which was a forerunner to the Works Progress Administration, divided the needy into two categories. Those who couldn't work would be cared for by charities. Men able to work would be given jobs on public projects. Funding for the plan was financed by contributions from the wealthy and another $1 million from employers. Those still working were asked to donate one day's pay. The money proved inadequate to continue the program because contributions evaporated.

The Democratic Party helped where it could. One committeeman deposited 15 tons of coal on a neighborhood street, allowing residents to scoop up what they needed to heat their homes since they couldn't afford to buy fuel. Oil drums were distributed to provide heat when utility companies shut off electricity to delinquent customers. The county allotted residents small plots of land to grow fruit and vegetables. Democrats also organized Relief Clubs and distributed 300 pounds of flour each month.[60]

The Democrats under a Republican administration could do little more because the GOP so thoroughly dominated the Democratic Party. Except for 1882, when the Democrats elected the governor, the GOP had controlled state politics since the Civil War. The Republican Party's control over the Democrats was so extensive that William Vare, the state's GOP boss, selected which Democrats could run for office and paid the rent for their party headquarters.[61] The corrupt GOP organization in Pennsylvania was viewed by a suffering public as being aligned with the railroads, public utilities, bankers and industrial barons who benefited from the tax breaks and use of the Coal and Iron Police to smash strikes in return for campaign contributions to Republican candidates.[62]

Governor Pinchot bucked heads with the GOP political machine led by the Mellons. Pinchot called for special legislative sessions four times during his tenure to address the state's economic problems. He proposed higher personal and corporate income taxes along with increased taxes on gas, food and tobacco, but his fellow Republicans blocked him each time. "The Republican Party must go progressive or stay bust ... the American people are sick of the old deal."[63] Pinchot asked the General Assembly in 1931 for $60 million in aid, but lawmakers only allocated $10 million. He went to Washington seeking a $35 million personal loan from Secretary Mellon, but Mellon rebuffed him.

A Pittsburgh newspaper criticized the Pennsylvania legislature for failing to undertake meaningful relief efforts to lessen the hardship on families and alleviate rampant unemployment. The state's unemployment rate was over 37 percent. An editorial took lawmakers to task, saying legislators do not "seem aware of the full intent of the crisis or it would have done more than make feeble gestures toward relief during the course of its extra session."

9

"Brother, Can You Spare a Dime?"

Empty is the cupboard,
No pillow for the head,
We are the hungry children
Who cry for milk and bread
We are all the workers' children
Who must, who must be fed.
—Song sung by 10 children and four adults
at the gates of the White House,
Thanksgiving Day, 1932,
shortly before they were arrested

Father Cox read with growing anger news accounts of Communist-led hunger marches on Pittsburgh's city hall, the state capital in Harrisburg, and Washington, D.C., in 1931 by protesters demanding federal aid for the unemployed. His anger intensified when the Communists displayed flags with the hammer and sickle and demonstrators singing the "Internationale."

"This is repugnant to me and I so stated casually in a radio talk," Cox said. "I remarked that, while I condemned all Red demonstrations, I believe a body of real American citizens should go to Washington and protest against unemployment conditions which exist without any reason in the United States today."[1]

The Communist Party was hoping the nation's economic problems would attract followers who had lost faith in capitalism and traditional American institutions. The party announced a series of marches on "Red Thursday" in major cities like New York and Chicago. In Pittsburgh, the Communist-led Trade Unity League scheduled a protest even though officials had denied them a parade permit. Vowing to defy police, more than

5,000 people turned out to watch the march, but very few were party members. They traveled a half block before their momentum petered out. The march ended in fistfights between the Communists and spectators.[2]

The Pittsburgh Unemployed Council, a Communist-front group, blocked evictions by preventing sheriff's deputies from removing people from their homes. It reconnected utility lines that had been turned off because of unpaid bills. In 1933, the Unemployed Council stormed city hall, demanding $250,000 to feed hungry children.[3] They demanded Mayor William McNair release $40,000 to buy shoes for destitute children.[4] The Communist Party viewed Pittsburgh as a test for its organizing efforts, particularly in the coal and steel industries, but party organizers in Pittsburgh and Allegheny County had difficulty convincing the unemployed that their economic salvation rested with Communism. Circulation of the party's newspaper, *Daily Worker*, was declining, and party organizers were falling short of their recruiting goals.[5]

In the decade of the 1930s, the party staged marches and protests but failed to generate much support. Their demonstrations usually were met with force by police who broke up their meetings or by city officials who refused the party permission to march. In 1930, a parade on behalf of the unemployed attracted fewer than 100.[6] In February 1931, the party staged a hunger march in Harrisburg demanding food and unemployment insurance. Gov. Gifford Pinchot couldn't promise help because he was embroiled in a legislative dispute with the Republican-controlled Senate over relief aid.[7]

In April, 75 members of the Communist-led National Miners Union arrived in Harrisburg to petition the state for help.[8] In November, Communists on their way to the nation's capital crossed through Pennsylvania, demanding food to feed 500 at stops in Pittsburgh, Uniontown and Philadelphia, but city officials rejected their demands.[9] In December, 400 protesters descended on Pittsburgh, demanding work as the unemployment rate reached 40 percent in Pittsburgh and Allegheny County.[10] The Helping Hand Association offered to lodge and feed them, but they were evicted after complaining about the food and holding a Communist Party meeting.[11]

When 5,000 demonstrators marched on City Hall, the mob found the building surrounded by police and firemen, who turned their fire hoses on the demonstrators and quickly dispersed the crowd.[12] In the spring of the following year, 150 unemployed men went to Harrisburg, again under the auspices of the Trade Unity League.[13]

That summer, miners from the coal patches of Washington County, south of Pittsburgh, marched on the county courthouse, protesting the starvation wages they were being paid. Between 8,000 and 9,000 men women and children walked silently past the courthouse as onlookers watched the haggard-looking miners and their families, mainly immigrants from Eastern Europe, parade by.[14] "Hundreds of people for the first time in their lives saw just what miners looked like—found out they were human after all, and underpaid, and hungry," wrote a reporter for the *New Republic.*[15]

A mob demanding food, clothing, jobs and money for rent stormed city hall in one community near the city. Pennsylvania state troopers had to rescue local officials who barricaded themselves inside the municipal building.[16] In the small town of Verona, just north of Pittsburgh, the mayor and council hunkered down in the borough behind a phalanx of police and firemen when Communists threatened to storm it.[17]

The Communist Party marched on Washington, D.C., in December 1931 as 1,500 people from twenty states arrived at the capital riding in two columns of old, battered vehicles.[18] They got out of the cars and marched in columns of four under a lavender-colored sky as sunlight poured through the city's leafless trees, making the patent leather visors on the caps of the police officers glisten in the sun. The marchers strolled past Chinese restaurants, flophouses and burlesque theaters that their owners had boarded up because the owners feared their windows would be broken if there were riots.[19]

The only attention the Communist Party received was from the 1,200 police officers who met their arrival with a cold shoulder reserved for unwelcome guests. One columnist wrote the communists were presented with a key to the city but it was for the back door.[20] They sang the "Internationale," then shouted their demands for unemployment insurance.

A U.S. Senator got caught up in the congestion and bawled out police officers for delaying him.[21] By summer's end, there were forty hunger demonstrations across the nation, but they failed to attract much public or government attention. The failure of the party's leaders to understand the plight of the jobless contributed to their lack of success. People who were out of work faced a daily battle to eat, stave off eviction and have enough money to pay their utility bills.[22]

Cox had been feeding the poor, hungry and jobless since the early days of the Depression, begging the owners of stores and bakeries in the Strip District for leftover food to feed the men who were showing up every day at his church. There were 160,000 people facing starvation in the region.

More than 28,000 families were on relief rolls and the emergency fund to feed them was nearly exhausted. Cox blamed President Hoover for turning a deaf ear to the nation's sufferings. He questioned how Hoover could save Europeans from starving after World War I, and Americans after the devastating Mississippi River flooding in 1927, but failed to come up with a plan to meet the Depression. "It seems to me that if President Hoover would set about and handle the depression in the same efficient manner as he handled relief in Belgium and other foreign countries he would go down in history as one of our greatest presidents," said Cox. "Relief is needed more here at the present time than it was needed in Belgium during the war."[23]

Cox said if he could muster the support, he would lead an army of patriotic unemployed men to Washington. "The idea caught fire. Immediately the telephone began to ring and letters came from all sides to make the march," he said.[24] Cox warned that quick changes to the economic condition of the country must come.

> The changes will come violently or smoothly. If we don't get on the job pretty soon and start cleaning house, according to the dictates of law, we won't have the chance. All revolutions have followed the same course, of either violence or revolution.[25] We are not Red demonstrators. We are real, honest American citizens. If Congress refuses us we are open to anything—in other words bloodshed. The country has everything but the heart to relieve the situation. It is like boys playing marbles and one boy winning all the marbles. He refuses to stake the others to a few in order that they may make a new start. The president seemed willing to listen only to the wealthy. His ears are not open to the cries of the poor and distressed. So we shall not try to gain an audience with him.[26]

Cox planned the march, scheduled for early January 1932, in the basement at St. Patrick's. The room was packed with so many people that Cox positioned loudspeakers outside so the overflow crowd could hear the discussions underway. Momentum began to build as newspapers and radio reported on plans. Cox warned the gathering the trip would be arduous because it was winter and the trek would take the contingent through the rugged mountains of central Pennsylvania, to Harrisburg and then to Washington, D.C. "Will you go? I asked the men. Their hands went up and their voices rang out. Yes, no matter what price we must pay."[27]

Ralph Balzar was captivated by Cox's enthusiasm. He was playing basketball in the gym at St. Mary's Church in Beaver Falls when he and his friends heard Father Cox talking about the march on a radio. "It sounded like a good idea and we wanted something to do. I was 20 years old at the time," said Balzar. "I doubt if we realized at the time what the real meaning and purpose of the march was except it might help us find

Cox addresses marchers and members of Congress in the Capitol Rotunda, 1932 (Dr. and Mrs. Mason, Father James Renshaw Cox Collection, Saint Patrick–Saint Stanislaus Kostka Parish, Pittsburgh, Pennsylvania).

work."[28] Balzar borrowed his dad's truck so he and eight friends could ride to the capital. A friend produced a phony police badge, and Balzar claimed he was a march official and moved his truck behind Cox's vehicle. For three nights, Balzar and his friends drove without sleep until they arrived in Washington. "We did realize that the reason for our going was serious. We didn't go as protestors but because it was a good cause."[29]

Cox's initial plans for the march on Washington were modest. He expected, at most, 1,000 men to follow him on a route that would take the marchers to the Tomb of the Unknown Soldier. "We are going to appeal to the Unknown Soldier to soften the heart of Herbert Hoover that he may be awakened to the need of giving aid to the jobless men of this country. The ears of our president seem to be open only to the bankers and the very wealthy and are not open to the cries of the poor and distressed. I'm not a radical so there will be no reason to stop the march," said Cox.

He banned women, guns and communists from the journey, but on the eve of the trip, the communists tried unsuccessfully to paint the priest as a tool of the city's wealthy and turn the men against Cox. A group appeared at the shantytown, bellowing that Cox represented the "bosses" and claiming the priest was "comfortably housed and getting rich by exploiting the misery and starvation of others." One resident of the shantytown began criticizing them and was beaten. A mob of homeless men attacked the communists as police arrived and arrested the agitators, who were mostly of Russian descent. They were fined $10 each. "I wish I could make the sentence more severe," said a magistrate who fined the men. "You are the kind of people we want to get rid of."[30]

10

Washington or Bust

I'm spending my night at the flophouse
I'm spending my nights on the streets
I'm looking for work and I find none
I wish I had something to eat
Soo-oop, soo-oop
   —"Soup Song" by Maurice Sugar

The murmur of thousands of men talking softly in the pre-dawn darkness filled the air around St. Patrick's Church in the Strip District as marchers began forming ranks for the march on Washington, D.C. Men climbed onto vehicles bearing banners reading "Cox's Jobless Army" and "Washington or Bust" as they waited for their leader to appear and lead them.

A sea of faces consisting of thousands of bystanders and well-wishers surrounded the church as Cox and his mother stood on the portico of the rectory watching as the men formed into companies led by their "captains" and "lieutenants." Men with grimy faces were ordered to wash before leaving. Men with beards were ordered to shave. American flags were unfurled. Men jumped to attention and bands began playing the National Anthem.[1]

More than 2,000 cars and trucks blocked the streets, creating a huge traffic jam that stretched for blocks as thousands of unemployed men flooded the sidewalks ready to follow Cox.[2] The procession included 15 trucks loaded with bread to sustain the men on the journey.[3] Cox advised the men to "bring soap, a towel, shaving cream, sandwiches or money. Those who have a truck, [bring] straw."[4] The marchers ranged in age from 17 to 70. Exactly how many men followed Cox is a mystery. One account said Cox started with 10,000 which grew to 25,000 as the ragtag army of the jobless slowly made its way through central Pennsylvania in the middle of winter.[5] Cox used 25,000 in his account of the march written for a

Pittsburgh newspaper.[6] The route the caravan followed took Cox from Pittsburgh in Allegheny County through small towns in Indiana, Cambria, Blair, Huntingdon, Mifflin, Dauphin and Adams Counties, and then into Frederick, Maryland, before it reached Washington.[7]

The men carried knapsacks and blankets. Some were dressed in ragged clothes and shoes while others wore parts of military uniforms and sheepskin coats.[8] Elmer Cope, a union organizer and socialist, was stunned by the turnout. He had little faith in the church's ability to help the poor, but Cope never doubted that Cox's intentions were sincere and "that he has the workers truly at heart."[9] Cope found himself caught up in the event. "When I left home, I had no intention of going more than to see the gang off but the turn-out was so intriguing that I went on to Wilkinsburg, then to Johnstown and later to Harrisburg and Washington as you know," said Cope.[10]

Father Cox emerged from the church rectory, jumped into the cab of a red truck, and sat down next to the driver.[11] "At eight promptly, a big red Ford truck, with myself beside the driver and 30 men behind, started the trek toward Washington and other cars followed."[12]

Men scrambled onto the backs of trucks and into cars. Others clung to the bumpers. Those who couldn't find a place to sit or stand had to walk as the massive army slowly began moving along Liberty Avenue in downtown Pittsburgh, creating a traffic jam that lasted for two hours. "The cars were filled like magic," Cox wrote.

Gov. Gifford Pinchot assigned a squad of state troopers to escort Cox to the Pennsylvania-Maryland border. The skies were overcast and rain began to fall as the men left Pittsburgh. The temperatures plunged, turning highways into sheets of ice. Then it snowed.[13] Cox's army made their way through city streets until the procession of men and machines reached the outskirts of Pittsburgh.

Pittsburgh's future mayor David Lawrence, then chairman of the Allegheny County Democratic Party, asked attorney Henry Ellenbogen to accompany Cox to Washington in case President Hoover ordered Cox's arrest, as Grover Cleveland had done to Jacob Coxey in 1894 for stepping on the Capitol lawn. Cox and Ellenbogen shared an interest in social issues. Ellenbogen, who was Jewish, became one of Cox's closest friends and advisors until the priest's death in 1951.

Ellenbogen came to the U.S. from Vienna in 1921. He and Cox attended Holy Ghost College, now Duquesne University in Pittsburgh, and worked in department stores to earn money while in school. As a congressman, Ellenbogen sponsored legislation that created pensions for the elderly, unemployment insurance, public housing for the poor, and 30-year mortgages for homeowners.[14]

The procession made its way out of Pittsburgh, going from the Strip District through the streets of Lawrenceville and Bloomfield, where thousands of people stood and watched in silence as the motorcade passed by. Allegheny County into neighboring Westmoreland County, where people in small towns along the way spilled out into the streets to see the army trudge pass by in the freezing drizzle. The contingent reached Delmont in Westmoreland County, where the men were fed sandwiches and Graham crackers by the Salvation Army. When the caravan resumed, 1,000 men were too tired to continue and stayed behind. By the time the men they reached Greensburg, they were soaked.[15]

Some of the marchers couldn't keep up the pace on foot, so they broke up into small groups along railroad lines, waiting to jump onto passing eastbound freight trains. Others tried to hitch rides with passing vehicles. Hundreds more men were stranded in Latrobe and Derry.[16]

The marchers made their way into Indiana County. V.L. Sedlak reached Indiana by a truck, which broke down, forcing him to hitchhike the rest of the way to Washington. He thumbed rides to Johnstown, then Windber, Bedford and Gettysburg before reaching the capital. When he reached Washington, a police officer paid Sedlak's street car fare and he slept under a pool table at a National Guard Armory where thousands of other men were bedded down for the night. The next day a woman gave him two street car tokens and fifty cents. "Buy yourself a good meal," she said.[17]

In one small town, the exhausted men slept on the floor of a municipal building. A few men couldn't go any farther and headed back to Pittsburgh. Others forged ahead despite their exhaustion.[18]

Pittsburgh radio stations interrupted their programs to deliver bulletins on the progress of the march.[19] By the time Cox reached Johnstown on noon of the first day, it was raining harder than it was in Pittsburgh, and the men stood in the cold downpour waiting for the food trucks to arrive. Cox's army had grown to more than 20,000 by the time they reached Cambria County. Cox received a telegram from Pittsburgh claiming another 20,000 men in the city wanted to join the pilgrimage but didn't have rides.[20]

Johnstown Mayor Eddie McCloskey, a redheaded former boxer, arrived to greet Cox. The two men had met a few days earlier in Pittsburgh when McCloskey asked Cox to pass through Johnstown in hope of attracting marchers from his city. McCloskey had been in office for only two

tumultuous days when Cox reached Johnstown. The man McCloskey succeeded, Joseph Cauffiel, had served two years in prison. The Johnstown
city clerk didn't know what to do because McCloskey was demanding he
was the rightful holder of the office. The clerk refused to act. Eventually,
he swore in McCloskey.[21]

McCloskey was a brawler and an anti–Semite who quit school and
worked as a messenger boy for a steel company. Then he became a heater
in the bolt shop and trained as a machinist. He had fought as a lightweight
and had a record of 10–9–3 including five knockouts. After a fight in
Detroit, he quit boxing and went to work for the Packard Car Co. before
moving back to Johnstown, starting a cab company and opening a dry-
cleaning business.[22]

McCloskey and his son, Eddie Jr., got into separate fights with the
same man on the same day.[23] McCloskey wrote J. Edgar Hoover, director
of the FBI, about a rich Johnstown businessman who allegedly had paid a
$500 bribe to a congressman to get his son deferred from the draft during
World War II. The FBI noted that McCloskey had a reputation in Johnstown as a "Jew baiter" because the businessman in question was Jewish.[24]
"It appears that Mr. McCloskey is somewhat of a fire brand," wrote an FBI
agent.[25]

The city of Johnstown didn't fare much better than the rest of the
state. From 1920 until 1929, the city enjoyed good economic times in the
steel and coal industries, but after the Wall Street crash, orders for steel
dried up. More than 11,000 steel workers lost their jobs, and 5,000 workers
left the city in search of work.[26]

When Cox reached Johnstown, McCloskey vaulted onto the truck's
seat next to Cox and drove with his fellow Irishman to Point Stadium,
located at the confluence of the Little Conemaugh, Conemaugh and Stony-
creek Rivers, where Cox delivered an impromptu speech. "I am going to
Washington to talk to Uncle Sam, not to fight with him," Cox said. "There
is plenty of money in the country but try and get it. The government sent
Al Capone to jail for cheating it out of $100,000 yet John D. Rockefeller
is giving $4,000,000 to his son to escape the inheritance tax. Our only
mission is to ask for jobs. We don't want to change the government. The
government is all right."[27]

Inside the stadium, the men were fed sandwiches as they listened to
Cox rail against Hoover's plan to loan money to banks through the Reconstruction Finance Corporation as a way of spurring the economy. The procession moved on to the Cambria County Fairgrounds, where the cars
and trucks were parked.

Father Cox stood for several hours at the entrance as cars zoomed past him. Jane Boyle, a nurse who served in World War I, greeted the men as she drove her truck along the highway picking up stragglers. She rounded up a total of 125 men, fed them, and provided shelter from the snow and rain. Then she gave the stranded men money to buy gasoline and tires.[28]

The procession of trucks and cars moved along a line of march that took them across central Pennsylvania. Men standing on the truck beds were pelted by rain, so they stood on their tiptoes peering over the canvas to escape the smell of exhaust fumes. They joked about the stock market, asking each other how their stocks were faring and then roaring in laughter at the black humor.

The trip was slow and tortuous. Drivers had to proceed slowly because men were hanging onto the backs of trucks or standing on the bumpers of cars and any sudden turn would send them tumbling off onto the pavement. Several men were hit by passing cars and suffered broken legs. Men began collapsing from exhaustion, but despite the hardships they pressed on, inspired by Cox, who urged the men to keep smiling and keep marching.[29]

The hard rain continued to pound the men as they made their way through the mountains to Altoona, home of the Pennsylvania Railroad. The rain turned to sleet, then snow, as the line of vehicles weaved through the twisting mountain ridges overlooking the Juniata River. They reached the small central Pennsylvania town of Huntingdon, where local restaurant owners brewed hundreds of gallons of coffee for the men. The city of 8,000 swelled to more than 12,000 as people from nearby towns came to see Cox.

The Rev. Owen Poulson, pastor of the Methodist Episcopal Church in Huntingdon, trudged through ankle-deep mud to greet Cox and tell him that breakfast had been arranged for his men.[30] Cox and Father Casimir Orlemanski went to a hotel, where they read their Bibles in the lobby. Orlemanski was a tall, broad-shouldered cleric who resembled the coal miner he had been before being ordained a priest.[31] He disagreed with Hoover's economic policies as much as Cox. Orlemanski wrote the president that social injustice was at the root of the nation's economic problems.

Dear President: They are crying and lying low now but down deep they are inscribing indelibly this injustice for future reference as the days go on the conditions are getting worse and worse. Now people want help from their government. The government does not belong to the president or any legislature. It belongs to them:

their good is to be the supreme good. A system which can in the space of a few days add ten billions of dollars to the worth of securities on Wall Street when in the same time thousands of men are thrown out of work and the industry as a whole added not one bit to the appreciation of the value of securities which cannot long endure.[32]

To take their minds off their discomfort, the men sang songs they learned in the Army and watched blind Pennsylvania legislator Matthew Dunn imitate John D. Rockefeller by handing out shiny dimes to everyone he met.[33] The men played poker and built bonfires until the rain extinguished the flames. Then they bedded down for the night, sleeping in cattle sheds or in their vehicles.

The men awoke in the morning to a bugle call for breakfast. They then began moving through a muddy cornfield to resume the march, but tow trucks had to pull out some of the vehicles that had become mired in the thick muck.[34] Cox got out of the truck and marched for a mile with the men. A reporter accompanying the marchers wrote the men looked to Cox "as their shepherd who will lead them to a place where there is hope for jobs."[35]

Cox halted the march near Lewistown in Mifflin County to give stragglers a chance to catch up with the main body. He walked up and down the caravan talking to the men. Marchers left behind in Pittsburgh hitched rides and caught up with Cox later that day. The newcomers were so determined that they started out on foot from the city, then walked 20 miles back to Pittsburgh to catch a ride.[36] The weather was beginning to take its toll. Some of the men became sick while others coughed in the cold air.

Cox reached Harrisburg on Thursday. As they approached the state capital, the eight-mile-long procession sped through the toll booths at Clarks Ferry that spanned the Susquehanna River without paying the 10-cent toll. Waiting in the rain for Cox on the steps of the state capitol was Gov. Gifford Pinchot, a thin, angular man who wore a bushy moustache. Pinchot had a love-hate relationship with the Republican Party and left the mainstream GOP during his first term as governor from 1923 to 1927. At one point he became a member of the Progressive League, but when the faction dissolved, Pinchot returned to the Republicans and was elected governor a second time in 1931.

Pinchot arranged to feed the men at the state cafeteria at his own expense. He was astonished by the size of the crowd facing him.[37] Some of the men fainted from hunger and exhaustion. Others rested their heads on the capitol steps and quickly fell asleep.[38]

Pinchot stood next to Cox and proclaimed, "Boys, here is a wonderful man."[39]

"Boys, here is the leader of America," Cox replied.[40]

"I wish I could offer you a drier welcome," said Pinchot. "Unfortunately, the only state building in Harrisburg which can begin to accommodate you is the state capitol. Come in and get out of the wet.[41]

"Governor, I want you to talk to my boys," Cox said. "We have a loud speaker apparatus on a truck outside. Will you talk to them there?" Cox asked.[42]

"I'll talk to them anywhere," Pinchot replied. "Command me! Whatever you want me to do, I will do; you are the master of ceremonies."[43]

Pinchot told the shivering men that "civilized government is a fallacy if men who are able and willing to work to support their families cannot get the chance. Pennsylvanians led astray by the Republican state organization failed lamentably in making provisions for both work and direct relief. You are right in asking for federal relief." Pinchot attacked U.S. Treasury Secretary Andrew Mellon for contributing a paltry $170,000 for relief when Mellon had an annual income of $10 million. He called President Hoover's unemployment relief plan "vicious. It takes money from the little fellow. It does not take money from the big fellows," Pinchot said.[44]

The marchers mingled with government workers who left their offices to watch the spectacle. Cox viewed the moment as historic and added to the drama by warning of the violence that loomed if relief didn't come soon. He mounted the steps as if he were a maestro waving his baton and the crowd were his orchestra. "Just as an orchestra director waves his baton, there was a spontaneous outburst of sincere applause which rang true and beautiful in the plaza. It was more like music than a shout," a reporter noted as Cox began to talk.[45]

> The thought came to me that this meeting of the people and their government had a double significance. The men who stood there realized more deeply than before the problems of government and the men who are entrusted with the administration of government appreciated more fully the responsibility of their work as trustees for the people instead of proprietors of the people. It meant that the artificial barriers which have grown up between the people and their government are being swept away, and that pretense is disappearing. There is no need for it among educated people.... Theirs [the marchers'] is a war that only has just begun—a struggle to free civilization from the curse of poverty and unemployment; a battle that will end in final victory when every man has a job that will permit him not only to exist but to enjoy a real American standard of living. The change will come violently or smoothly. If we don't get on the job pretty soon and start cleaning house, according to the dictates of law or reason, we won't have the chance. All revolutions have flowed the same course, either violence or revolution.[46]

Cox's Army departed Harrisburg and headed for Gettysburg, trudging past the Civil War battlefields in a column that stretched for 40 miles, according to newspaper accounts. Darkness cloaked the monuments and farmhouses that dotted the landscape. The men were wet, their clothes splattered with mud. Some wrapped themselves in blankets, burlap bags and newspapers to ward off the cold. A reporter jumped onto the truck carrying Cox and asked where they would camp for the night. "God only knows," Cox replied.[47]

After two days on the road, Cox's army reached the outskirts of Washington, D.C., on January 7. He got out of the truck, walked into a drugstore and ordered a sandwich and glass of milk. After eating, he called the police to tell his army had arrived.

11

Invasion

Cox's Army reached the outskirts of Washington after traveling through the night in fog and heavy rain. The column halted in a muddy cornfield as the men formed ranks. Some had no shoes and wore three pairs of socks to protect their feet. Others, with holes in their shoes, wrapped rubber inner tubes around their feet to keep them dry.[1] "Boys, I know how tough it's been but can you still smile?" Cox asked the men.[2]

A musician in the band accompanying Cox collapsed as the contingent moved down Wisconsin Avenue. Police found more than $1,000 in the man's pockets. "I had some money. I had it saved in a bank," he said. "And then I found myself out of a job, and I've got a wife to take care of, too. I drawed it out and had it in my pockets ever since."[3]

There was no food for the men when they reached Washington, but police found shelter for them in National Guard armories around the city.[4] Officials promised Cox they would feed his men the next morning.[5] "Father, we are going to look after your men the right way," said Police Chief Pelham Glassford, a retired brigadier general who had been appointed the city's police chief a year before. "We want them to have breakfast and lunch with us tomorrow and we're going to give them a real feed."[6]

A police escort steered the silent marchers through the streets until the column reached a field in the southwest part the city where tents had been erected for the rest of the men. The men were fed a breakfast of coffee, bread, doughnuts and cereal at U.S. Army field kitchens the next morning. For lunch, they dined on wieners and sauerkraut. By the time they departed the city, they had consumed 11,000 apples, 16,000 doughnuts, 650 gallons of beef soup, 500 hot dogs, 2,800 pounds of sauerkraut, 450 loaves of bread, and 300 pounds of sugar, and had drunk 100 gallons of milk and 500 pounds of coffee.[7]

Exhausted marchers slept in the lobby of a Washington hotel, 1932. Others were housed in National Guard Armories around the city (Dr. and Mrs. Mason, Father James Renshaw Cox Collection, Saint Patrick–Saint Stanislaus Kostka Parish, Pittsburgh, Pennsylvania).

The men referred to hot dogs as "Hoover turkeys." They "taste swell when you are hungry but a good beefsteak would look good to me," said William Brozek. "I ain't seen one in five years except through windows of restaurants."[8]

Some of the men hadn't eaten for two days by the time they reached the city. "Hungry? I'm so hungry I could eat the ears off a skunk," said one marcher. Other men were concerned about how they would care for their families once they returned to Pittsburgh. Stephen Foley was 19, married and about to become a father. "Here's the kid coming and we have hardly enough to take care of ourselves."[9]

Cox ordered his men the next morning to line up in formation eight abreast. At 11 a.m. he issued marching orders and the men began walking along Maryland Avenue toward the Capitol. "What a difference this was compared with the un-orderly Red group a few weeks before, uttering all kinds of epithets against the government and its officials," wrote Cox.[10]

Cox's Army marches down Pennsylvania Avenue upon its arrival in the capital, January 1932 (Dr. and Mrs. Mason, Father James Renshaw Cox Collection, Saint Patrick–Saint Stanislaus Kostka Parish, Pittsburgh, Pennsylvania).

The demonstration was political theater and Cox was the star of the production. As the men walked toward the Capitol, Cox's mother, Julia, appeared on cue and approached her son. Immediately the marchers stopped as the two embraced.[11] "I have been proud of my son all his life but never as much as today," said his mother. "I am heart and soul in accord with this movement and I pray to God it will yield fruit."[12] When the contingent reached the Capitol's steps, they formed a large bloc.

The North Braddock Firemen's Band led the march as bystanders cheered the ragtag group.[13] Waiting for Cox on the Capitol's steps were Pennsylvania lawmakers Sen. James Davis and U.S. Rep. Clyde Kelly. The men cheered as Cox ascended the steps. He said, "I know how hungry and cold you have been and how you have suffered on this trip. You will live to tell your grandchildren of this event, of the courteous treatment you have been accorded by everyone in the city. This is God's country and under God we are going to keep it that way. Today you have asked only for your God-given right to work. So long as I live and have a tongue and can breathe, I will work for you and all the common people."[14]

Some of the men were so overcome by emotion they began crying while shivering in the cold. Cox complained the Hoover administration was "acting like an ostrich that sticks its head in the sand believing that if he cannot see the hunters pursuing him or that trouble is nearby, that the hunter or the trouble does not exist."[15]

Aides to President Hoover were searching for derogatory information about Cox and investigating whether he had ties to the Democratic Party.

They scoured newspaper articles and questioned critics. "We will not see this man: if he has a petition we will be glad to receive [it] but he cannot see the president," said Hoover's secretary, Lawrence Richey.[16]

Cox had been warned by Vice-President Charles Curtis that he would not be able to speak with Hoover, so Cox was surprised when he and a small group of supporters were ushered into a White House reception room for a six-and-half-minute meeting with the president.[17]

Cox was accompanied by Matthew Dunn, and by Chester "Happy" Waddle, a Pittsburgh cabbie who was wearing a leather jacket and black fur cap. Another cabbie, Huckleberry Burns, wore a battered derby. E.R. Frane was dressed in a costume as Uncle Sam. Father Orlemanski, Henry Ellenbogen, Earl Dean and George Ewing tagged along. A smiling Hoover greeted the men, who formed a semicircle around the president.[18]

He stood before the men with his hands in his pockets. Hoover told Cox the Depression was nearing an end, but Cox remained skeptical.[19]

I am glad to receive you as the representatives of Pennsylvania unemployed. I have an intense sympathy for your difficulties. I have considered that the vital function of the President and of the federal government was to exert every effort and every power of the government to the restoration of stability and employment in our country, which has been so greatly disturbed largely from abroad. The federal government is now spending half a billion a year above normal to give employment. World-wide depression and their result in unemployment are like great wars. They must be fought continually, not on one front but upon many fronts. It cannot be won by any single skirmish or any panacea. In the present, and what I believe is the final campaign against the depression, I have laid a program before Congress and I trust we will secure its early adoption. The real victory is to restore men to employment through their regular jobs. That is our object. We are giving this question our undivided attention.[20]

Cox left the White House and delivered a national broadcast over the CBS radio network, saying he hoped Hoover "will rise to the occasion and recommed to Congress the enactment of the measures we have proposed."[21] "I told the president in my most earnest manner why 25,000 men had crossed the mountains to the Capitol. I told him of the sad plight of the unemployed in all parts of the United States—hungry children, distressed men and women, broken-up families—all due to the Depression that has no reason to exist, according to economic law."[22]

The nation was sitting "on top of a volcano that might erupt at any time that the danger exists of rioting and bloodshed every day."[23] The *Pittsburgh Courier*, the largest and most influential African American newspaper in the country at the time, echoed Cox's warning in an editorial: "When a man is hungry, he asks not the creed, nor the color of the leader.

The 'army' following Father Cox over the highways of Pennsylvania is following an idea rather than a leader. If the idea fails, if they find no gold at the end of the rainbow, what then? There is no telling what a man will do when he is hungry."[24]

Cox gave Senator Davis a copy of the "Resolution of the Jobless." Davis had the document placed in the Congressional Record. It began: "In this land of ours the soil is rich, the earth is bursting with abundance, bins are filled with grain, the storehouses are filled with goods, the shelves are overflowing with merchandise, the vaults are stacked with bars of gold, and the very channels of trade are choked by the undistributed surplus of the products of mill, mine and farm."[25] The resolution called for appropriating $5 billion to create public work jobs, plus funding for food, clothing and shelter. Cox demanded loans for farmers and a 60 percent income tax rate on the rich. He also wanted Congress to implement a 70 percent inheritance tax and a gift tax.[26]

Cox led the men to the Tomb of the Unknown Soldier. "We do not know who this unknown soldier we are honoring, is. We do not know his face, his religion, only that he kept the faith. And that is what we ask all public officials to do with their countrymen."[27]

Cox gave the order to return to Pittsburgh at the end of the ceremony, but every man had to get home on his own. After the main body left Washington, 276 men remained stranded. Washington newspapers said they were glad to see Cox depart. The *Washington Post* demanded to know how Cox financed the trip. An editorial noted that Governor Pinchot also had made "a couple of mendicant trips" to Washington seeking aid for his state: "The governor's begging trips were even more to be deplored."[28] The editorial said Pennsylvania was a wealthy state and questioned why it couldn't take care of its own people like other parts of the nation and reject government assistance. The *Washington Star* warned future groups not to expect a similar welcome as Cox's army.[29]

The returning hunger marchers didn't find the welcoming crowds as they made their way back to Pittsburgh. Local police departments refused to let the men stop or rest. The men were to rendezvous in Uniontown, Pennsylvania, so they could march together into Pittsburgh, but 2,000 were scattered between Washington and Pittsburgh. Cox sent telegrams to police departments asking for help in rounding up the exhausted stragglers. He said he was sending trucks to pick them up. The telegram read: "Try today to send trucks to pick up stranded. Do as they request. Take care of these men."[30]

More than 4,000 bone-weary men staggered into Johnstown. Another

Cox and "Uncle Sam" address a crowd at the steps of the U.S. Capitol, 1932 (Dr. and Mrs. Mason, Father James Renshaw Cox Collection, Saint Patrick–Saint Stanislaus Kostka Parish, Pittsburgh, Pennsylvania).

150 men stopped in Ebensburg. Some men tried to commandeer rides on passing cars, hoping the drivers would take pity on them. State police had to free one woman from a mob who had surrounded her vehicle. Two men forced their way into another motorist's car, but when the driver refused to move, the men finally gave up.[31]

Stragglers reached Delmont in Westmoreland County, about 15 miles from Pittsburgh. The Salvation Army again rushed to help, distributing 800 sandwiches and apples. When Cox and the main body finally reached Pittsburgh, thousands of people cheered the men as they marched from the Golden Triangle toward the Strip District in a caravan of vehicles. Police officers saluted at attention as Cox drove past.[32] "God bless you, father. We prayed for you," shouted a woman in the crowd.[33]

In front of St. Patrick's, a larger crowd awaited Cox's arrival. As the cars slowly moved through the crowd, trucks filled with men arrived at the church every half hour. Their eyes were red from a lack of sleep. They were cold and hungry and there were holes in their clothes. The men ate

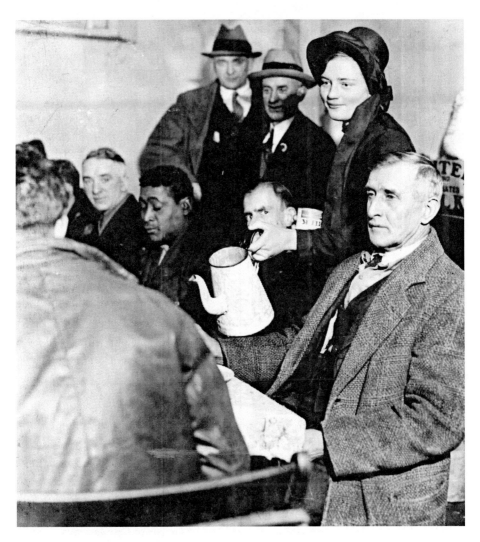

The Salvation Army came to the rescue of stragglers and stranded men who couldn't complete the march. Army members pour coffee and distribute sandwiches to weary men, 1932 (Dr. and Mrs. Mason, Father James Renshaw Cox Collection, Saint Patrick–Saint Stanislaus Kostka Parish, Pittsburgh, Pennsylvania).

sandwiches, hot dogs and sauerkraut, and coffee.[34] An exhausted marcher passing a barbershop received a quarter from the barber. "I came home with more money than I had when I left home," he said.[35]

People in the welcoming crowd looked as ragged as the marchers as they jammed the sidewalk in front of the church. Women held babies aloft and surged toward the truck carrying Cox. He got out of the truck, made his way through the crowd to the church's portico, and stood before a microphone set up by a Pittsburgh radio station.[36] Cox appeared haggard. His clothes were wrinkled, his voice was hoarse.[37]

> People wanted to know why we were going to Washington. We went to impress upon the government the need for unemployment relief. I feel that our mission has not been in vain. I feel our mission has not been a vain effort. I think it will do more to restore prosperity to America than anything that has been done. I consider myself a shepherd and a shepherd must look for his sheep. I come from the people. I belong to the people and I intend to die among the people.[38]

A Pittsburgh newspaper wrote that even critics of Cox's march would have loved to have been part of the historic event. "Even those who are most critical of Father Cox, and those who believe that such movements can serve no practical purpose, must know in their hearts that there were untold numbers in the county who would have welcomed the opportunity to appear in the host outside the Capitol at the time the priest was presenting his petition to Congress. It is one of the misfortunes of the Great Depression that there is no agreement regarding ways to end it."[39] The editorial writer said hungry children, evictions, disease and the breakup of families were undermining American society. The march focused national attention on the need to aid their fellow Americans.[40] The *Jewish Criterion* defended Cox from criticism that he was upsetting the *status quo.* "Any man of any church who is courageous enough to speak in the name of social justice is looked upon with suspicion by those who have."[41]

Some Pittsburghers thought the march was a waste of time and just a publicity stunt. "This observer is fully aware of the useless expenditure of money to make this march of the jobless possible," wrote A.C. Burke in a letter to the editor in the *Pittsburgh Press.* "Thus, from a standpoint of benefit deriver, the march of Rev. Cox was a failure."[42]

A truck driver questioned the political motives of Cox's critics: "Did you ever have six or seven children nag at your coattails asking for food when the cupboard was empty? Probably you are one of those who think Father Cox marched to Washington to embarrass the president. Does a child embarrass his father when it asks for a piece of bread?"[43]

"I say more power to Father Cox, a man for the people, and I am a Protestant. He's a fearless representative of 98 percent our people and that is why they will vote for him. Protestants, Catholics, Jews and persons of no religion will unite to vote for this fearless representative of the people," wrote Roy Greene[44] in an editorial for the *Press.*

Catholic newspapers around the country praised Cox. The *Pittsburgh*

Catholic wrote "the pilgrimage ... if it does nothing else, brought to the nation's attention the fact that Catholic priests are vitally interested in the social and economic welfare of the people of all faiths, and that the downtrodden and oppressed will continue to find as they always found, a true friend and champion in the parish priest."[45]

A publication in Nebraska wrote the march was a "rather unique way of calling attention to massive unemployment."[46] A diocesan paper in St. Louis wrote Cox's army should have stayed longer in Washington "and slept on the White House lawn. It should have made its presence felt to the discomfort of the president, the legislature and the citizens."[47]

The economic situation in Pittsburgh was growing more desperate by the time Cox returned to Pittsburgh. The Welfare Fund and Emergency Association raised $5.4 million, but officials said that the money would last only till summer and twice that amount was needed to care for the needy. Families were surviving on ninety cents per person a week.[48]

Monsignor John Ryan of the National Catholic Welfare Conference said Hoover's lack of action "is almost criminal negligence. Congress needed something to break up the mood of complacency and I think Father Cox and his men have done just that."[49]

The Rev. John Ray Ewers of Pittsburgh, writing in *The Christian Century* magazine, said, "Millions will not suffer in silence; today after more than thirty months of inarticulate deprivation, they seem to be finding a voice in Father James R. Cox...."[50]

Cox threatened to stage protests at the Republican and Democratic national conventions later that year if the two parties didn't take legislative action. "I don't mean this as a threat to President Hoover and Congress. We have given our position. We must have relief. I don't want to see any further growth of Communism. If something isn't done, we're headed for trouble."[51]

Cox said the march was the first step in bringing the plight of the hungry and jobless to the leaders of the government. "We received all sorts of encouragement for our program and we feel more convinced than ever that, if property presented, what we must secure from legislation in most instances will be cheerfully accepted, investigated and, if possible given prompt action.... After all, the state is ours, and the heads of the state are our public servants. We ask only what is reasonable, the right work."[52]

Cox already was planning to create a third party to run for president, blaming both parties for failing to help the poor. "If both the Republican and Democratic leaders of government do not provide employment relief that people deem necessary, they [the unemployed] will put their own candidates in the field at a convention of the jobless to be held in some large city."

The march put Cox $15,000 in the red. "What were we going to do with the men stranded along the road for lack of food or gasoline?" Cox asked. "We couldn't leave those men there. We used my name to secure credit for thousands of gallons of gasoline and to get food. They'll be paid somehow. They always are. We're thousands of dollars in the hole but we'll get out some way."[53]

Republicans viewed Cox's march as a publicity stunt instigated by Democrats or the Catholic Church to embarrass Hoover. The GOP National Committee accused Cox of working for a powerful political figure opposed to President Hoover, in a thinly veiled political reference to

Vehicles created a traffic jam along the route as men stopped for gas. Treasury Secretary Andrew Mellon ordered Gulf gas stations owned by his nephew, William Larimer Mellon, not to charge the men for fuel. Mellon later paid for train tickets so stranded men could return to Pittsburgh, January 1932 (Dr. and Mrs. Mason, Father James Renshaw Cox Collection, Saint Patrick–Saint Stanislaus Kostka Parish, Pittsburgh, Pennsylvania).

FDR.[54] "Any child should know that the first unemployment march was inspired by Communist agitators and the second had its genesis in the activities of a power figure opposed to President Hoover."[55]

There was a force behind Cox that aided the march, but it wasn't Roosevelt. Treasury Secretary Mellon of Pittsburgh arranged for the drivers to get free gasoline for their vehicles at Mellon-owned Gulf stations. Mellon also paid $1,242 for tickets on the Baltimore & Ohio Railroad so the stranded men could get home.[56] Catholics were not happy with GOP suspicions. "It seems as though some stalwarts in Washington sensed some sort of papal plot or a least a dirty Democratic trick to discredit the Hoover administration," wrote the *Pittsburgh Catholic*.[57]

In an editorial in *The Militant*, a publication of the Trotskyite wing of the Communist Party, Cox was accused of exploiting the unemployed.

> The exploits of this clever sky-pilot are crowding the legitimate workers' movement out of the daily news. While this can be attributed, in part, to a more or less deliberate policy of the capitalist press, it must be admitted that his methods and program have a superficial attraction for many workers. He stole the thunder of the Communists with his "hunger march" to Washington and, from all reports, made just as good a showing. He demands "immediate relief," government appropriations and similar measures, which have a practical sound and make a certain appeal to the desperate workers who are staggering under the heavy blows of the crisis. This is indicated by the attendance of fifty thousand at his Pittsburgh mass meeting. It is not altogether out of question that his project for a national convention at St. Louis should arouse widespread hopes and attain a measure of success. One thing is incontestable: The intolerable burdens of unemployment are arousing millions who can no longer bear them in silence. They are moving with irresistible force toward some form of expression. Whether it will be a fighting program or a compound of reformist and religious illusions, whether it will be led by revolutionists or demagogues—this remains undecided. It is not written anywhere that the workers, in the first stages of their awakening, will take the road of militant struggle. Neither is it precluded. The policy and methods of the party are the deciding factor in this question. The conditions work in a progressive direction, but the leadership fumbles every time and turns the movement back. Time is vitally important. Every error and every delay increases the danger that the course of the movement will be turned aside. The spectacular successes of Father Cox are a sharp warning of the reality of this danger.[58]

The march, and the publicity it generated, had no effect on President Hoover, who demanded the federal government curtail spending. Hoover said pending legislation that would have allocated $40 billion in new government spending "will never see the light of day."[59] "We cannot squander ourselves into prosperity," he said.[60]

12

The Bonus March

More than 20,000 unemployed World War I vets began assembling across the country in the summer of 1932 to rendezvous in Washington, D.C., to demand that President Hoover pay a promised bonus for their military service during the war. The only problem was the bonus wasn't payable until 1945. The World War Adjustment Compensation Act of 1924 pledged payments for every day a man served during the war. The beleaguered veterans needed the money to help their families who were struggling to make ends meet. The men felt abandoned by their government and couldn't understand why Congress couldn't agree on immediate payment.

These veterans called themselves the Bonus Expeditionary Force after the American Expeditionary Force they were part of in Europe. The former soldiers, sailors and Marines would be paid $1.25 for every day they served overseas up to a maximum of $625. Servicemen who were not deployed would receive a dollar for each day in the military.[1] More than 3.6 million were eligible, and if the government paid the bonus immediately, it would cost the federal government almost $4 billion. Hoover and the Congress opposed an early payment because of the nation's economic problems.

Father Cox supported the bonus payment and entered the controversy on the veterans' behalf. Cox's support for the veterans was sincere, but he also saw an opportunity for political gain. When he spoke to veterans' organizations in western Pennsylvania, he was looking ahead to a presidential campaign in the fall as the head of the Jobless Party. In a speech that summer before 2,000 members of the Veterans of Foreign Wars in Pittsburgh, Cox attacked war profiteers who made fortunes during the war.

Suppose the government had promised the war millionaires that they would reap their profits 20 years after the war? They would have refused absolutely to furnish

ammunition to the government unless paid immediately. The man or woman who
has fought for his or her country, has always had first place in my heart and should
have first place in the hearts of the American people. The Bonus Army should be
paid in full and immediately. If the multimillionaires who made their millions
through the bloodshed and hardships the solider endured, paid their proper and
proportionate share of taxes, there would be plenty of money in the United States
Treasury to pay the bonus.[2]

Cox told reporters Pennsylvania veterans asked him to come to Washington and serve as their spokesman.[3] Shortly after the interview, he appeared for photographers at an airport outside Pittsburgh dressed in his Army uniform while standing next to an airplane. He flew to Washington and was greeted at the airport by more photographers and reporters. Cox was in his element. A police escort drove Cox to Camp Anacostia, which served as BEF headquarters. Cox climbed atop the roof of a shack and, standing beneath a hot, glaring sun, castigated the federal government for refusing to pay the bonus while giving tax refunds to steel companies and their multimillionaire owners. Cox said he hated to use the word "bonus" to describe the payment, since the amount of money they could get was a pittance. "I hate the word. Why, it isn't even good back pay."[4]

The impetus for the Bonus March began in November 1931 when a group of vets from Oregon hopped freight trains and traveled cross country to Washington to meet with their home state congressmen. In April 1932, the Veterans of Foreign Wars dispatched 1,200 men to Washington carrying petitions bearing the names of 2.2 million veterans demanding payment.

Walter Waters of Portland, Oregon, a former sergeant who served in France, emerged as their leader. Waters had fought Pancho Villa in Mexico as a member of the Idaho National Guard. He later joined the Oregon National Guard after it was federalized and sent to France. Speeches had little impact with veterans until the men realized that neither Hoover nor Congress would allow the bonus bill to become law.

Waters said the veterans didn't need Cox's help. He charged that Cox invited himself for political purposes. He said Cox got onto the back of a truck and began urging the sleeping men to merge the BEF with his Jobless Party and the fascist Khaki Shirts. Cox admitted that was his purpose and offered the slot of vice-president on the Jobless Part ticket to any member of the BEF that the veterans chose. "I prefer to put up a united front as a political organization but if you prefer to continue the Khaki Shirts in a semi-military manner as I understand they now exist, I am willing to take over leadership of that group," Cox said.[5]

Cox boards an airplane in Pittsburgh for a flight to Washington to speak on behalf of the Bonus Expeditionary Force in the summer of 1932. Cox used the trip to increase his support for the Jobless Party, but the veterans wanted no part of his politics (James R. Cox Papers, 1923–1950, AIS.1969.05, Archives & Special Collections, University of Pittsburgh Library System).

Waters said Cox come to the encampment uninvited and the sleepy men told Cox they preferred Waters as their leader. "At three in the morning Father Cox and the Jobless Party came to the camp and roused the men and began a political speech. The men jeered him down and went back to sleep," Waters said.[6] Cox fired back at Waters, claiming he went to Washington because he had been asked by the veterans to replace Waters as their leader. "They've been trying to get me back for a long time, but I held back," Cox said. "Waters was afraid of me right then and I could have put it over like a flash but I didn't want to."[7]

Cox claimed the men readily accepted him. "There was only one man objected [sic] to me in making a talk and he was drunk."[8] He called Waters a "chiseler" adding, "Waters was a traitor to the whole cause. He played right into the hands of the officials at Washington."[9]

Cox and a small group of veterans presented their demands to Vice-President Charles Curtis. Curtis took Cox aside and told him: "Father, I had no idea back in 1925 when I helped pass this bonus bill over the president's veto that it would stir up all this fuss."[10] After meeting with Curtis, Cox rested, ate a hot dog and drank three bottles of root beer before flying back to Pittsburgh.

Cox initially told the men to return home and vote against any legislator who refused to approve the bonus. He may have underestimated the determination of the men. They jeered him and rejected his advice. "You are Americans, not radicals. We have a legitimate way out of this trouble. It is through the ballot. If Congress rejects your demands, go on as orderly soldiers and through the November ballot turn out of office all those who have refused your demands."[11]

The reaction of the veterans forced Cox to do an about face. He urged the men to persevere. "You will never get what you want unless you stick. Men are coming from every corner of the country and if you stick it out, before this is over, there will be 500,000 to one million of you. There is a false impression that I am going to advise you to go home. I am, but only after you have got what you came here for."[12]

To add some drama to the moment, Cox added: "I know every one of you is as much a soldier prepared to protect his country as he was in 1918."[13] Then speaking in a soft voice, Cox folded an American flag he had taken down from a nearby standard. "There is no place for the man or woman who would tear down that old red, white and blue and what it represents."[14]

Waters tapped into the reservoir of desperation among the out-of-work former soldiers. He led a contingent on a 3,000-mile cross-country trek, setting up camp in the shadow of the Capitol on May 3, 1932. U.S. Rep. Wright Patman sponsored payment legislation, but the bill died in committee. In June, Patman's bill got out of committee for a vote. The House passed the bill 211–176 but it was defeated in the Senate.

More veterans began mobilizing across the county. More than 1,200 men massed in Cleveland, blockading freight traffic from leaving the rail yards. The men wanted the railroads to allow them to hop freight trains so they could reach Pittsburgh, a major way station for men moving across the country on their way to Washington. The veterans paralyzed rail traffic until 300 police officers broke the blockade. The men resumed their journey to Pittsburgh on foot, but they found their arrival unwelcome. Pittsburgh police marched the men through the city. Gov. Gifford Pinchot refused to provide any aid for the veterans, and they were denounced by the American Legion and the Veterans of Foreign Wars, who kept their distance because of suspicion that the march was backed by the Communist Party.

As the veterans surged eastward, they played a cat-and-mouse game with the authorities. More than 800 vets arrived in Pittsburgh from Chicago. Another 450 came from Missouri. More than 700 more came from the Monongahela Valley in southwestern Pennsylvania. Just north of Pittsburgh, 60 men tried to board a train in Sharpsburg despite efforts of railroad detectives to stop them.

In Connellsville in Fayette County, 600 men brought freight traffic to a halt. With the trains grounded, the marchers sunned themselves atop Pullman cars or swam in the Youghiogheny River. Others lounged on the tracks, their bodies draped across the ties with their heads resting on the rails to prevent trains from rolling. Railroad officials spread rumors that a freight train was ready for travel. Several hundred men climbed atop boxcars, but the train simply backed into the yard and stopped as a freight train rumbled by them.[15]

On June 6, 1932, the first contingent of 5,000 veterans paraded past 100,000 spectators in Washington, D.C., who saluted the men as they marched past. Some of the ex-soldiers wore tattered shoes and threadbare clothes. Others wore their military uniforms. At a pace of 90 steps per minute, they filed along carrying American flags that were grimy from the long, cross-country trip.

President Hoover had been informed July 27 by military officials that the situation along the Anacostia Flats was out of control. Hoover ordered a grand jury investigation into the BEF because he suspected communists were behind the movement.[16] The Bureau of Investigation checked 4,364 sets of fingerprints for criminal records among the veterans. The bureau discovered 1,069 had records for murder, manslaughter, robbery, assault, car theft, assault and burglary. Thirty-eight men had been convicted of crimes at least four times.[17]

General Douglas MacArthur ordered soldiers to move in on the encampments on July 28 and push the veterans across the Potomac. Infantry units, led by Majors Dwight Eisenhower and George Patton, approached the campsites, firing tear gas and forcing the men to retreat. They were followed by cavalry with sabers flashing in the sunlight. Vets and their families were caught in the confusion of rearing and kicking horses and the effects of the tear gas on the nose and eyes.[18] The next day, MacArthur ordered the camps burned. The treatment of the vets enhanced the public's perception that Hoover had disregard for the suffering of

Americans. Cox called the removal of the veterans "barbarous,"[19] charging that "King Herbert the First had blood on his hands. He has the blood of soldiers on his hands and I say that any man who supports him will not only have blood on his hands but on his soul."[20]

America must reject Herbert Hoover and all that he represents if she means to continue as a democracy. Herbert Hoover lost trust with the American people. Not only was his the most inefficient administration in history, but he now adds to his infamy by asking the American people to forget that he unnecessarily sacrificed the lives of World War vets in the debacle at Anacostia. America has always stood for justice and a square deal. America will never forget. America will never excuse the barbarous treatment of the World War heroes.[21]

After being routed, the dispirited veterans left Washington. They were driven out of Virginia and Maryland as the men made their way on foot or automobile to Johnstown, Pennsylvania. Mayor Eddie McCloskey came to the capital and told the men they would be welcome in his city, although he later denied issuing the blanket invitation. The bonus marchers soon wore out their welcome in Johnstown. After the final 400 men eventually left Johnstown's Camp McCloskey, named after the mayor, the encampment was set on fire. The Pennsylvania and Baltimore & Ohio railroad sent 80 cars to pick up 6,000 marchers as volunteers passed out 2,500 sandwiches and poured 60 gallons of milk. The dispirited men pledged: "We're not done. We'll be back."[22]

Immediately upon his return from Washington, Cox and 60 others embarked on another pilgrimage to Lourdes, France. When he returned, he would begin his quest for the presidency of the United States.[23]

13

Cox for President

More than 55,000 people jammed Pitt Stadium in the Oakland section of Pittsburgh in February following Cox's return from Washington. "I'm going to run for president," he told reporters. "The principal point will be a job-for-every-man, as outlined in the petition I presented to Congress and President Hoover.[1] A Jobless Party could rally millions right now in this country," Cox predicted.[2]

The *Pittsburgh Catholic* wrote that given the degree of discontent simmering in the nation, Cox might easily lead three million supporters in the creation of a third party. "The idea is not entirely without the realm of possibility, not if one is to judge by the comments on the street," noted the paper in an editorial. "There are men in high places who will laugh [at] such a suggestion to scorn, but they are men who have no idea of the state of mind of hungry men and women."[3]

Oakland was the home of the University of Pittsburgh and the stadium was the home of the school's football team, the Pitt Panthers. Hundreds of cars and trucks created a logjam as the unemployed from the coal patches and mill towns of southwestern Pennsylvania flooded the stadium under a gray sky that spit hailstones on the crowd from a rainstorm. Thousands more stood outside hoping to catch a glimpse of Cox or shake his hand.

The crowd was a mix of women dressed in fur coats sitting next to coal miners wearing tattered sweaters and unemployed men with gaunt looks, all cheering for Cox.[4] "I also especially invite the old families, the society leaders, the industrialists, the bankers who are interwoven in all life in western Pennsylvania to attend alongside their unemployed neighbors," said Cox.[5]

The crowd was in a frenzy. Each patriotic song played by the several bands brought volley after volley of cheers from the crowd. Cox entered

Cox addresses crowd at Pitt Stadium after his return from Washington, D.C., in 1932. Just a month after his historic march, Cox already had his sights set on the White House, as 55,000 people filled the stadium for the rally (James R. Cox Papers, 1923–1950, AIS.1969.05, Archives & Special Collections, University of Pittsburgh Library System).

the stadium and walked along the cinder track in front of his "army" seated by the speaker's stand. A rabbi delivered the invocation. A Lutheran minister performed the benediction. E.R. Frame was dressed as Uncle Sam. "I'm not interested in any political office," Cox told the crowd. "I am interested in the people and their needs.[6] We have no respect for either party,

Cox meets with supporters after returning to Pittsburgh from Washington in January 1932 (Dr. and Mrs. Mason, Father James Renshaw Cox Collection, Saint Patrick–Saint Stanislaus Kostka Parish, Pittsburgh, Pennsylvania).

the Republican or Democratic Party. Both have failed. They had had two years in which to act and have done nothing while conditions grow steadily worse."[7]

Cox created a stir by rushing to the front of the platform, grabbing a large American flag from the hands of a band member, and waving the flag to the cheers from the crowd. Cox announced his Jobless Party would hold a nominating convention in St. Louis that summer in the hope of forcing the major parties to enact legislation that would lessen the nation's suffering. The Great Depression continued its stranglehold on the city as relief organizations were running out of money and patience waiting for Congress and Pennsylvania to act.

More than 500 people were seeking help each day in early 1932, straining the resources of relief agencies. The Allegheny County Emergency Association had spent nearly $2 million of the $3 million it had

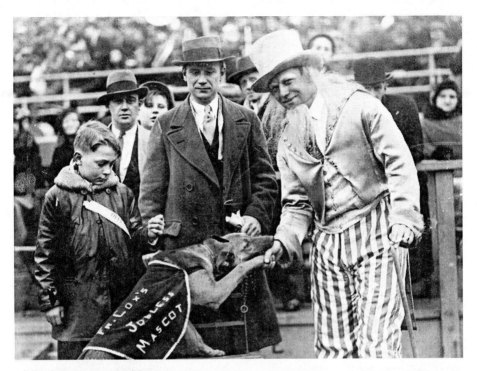

E.R. Frame portrayed Uncle Sam at a rally at Pitt Stadium, touting Cox's campaign for the presidency, ca. 1932 (James R. Cox Papers, 1923–1950, AIS.1969. 05, Archives & Special Collections, University of Pittsburgh Library System).

raised from various corporations.[8] The heads of city and county relief agencies begged for help. Pittsburgh and Allegheny County were running out of money for relief as more than 160,000 people faced starvation by March unless money was found to help feed them.

The Pittsburgh Emergency Association was broke and the Allegheny County Welfare Fund needed an immediate infusion of cash.[9] Pittsburgh Mayor Charles Kline asked city council to declare an emergency and authorize spending $500,000 that council had been withholding as a "last resort." But councilman W.Y. English, chairman of the Finance Committee, said the city hadn't reached a crisis yet and hoped the state legislature would come to the city's aid.[10]

The Poor Board announced it no longer would provide help to the unemployed, only the poor, and passed the buck to the Emergency Association. Attorney Harry W. McIntosh said, "We decided we exist only to care for the poor and any measures to care for the unemployed be taken care of by the Emergency Association."[11] Cox sent a telegram to President

Cox relaxes on the deck of an ocean liner during one of his pilgrimages to Lourdes, France, ca. 1932 (Dr. and Mrs. Mason, Father James Renshaw Cox Collection, Saint Patrick–Saint Stanislaus Kostka Parish, Pittsburgh, Pennsylvania).

Hoover reminding Hoover of the consequences of failing to act to alleviate unemployment: "Told you last January there would be riots and probably revolution because of your attitude toward unemployed."[12]

Cox sailed for Europe to attend the Eucharistic Conference in Ireland in July before starting his presidential campaign. He planned to visit Italy and Germany, but before leaving Pittsburgh, Cox gave reporters his views on national politics that made him sound more like a despot than a priest. He wanted the U.S. Army and Navy to stage a military coup and make the president a dictator, "and in 12 or 15 years this country will be fit to live in."[13]

Let him actually assume the tradition [sic] power of the president as commander-in-chief of the armed forces of the nation. But don't hamstring him with a Supreme Court. This all sounds like Fascism but it's more than fascism: It's the only to bring some sense out of chaos. We believe the capitalists who are in control must be

Cox chartered a train car for his annual pilgrimage to the Shrine of Ste. Anne de Beaupré in Canada, 1932 (James R. Cox Papers, 1923–1950, AIS.1969.05, Archives & Special Collections, University of Pittsburgh Library System).

ousted. Wall Street is not an American institution but a capitalist institution. We have had Wall Street control for too long. Hoover, like Nero fiddling while Rome burned, is asking for confidence while thousands are starving.[14]

Before arriving in Ireland, Cox stopped in Canada, where he continued to criticize American politicians. "Until we produce statesmen, such as England and Canada have produced, rather than a horde of crooked politicians and grafters, conditions in the United States, as they are today, will not improve," he told reporters.[15]

Cox said he would seek meetings with Hitler and Mussolini to ask their advice on how to run the nation after he was elected. A Protestant magazine attacked Cox for seeking advice from the Fascist dictators while other critics called him a Nazi sympathizer. Cox later denied ever seeking their advice, but he conceded that he met with one of Hitler's representatives during a previous trip to Munich.

After reaching Ireland, Cox handed out food to the poor as he traveled around Dublin. Cox passed out pennies to the children who pushed and shoved to get close to the priest and scrounged on the pavement for coins that fell from his hands. Cox noticed the legs of the children were so thin that they resembled a child's wrist.[16]

"I have been among the poor all my life and I can look at a child and tell whether it has had enough to eat. These children were terribly undernourished; some of them were actually starving. I felt sick at heart because I knew that these few pennies meant not candy or soda but food.[17] I made it my business to visit every slum in every city I was in," he said.[18] Cox went to one of the poorest sections of the Irish capital where Irish flags flew in every window of the tenements. He walked past the buildings where the living quarters of the residents consisted of a bed, a table and three chairs.

The crowd attending the Eucharistic Conference was estimated at 500,000. Cox chartered a plane and flew over the throng, marveling at the sea of scarlet and purple robes of the bishops and cardinals who were present.[19] Back in Pittsburgh, his supporters were making arrangement for a meeting between Cox and William "Coin" Harvey, leader of the Liberty Party, at the Creve Couer racetrack near St. Louis. The goal was to merge Cox's Jobless Party with Harvey's Liberty Party and nominate a presidential candidate to challenge Hoover.

Cox left Ireland, traveled to Rome and began talking publicly about his plans for his presidential campaign that he convinced himself he could win with the help of the nation's unemployed. He boasted to a reporter for the Italian newspaper, *Tevere*, he expected to receive at least 17 million votes. He was so confident of winning that he invited the correspondent to lunch at the White House after he was elected.[20] In Rome, Cox claimed he met privately with the Pope to gain his blessing, but a Vatican spokesman was quick to say that Cox was only a part of a group of pilgrims touring the Vatican. "He neither had a chance to talk with the Pope nor receive the Pope's approval. He has not spoken with anyone at the Vatican regarding his candidacy. Neither is anyone at the Vatican interested therein," said a spokesman.[21]

"I didn't have a private audience with the Pope," he conceded. The issue of a priest seeking public office was not an issue, he said. "He [the Pope] would no more have anything to do with my candidacy than I would with his rule of Vatican City," Cox said.

"The bishop is my spiritual father and I have his permission to run. Bishop Boyle said he would not interfere with my plans. There is no law in the Catholic Church which prohibits a priest from running for public office and I shall accept the nomination of the Jobless Party if the honor is offered me."[22] Boyle said he had no problem with Cox running. "If Father Cox wants to be president of the United States, his bishop will not interfere," Boyle said.[23]

After leaving Rome, Cox traveled to Munich, Cologne, Paris and Cherbourg before returning to New York on the SS *Majestic*. Cox told reporters how he planned for the government takeover of banks and utilities after he was elected.

> Whatever influence I have will be used to preserve this great government given to us by our forefathers that has been appropriated by the *plunder bund* and used for their selfish interests and against the many.[24] The government ought to control the banks just as it controls the army and navy put together. Why should the government print money and then turn it over to the private bankers to profit by? The people of this country are not going to stand another winter like the last one. There will be bread riots all over the country.[25]

Cox got into an argument with his traveling companions on the return trip to the U.S over statements he made about wanting to meet Hitler and Mussolini.[26] "There may have been some little bickering and squabbling among the men occasionally but that is to be expected," he said.[27] When the ocean liner docked in New York, Cox changed his story claiming he only wanted to pay his respects to them as important figures, but changed his mind. "I almost fell over when I found out that, according to the newspapers, I was going to get tips on how to run the United States. Of course, that's absurd. Furthermore, Mussolini and Hitler are the last people on earth I'd want any advice from. They are the direct antithesis of what I represent. I'm sorry there was so much of a mix up about the whole business."[28]

Cox prepared to campaign when he returned to the city. Andrew Krupnick, who served as Cox's secretary, filed the papers in Harrisburg creating the Jobless Party, which also fielded candidates for the U.S. Senate, Pennsylvania Auditor General, Treasurer, and two judges for the Pennsylvania Superior Court. Cox planned to hold conventions in Chicago and St. Louis to coincide with the Democrat and Republican Party conventions, but decided to hold one session in St. Louis.

Before leaving for St. Louis, Cox spoke to a crowd in Monongahela in southwest Pennsylvania and attacked fellow Catholic Al Smith, accusing him of being a tool of Wall Street. "I have no regard for Al smith," Cox said. "He represents Wall Street and the money interests as much as Republicans. Don't you believe anyone who tells you my speech making is camouflage for the political campaigns of either Republicans or Democrats. You know what I think of the Republicans and Democrats.[29]

Cox became more strident in his criticism of both parties. "The old parties have a chance now," he told a crowd at St. Patrick's. "They have been shown the situation. The demands of the people are apparent to all."

14

"No Weapons,
No Grouches, No Liquor"

Cox devised a grandiose scheme to end the Great Depression. He built an agricultural commune outside of Pittsburgh to allow its residents to become self-sufficient by growing their own food. Coxtown was built on 36 acres 10 miles north of the city in O'Hara Township on land that he purchased for $75,000. Jobless men hacked out the community from a heavily wooded area using axes and saws to fell trees and clear thick brush.[1]

The men built public baths and a jail. Since money was scare, Cox printed scrip with a picture of himself to serve as currency. Quarter-acre plots were given to families who lived in two-room bungalows.[2]

More than 10,000 people turned out for the dedication ceremony, but the experiment was a failure because the lots were too small to grow enough crops to be self-sustaining. A bank foreclosed on the property in 1937 after Cox failed to pay off the remaining $13,000 debt and it was sold at a sheriff's sale.

Cox used Coxtown as a launching pad for his presidential campaign before leaving for St. Louis. Cox hoped 25,000 would attend the campaign kickoff, but only 2,500 showed up. His expectations for a million people to follow him to St. Louis also failed to materialize. People huddled around the speaker's platform or sat on the hillside to listen to the angry priest who was itching for a fight. He referred to millionaires as "rats" and attacked charities, the wealthy, newspapers and politicians. He removed his clerical collar, whipping himself into a fever pitch.

Cox raised ethnicity as a campaign issue by referring to Herbert Hoover's Anglo-Saxon background. Pointing to a reporter in the crowd, he accused journalists of refusing to mention Hoover's ethnicity in their

119

Homeless men build an experimental community of Coxtown outside Pittsburgh that Father Cox hoped would be a self-sustaining town populated by
homeless families. The plan was doomed from the start because the plots were
too small to grow enough crops to be self-sustaining. Circa 1930 (James R. Cox
Papers, 1923–1950, AIS.1969.05, Archives & Special Collections, University of
Pittsburgh Library System).

stories.[3] In the 1920s and 1930s, people were often defined by their ethnic
background, their religion, or where they lived. The working class viewed
the Scotch-Irish Presbyterians as their overlords because these white,
Anglo-Saxon Protestants controlled banking, finance, government and
the legal professions to which the poor had no access.

The longer Cox talked, the more strident his speech became. Words
flowed off his lips without much thought. Instead of preaching nonvio-
lence as he did during the hunger march, he urged supporters to use their
fists if they had to. "If they try to cheat Father Cox at the polls, I ask you
to literally knock their heads apart. It's the first time I've asked you to be
pugnacious or militaristic."[4] Cox challenged FDR and Hoover to a debate.
"I will at any time debate any issue with Roosevelt or Hoover matching

Supporters listen as Cox delivers a blistering speech criticizing Herbert Hoover at Coxtown before he departed for the Jobless Party convention in Missouri, August 28, 1932 (James R. Cox Papers, 1923–1950, AIS.1969.05, Archives & Special Collections, University of Pittsburgh Library System).

my brains with theirs and then you will see if I have a right to oppose them," Cox said.[5]

Cox departed for Missouri after the speech, wearing a silk blue shirt with a banded white collar and the words "National Chief" embroidered in yellow thread.[6] His blue-shirted followers trailed him in their cars and trucks. His only orders were there be "no weapons, no grouches, no liquor."[7] As more than 200 cars and trucks headed west from Pittsburgh, Communist Party members passed out pamphlets to the passing vehicles. The literature was torn up and discarded.

The caravan that escorted Cox to St. Louis was much smaller than the one that accompanied him on his march to Washington, but Cox expected more people to greet him when he arrived in St. Louis. "There'll be a big crowd there. Lot of Pittsburghers have gone there already." He added, "I have reports from my office that many left Sunday after we did and that a lot more will leave today. You'll see something really wonderful in St. Louis. It's going to be a revelation to everybody."[8] He told reporters he expected between 40,000 and 50,000 to make the trek to St. Louis. Cox believed that his campaign was a national cause and naively expected one million people from across the nation would rally behind him. Cox overestimated his popularity. "This is serious business—a sacred crusade—and it is no time for levity."[9]

The threat of massive crowds triggered fears among St. Louis officials, who worried the influx of so many people would create health problems because of the lack of sanitary facilities.[10] St. Louis Police Chief Joseph Gerk said he had received a telegram warning him that 400 communists planned to infiltrate the Jobless Party to get communist candidates on the Jobless Party ballot. Cox claimed that Gerk had sent the telegram to himself to prevent the march.[11] "If there is anything a Blue Shirt despises more than a capitalist, it's a communist," Cox said.

The caravan moved along 17th Street in the Strip District to Penn Avenue, then down Grant Street past the Allegheny County Courthouse and City Hall before heading west toward Ohio. Cox led the motorcade riding in a Packard, followed by a blue pickup truck. The caravan headed for the suburbs of Mount Lebanon and Dormont until it reached Washington, Pennsylvania, 20 miles south of Pittsburgh, then headed west.

Stragglers were to rendezvous in Cambridge, Ohio, before heading for Columbus. They stopped to rest as Cox's supporters spent the chilly night sleeping in their cars or on the ground in rolled-up blankets. From there they traveled to Indianapolis. About two dozen supporters hopped Chicago-bound freight trains hoping to meet Cox in St. Louis. Through southwestern Pennsylvania and eastern Ohio, well-wishers swarmed his vehicle, kissing his hand and offering money for his relief work.

Cox hoped to merge his Jobless Party with the Liberty Party led by "Coin" Harvey, an eccentric 81-year-old populist lawyer and author whose support for the free coinage of silver had earned him his nickname. He hoped the two would hold a joint convention to nominate candidates for president and vice-president. Harvey was known as the "Tom Paine of the Free Silver Movement" and wrote a successful book, *Coin's Financial School.*

In the early 1890s, the country experienced a depression that was followed by bank failures, farm foreclosures and business bankruptcies. Harvey ardently believed the nation should abandon the gold standard and return to silver as a basis for currency to restore economic prosperity. He formed the Liberty Party in 1931, and like Cox, saw no difference between the Republicans and Democrats.

The joint convention was held at the Creve Coeur Lake Speedway outside St. Louis, but a rift developed between the two men over who should be the party's nominee for president. Cox brought 800 delegates to the convention plus 60,000 proxies. Harvey's followers numbered a hundred. The two men sat down to settle the dispute in a small, one-room cottage near the race track.

Harvey was a tall, lean man who sat on the edge of the bed smoking a corncob pipe. Cox got right to the point. "The one big question before us is whether we are willing to fuse. You represent the west. I represent the east. We can succeed if we get together."[12]

Fred Burch was an aide to Harvey. "You are undertaking, for Cox, to put this campaign over on a sensational and spectacular basis and on an appeal to the sentiment," said Burch. "We do not approve of that sort of campaign. We want to reach homes by a careful education program. Remember, the religious question beat Al Smith."[13]

Cox jumped to his feet and said such whispering campaigns about Catholic candidates being tied to the Pope appealed to bigots. "Don't forget that in 1928 the religious issue was not the only one. There was Tammany Hall and Wall Street. They will not figure in this battle."[14]

Burch questioned whether nominating Cox to head the ticket would be a smart move. "I'm not fighting you because you are Catholic," added H.G. Easteridge of Odessa, Texas, another Harvey supporter. "But how are you going to get it out of the people's mind?"[15]

Harvey was indignant that Cox would presume that he should head the ticket. You're asking me to step aside, while you, a new man, comes in and takes my place?" Harvey told Cox. "I've given my life to this work. I don't really want the nomination; I'm only taking it because of suffering humanity. Now you, who have been in this movement only two months, and bring this religious issue with you, want me to step aside. I'm disgusted."[16]

A reporter covering the convention wrote the disagreement between the two men was much more serious. "There were angry words. The religious issue was raised. Neither was ready to allow the other to become the joint party presidential nominee. Cox thought Harvey had agreed to campaign as vice president on the ticket until the religious issue surfaced. Cox's supporters accused Harvey of religious bigotry as Austin Staley, Cox's campaign manager, nearly came to blows with the elderly Harvey." "Because the Liberty Party raised the religious issue, the Jobless Party cannot consider a fusion [with the Liberty Party]," added Staley.[17]

Staley claimed that Harvey had agreed that Cox should head the ticket. "That's not true. It's false, it's false," said Harvey.[18] "It's not a question of religion but of bread and butter and jobs," Cox said. "If anybody suggests to me that I step aside because I am a Catholic priest then I am through. I am an American citizen."[19] Cox couldn't see why his Catholicism was an issue since he had family members who were non–Catholics.

> My forbearers were members of the Catholic and Protestant religions. I know them all and love them all and they love me because we are all Americans and all members of a great American family. If we choose different routes to heaven that is a matter which concerns us as individuals and not as American citizens. I am disappointed in the action of the Liberty Party.[20] If anyone wants to bring up the religious issue, he does so to his own detriment. If he turns the thing down because I am a Catholic priest, he'll raise an issue that he'll never live down.[21]

Liberty Party supporters were concerned about statements Cox made that he would seek the advice of Hitler and Mussolini on how to run the United States after he was elected. Harvey's supporters asked, "Do we want a dictatorship fashioned on the pattern Father Cox will cut with Rome and Berlin?"[22] Harvey said the question facing American voters in the fall was "the flag of Washington, Jefferson and Lincoln or the blue shirt of Father Cox."[23] The Communist Party called the Jobless Party "quasi-Fascist" and referred to Cox "as the blood brothers of Hitler and Mussolini." It said its creation was the "first aping of the European Fascist movement in the United States."[24]

Since Cox and Harvey couldn't reach a compromise, each party held their own convention. "The desertion of Harvey was just another sign of religious prejudice. I am glad it came out so quickly," Cox said. "I valued Harvey's ideas more than I valued Harvey. But I shall not miss his support. He has very few followers, only a handful attended the convention. If I went to the polls tomorrow, I believe I'd poll 100,000 votes but, by November, there may be a change."[25]

When the convention started, Cox's nephew, George Mason, nominated his uncle for president. Earl C. Dean seconded the nomination as more than 800 blue-shirted supporters cheered for 15 minutes and drivers honked their horns continuously. "Is that all the noise you can make?" Mason shouted.[26]

Cox said he never would have run if Hoover had met his demands when they met in Washington in January. He said the Depression that had settled upon the country "and throughout the world is not something that has come because any breakdowns of business in the last two or three years. It is the culmination of efforts of the last 50 or more years to place control of the government and business in the hands of a few."

His fellow Catholics were not impressed by Cox's rhetoric. The Catholic Archbishop of St. Louis, John J. Glennon, was less than enthusiastic about Cox's campaign for the presidency. "I am afraid that Father Cox, finding his efforts successful in helping the poor let his judgment be overcome by his enthusiasm. He is a man of little political sense, I understand. In fact, who has any political sense nowadays? I am neither an apologist, defender nor accuser of Father Cox," Glennon told reporters.

Glennon said he had no authority to stop Cox from coming to St. Louis. "Well, why should I? He didn't preach heresy, he was against communism as everyone knows, and he was striving in his way to help the unemployed. He used the word 'jobless,' that, I think, is a cheap word."[27]

The convention may not have been successful, but it did have some value. Cox's candidacy drew people back into the political arena. Cox sounded a death knell for Hoover's brand of capitalism as he left Missouri for Pittsburgh.

> Justice will have the bandage removed from her eyes, and America will be happy again if decentralization should be the order of the day; if we provide for our own protection and keep in mind that while the largest and most powerful nation on earth, we may become an easy victim to the avarice and cupidity of greedy enemies. Every attempt at monopoly or unfair trade practices should be, in the interests of fair trade, secretly prohibited and punished. We have come to the end of an economic era. As a nation, we are groping in the dark, awaiting the dawn of a new day. When that dawn comes, it must bring a better era than that which has passed. It must provide equal opportunity to all men, regardless of wealth.[28]

Most political analysts and writers didn't believe Cox was serious about running for president, given the fact that his campaign was hastily cobbled together. He had no organization, no staff and no money. Others weren't so sure about the militant priest. Democrats worried that a third party would help Republicans and Hoover win reelection. "Politicians who failed to appreciate the significance of the march of Father Cox's Army on Washington are making a grave political mistake," wrote one analyst. "The portents of that orderly petition of the dissatisfied to the government cannot be laughed off."[29]

15

Shepherd-in-Chief[1]

Father Cox began his quixotic campaign for the presidency at 1:10 p.m. on August 29, 1932, on the steps of St. Patrick's Church. A small group of supporters waited outside for him to begin his westward journey seeking votes among the nation's unemployed that Cox hoped would put him in the White House. Cox naively believed he could win the presidency by amassing more votes than any other third-party candidate in American history based on his perception of his popularity. He saw the nation's jobless as his flock and he was their shepherd.

Cox envisioned large crowds awaiting him at every stop as he headed west, cutting a jagged line across the country in a motorcade consisting of two cars and a trailer equipped with a loudspeaker. His campaign team consisted of his Sancho Panza, Andrew Krupnick, and John Obermeier, who served as Cox's driver. Two advance men, brothers Al and John Fabie, arranged speaking engagements at cities along the campaign trail. Attorney Donald Perry of Johnstown, Sarah Voit of Huntingdon, West Virginia, and Cox's uncle Will Mason also came along.

The team would soon be on each other's nerves during the arduous cross-country trek to California and back. They had to contend with car problems, petty squabbles, no money, hunger, spiders, humidity, heat, a near electrocution and a dearth of campaign donations that at times reduced the party to begging. Everywhere they traveled, the people they met were poor or just getting by. They relied on the kindness of locals and priests they met along the way for a meal and occasional lodging.

When Cox returned to Pittsburgh from Kansas City, he said surviving on the campaign trail nearly led to starvation. "Well, I very well nearly went hungry," he said. "We ate sandwiches and were glad to get them."[2]

Krupnick's diary is the most inclusive account of the campaign. Newspapers along the campaign trail gave little coverage to Cox despite all the stories about his hunger march earlier that year on Washington. The document, at times, reads like a travelogue, as Krupnick describes the sights, towns and people where they stopped. He writes little about the poverty he witnessed or how the residents of these widespread communities viewed Cox's candidacy.

Krupnick was a 40-year-old bachelor when he hit the campaign trail and lived with his sister and brother-in-law in Pittsburgh. He served as Cox's "Man Friday" and accompanied Cox on his pilgrimages to Lourdes.[3]

Traveling cross country wasn't easy in the early 1930s. America's roads were not in the best condition. There were no superhighways, so it took a driver between one and two months to drive from New York to San Francisco.[4] Krupnick didn't realize the distance between campaign stops, especially as they traveled farther west. "I had no idea about the wide-open spaces, miles and miles of it, and not seeing a human being or a house for miles and such straight country as far as your eyes could carry your [sic]," he noted in his diary.[5]

Cox was a part-time candidate and escaped much of the hardship because he returned to Pittsburgh between campaign appearances and caught up with the group at the next campaign stop. His frequent flights to and from Pittsburgh were a financial drain on the campaign. A flight from Pittsburgh to San Francisco cost $139 that the campaign could ill afford since the campaign spent $1,731.04 but only raised $478.88 in contributions.[6]

"I'm not departing my companions," Cox said. "It's imperative that I get back to Pittsburgh to see what can be done about replenishing our campaign chest. I am more convinced and determined than ever that the Jobless Party must carry its fight, the people's fight to the finish."[7]

By the time Cox ended his campaign, he and his supporters traveled 7,795 miles in six weeks through Ohio, Indiana, Illinois, Iowa, Nebraska, Missouri, Kansas, Oklahoma, Texas, New Mexico, Arizona and California. Cox spoke before crowds ranging in size from 8,000 in Elk City, Oklahoma, to a handful in the sparsely populated towns of the southwest.[8]

The first stop after leaving Pittsburgh was in Ohio. Cox arrived in East Liverpool, where he was greeted by 400 people. Krupnick passed the hat and collected $14.59 in donations.[9] Cox repeated his campaign promises at every stop.[10] "In 1917–18, we spent $40 billion in a war which resulted in nothing but the deaths of millions of brave men," he told his audience. "We should not hesitate to spend $5 billion to aid the needy. God never intended man to be a slave. Mr. Hoover has a good time and the many other rich men have good times. Why shouldn't the poor man at least be permitted two days out of the week in which to enjoy the beauties of the United States?"[11]

Cox reached Youngstown that evening and went to a minor league baseball game between teams from Youngstown and Dayton. Cox was introduced to the crowd of 6,000 by one of the umpires. "The empire [*sic*] introduced Father Cox and believe me there was a wild applause from the audience through the whole ball park," Krupnick wrote.[12] "I say my friends, we are not living, we are starving," said Cox as he shook hands and signed photographs of himself.[13]

Cox sat atop the car and told well-wishers about being a former newsboy, steel worker, cabbie, and baggage man for the Pennsylvania Railroad. Cox stayed overnight in Youngstown and shared a bed with Krupnick and Obermeier, who had to contend with Cox talking in his sleep. "We could not stand it much longer so I woke him up and told him to stop and let us get some sleep," Krupnick wrote in his diary. "He opened his eyes and siad [*sic*] 'What's the matter?'"

Cox and the others pressed on through Ohio. They reached Wooster, where the turnout was so sparse that Krupnick advised Cox to keep driving. "Note. Wooster is a Presbyterian town," Krupnick wrote.[14] In Massillon, Cox was greeted by Mayor Jacob Coxey, who also was running for president on the Farmer-Labor Party ticket. It was Coxey's 1894 march on Washington that inspired Cox to make his hunger march. About 2,500 Massillon residents turned out to hear Cox on a hot and humid night.[15] "Father Cox said to Mayor Coxey, 'You and I have made the greatest trips to Washington, D.C.—you had to walk over the mountains and we traveled by automobiles.'"[16]

Cox marched on to Mansfield, speaking to 2,500. It was still very hot when he arrived. Krupnick made the introduction to the crowd. "He is a man of the people [who] knows what it means to be poor. He knows what it means to have a mother struggle to educate him. He was a newsboy, a mill worker, a department store clerk, a taxi man, a baggage man. He is the father and shepherd of the jobless and last but not least he is the mayor of shantytown. It is our hope that the road from shantytown will lead directly to the White House in Washington, D.C."[17]

Local officials in Portage, Ohio, were not so hospitable and withdrew the welcome mat when county officials refused to allow Cox to speak on the courthouse steps.[18] Cox pushed on to Bucyrus, Galion, Upper Sandusky and Lima. The hot weather continued as Cox traveled from town to town.[19]

By the time the party reached Fort Wayne, Indiana, Cox already was back in Pittsburgh and his return flight to Indiana was late. Krupnick stalled for time and warmed up the crowd by telling a joke of how Lincoln freed the slaves, how Henry Ford freed the horses and how Herbert Hoover freed the working man. By the time Cox arrived, the crowd had dissolved.[20] "The crowd was sure disappointed in not seeing Father Cox," Krupnick wrote.[21]

Krupnick and others couldn't afford the cost of a hotel room, so they rented cabins at the Westwood Tourist Camp. It rained hard, increasing the humidity, which brought out the spiders and mosquitoes.[22] The rain was still coming down when they reached the cabins. It was damp inside so Krupnick took off his socks and placed them over a line to dry. A barefooted Krupnick touched an electrical cord and was jolted by a surge of electricity. "They tell me I gave out one awful yell for it was an agonizing sort of cry," he wrote of his near-death experience."[23] The shock knocked Krupnick unconscious. He collapsed on the wet concrete floor. A sparking electrical wire lay near him. His traveling companions thought he was dead. "My, what a feeling I had when I came too [*sic*]. It was like looking back to earth from another world."[24]

They reached Joliet, Illinois, where Cox attacked the two major parties. "Shoot me if you like. Do what and say what you will about me. It makes no difference. As long as I have a tongue, I will shout the truth about the Democrats and Republicans and the capitalists who are strangling the freedom out of America."[25]

In Iowa, the home state of Herbert Hoover, Cox's reception was downright cold. Local officials didn't take kindly to Cox's criticisms of Hoover's economic policies, so Davenport officials refused to issue a permit so Cox could speak.[26] A Cox supporter explained that Davenport mayor George Tank, a Democrat, was a "lukewarm Catholic."[27]

Davenport had been hit hard by the Depression. Thousands of residents were out of work and on relief. The homeless erected a shantytown along the banks of the Mississippi River. The local radio station also barred Cox from speaking because of the mayor's influence. "Whole town is stirred up about the city officials not allowing Father Cox to speak,"[28] Krupnick wrote.

During a stop in Davenport, Sara Voit read the diary that Krupnick was keeping and became angry when she read his unflattering description of her.[29] "The old she-devil started to pick on me and accused me of trying to blackmail her and ruin her character. I'm sick and tired of it all. I did not eat any breakfast.[30] Cox was angry when he learned of Voit's snooping and lectured her about her behavior and ordered her to return home. "It was a Battle Royal when we were all gathered in the room," Krupnick wrote. "But Father Cox had it all thrashed out before he left. It all lasted about an hour and a half and it was some battle,"[31] Later, when tempers cooled, Voit asked to stay. "Well, I guess you're sorry for what you said to me and what Father Cox said?" Voit said.[32] "No, I'm not," Krupnick replied.[33]

Despair began to engulf the contingent when Cox flew back to Pittsburgh. They were hungry, broke and tired. "This is the first time in my life that I can recall that I was broke without a penny to my name and so far away from home. It's tough. I called Father Cox on the phone and told him we were penniless he said that he was sorry but could not send any money as he himself was broke."[34] They hunkered down in a tourist cabin wondering how they would pay for the room and eat. "It was a terrible night out—raining very bad—the end of a terrible, lonesome day for all of us."[35]

Cox rejoined the group in Omaha, then rode with them through Missouri until they reached Kansas City, Kansas, where Cox met with Roland Bruner, national chairman of the Liberty Party. Bruner told Cox the party was disenchanted with Harvey and wanted Harvey to withdraw as their nominee.[36] Harvey, according to Bruner, "was nothing but a liar." Cox told Bruner that if Harvey accepted Cox as the presidential nominee, he pledged he would name Harvey Secretary of State after Cox was elected president.

Cox reached Oklahoma on September 19, where he met Dr. Victor C. Tisdal, an Elk City physician who was Cox's running mate. The two men made quite a pair. Cox was a rotund Catholic priest, and Tisdal was a Protestant, a 32nd Degree Mason and Shriner, who owned a hospital. The two candidates delivered their acceptance speeches at a banquet held at the Casa Grande Hotel. Tisdal delivered a five-page speech. When it came time for Cox to speak, the crowd seemed uninterested.

Cox downplayed the fact that he was a Catholic priest. The *Elk City Morning Times* reported that Cox said "he would fight to the death to see that every man worshipped God to the dictates of his own conscience and that he had been free to select his route to heaven and granted everyone the same privilege."[37]

"They sure were very hard boiled," Krupnick noted.[38] Cox spoke about the Blue Shirts and said his organization was not modeled after the Black and Brown Shirts of Mussolini and Hitler. Cox told his audience he never met either dictator but said Hitler's personal representative did interview him while Cox was in Germany.

I am a Catholic priest and I am doing my duty as a Catholic priest and I am doing my duty as a Catholic in a way that I know best to save my soul. But that does not hinder me from helping you regardless of your faith—which you know is right to save your soul. I am a shepherd. We are taught in school that we are shepherds and whoever thought of a shepherd sitting under a tree while his flock was being fleeced? So long as I live and God gave me my tongue, I will use it to what it best for humanity.[39]

Traveling through the vast, unpopulated areas of Texas, Arizona and New Mexico made Krupnick realize just how difficult campaigning in the west would be. When Cox reached Tucumcari, New Mexico, the local newspaper wrote that Cox's appearance was "unannounced, unheralded and unexpected."[40] The editor wrote that Cox was really a political shill for FDR and "living off the land and the people thereof while on tour."[41] Cox "was just one of the many characters who spring up during elections and panics but he was probably not as nutty as some of us think then, for they generally wind up with a nice little stake and a lot of prominence."[42] They reached Albuquerque, New Mexico, and were stranded. A crowd of 500 gathered in McLean Park but Cox couldn't leave Pittsburgh by plane because of high winds. The spectators were disappointed. Krupnick was only able to collect $8.40 in donations. "It sure did look like a lot after being broke," he wrote.[43]

In Arizona, the party stopped at a Navajo settlement where Krupnick went to confession and then Mass. He was surprised to find the church filled with Navajos and several "Chinamen."[44]

The party pressed on to California. They reached Needles on September 26 after traveling through the night along the narrow mountainous roads. "The least wrong turn of the wheel the wrong way meant certain death, a drop of thousands of feet and not a single person would ever know about it. We all sure were scared."[45]

Cox was to fly to San Francisco to rejoin the campaign team but expressed concern that the campaign was floundering. "We found a great deal of interest and enthusiasm everywhere we went and if I had enough money to put on a real campaign I could get results."[46] Cox's public statements were more optimistic than Krupnick's account. While Cox did speak to several large crowds, most of his appearances were either unattended or he was greeted by sparse turnout.

Next on their itinerary were Ludlow, Victorville, Cajon, San Bernardino, Cucamonga, Los Angeles, Azusa, Santa Anita and Pasadena. They reached Hollywood and waited near a movie studio hoping to see movie stars. They stopped to rest and resumed their journey later that afternoon along Route 101 until they reached San Francisco. They had been on the road for 31 days. Cox rejoined the campaign in San Francisco on October 1 and told a reporter that he had enough money "for one more week" of campaigning.[47] His arrival attracted 500 people at a speech after the two San Francisco newspapers, the *Examiner* and *Chronicle*, did stories on his arrival.[48] Another reporter asked Cox if he still wanted to get advice on running the country from Hitler and Mussolini if he was elected. "Father Cox said yes and the next morning had it that Father Cox was going to see Mussolini and Hitler to find out how to run the United States."[49]

Cox returned again to Pittsburgh, leaving Krupnick and the others to make the return home without him. They reversed course in California and reached Arizona. In Flagstaff, they didn't have money to pay the hotel bill, so they sat around in the hotel lobby playing checkers.[50] "No one has eaten anything since last night and it is now 1:30 p.m. We are playing cards and checkers. Everyone is suggesting one thing or another about getting some money or something to eat. We cannot leave the hotel. We have no money to pay for last night's lodging and furthermore, we have no gasoline for the car. What can we poor stranded nine people do but wait."[51]

Krupnick wired Cox of their predicament. "Stranded—no money— gassed yesterday—18.00 eaten up—all ate yesterday one fourty [*sic*] all day—need $100.00—Pine Hotel—Flagstaff—Arizona—Andy."[52] Krupnick managed to scrounge $2.25, which was enough to pay for a meal of pork, potatoes, corn and coffee. "Did we enjoy the meal. This is the first real meal in two days."[53] They were forced to sell one of the cars for $100 to raise cash for the return trip. The campaign officially ended in the scrub grass of New Mexico. They had been on the road for forty difficult days.

A woman dropped $100 in the collection plate during mass at St. Patrick's, allowing Cox to enable Krupnick and the others to finish the trip.[54] They pressed on through Oklahoma, Missouri and Indiana, reaching Columbus, Ohio, on October 9. They pushed onto West Virginia, where they had their seventh flat tire and spent their last $3.80 to fix it. "I prayed like I never prayed before that we would not have any more trouble for I had no money left," Krupnick wrote.[55]

Despite the hardships and lack of interest in the campaign, Cox told reporters he added supporters for the Jobless Party at each stop. "We feel that our trip so far has added 250,000 followers to our cause," he said.[56]

At 3 p.m. on Sunday, October 9, the party reached Pittsburgh. "It was like a new world and we were glad. Words cannot express how I felt after all that trouble. This was an ideal way of seeing the country even with all the trouble I had with all the money and dislikes of one another and the fights. It was the most unique way of getting to the people. My, but I am tired, very tired."[57]

16

"Roo, Roo, Roosevelt."

Cox told reporters he was abandoning his campaign for president while he sat at the kitchen table in the rectory of St. Patrick's Church sipping a cup of coffee. Getting out of the race was a bitter pill to swallow after believing that millions of unemployed would rally to his cause. Now he faced the reality that the jobless weren't listening to him. He claimed that it was not personal ambition that drove him to run. His presidential campaign had one goal, he said: to force Hoover and Roosevelt to focus on economic solutions to the Depression. In that regard, he said, his campaign was a success. "The nation's awake to the real issue of the election.[1] Tell the people the truth. I haven't the funds to carry on. Besides, it's a strain on my health. But don't get the wrong idea. I'm still in the race. Only it has come to me that the people of Pennsylvania know what I stand for. Those who will support me will do so without any last-minute effort on my part," he said.[2] "I realize that many ballots would be cast for me if I remained as a candidate but our political system is so ordered that I cannot be elected. It is so arranged that Roosevelt or Hoover must win."[3]

Cox was stunned by the poverty he had seen on his journey through the central and southwestern part of the country. "I have found conditions intolerable, worse than they are experiencing in the east and I experienced them in a first-hand way. In one state I found a farmer's family of five living on less than $50 a month while the state allows each prisoner in the penitentiary $18 a day," he told reporters.[4]

Cox's withdrawal drew more news coverage than the campaign itself. Newspapers, large and small, carried stories about his decision to quit and support Roosevelt for president.[5] The end of his candidacy didn't end the drama, but exposed the depth of Cox's political ambition. Socialist candidate Norman Thomas accused Cox of trying to persuade him to merge the Jobless and Socialist Parties just as he tried to merge with the

Liberty Party. Thomas said Cox made the offer after the Jobless convention in Missouri. Cox denied the claim, calling Thomas "a prevaricator of the first order."[6]

Thomas claimed Cox had approached him after the convention and said the two men could decide between themselves who would lead the ticket. Thomas came to Pittsburgh immediately after the controversy surfaced and took the offer as a joke.[7] Cox wasn't laughing. "It's a huge joke to think that fusion between a Socialist and a Catholic priest could be possible. I could no more endorse Socialism and Norman Thomas than I could endorse Stalin or Communism."[8]

Cox endorsed Roosevelt for president and the next day FDR accepted an invitation from David Lawrence, chairman of the Allegheny County Democratic Committee, to speak in Pittsburgh.[9] Roosevelt's train pulled into the city after traveling through small towns in Ohio and West Virginia. Thousands of people lined the streets to see the future president. Public schools gave students the day off. More than 12,000 turned out to hear Roosevelt in Wheeling, West Virginia, and another large gathering in Washington, Pennsylvania, as he made his way to Pittsburgh. Roosevelt accused Hoover and the Republican Party spreading the "gospel of fear."[10]

Roosevelt arrived at Forbes Field in the city's Oakland neighborhood to a 15-minute-long ovation. A car carried him to the speaker's platform. He walked up an incline holding onto the arm of his son, James. City and county officials were waiting to greet him as Democrat loyalists dressed as donkeys led the crowd chanting "Roo, Roo, Roosevelt."

Lawrence waited on the stage for Father Cox to make his dramatic entrance a few minutes before the speeches began. Cox excoriated Hoover, charging that Hoover favored the wealthy and that the president was "a man bent on making the rich richer."[11]

Mr. Hoover stands for special privilege. He stands for the protection of a few who have amassed swollen fortunes and who desire to dominate the country and its government for their own selfish gains. Mr. Hoover has forgotten 120,000,000 American citizens.[12] The opportunity to help was presented to Mr. Hoover a thousand times but never did he lift a hand nor raise his voice to relieve the suffering of the American people.[13]

Cox heaped lavish praise on the New York governor, who cited the encyclical written by Pius XI, *On the Reconstruction of the Social Order*, during his speech.[14] "Mr. Roosevelt has pledged himself to the protection of the interests of the common man. He has pledged himself definitely to the policies which will aid in the economic recovery and re-creation of work."[15] When Roosevelt began to speak, 55,000 people in the stadium cheered as floodlights focused on the speaker's platform.[16] At the same moment FDR was speaking, Hoover's running mate, Frank Knox, was speaking in Oakland to a much smaller crowd of Republicans at the Duquesne Gardens.[17]

Roosevelt discussed the daily struggles families faced making ends meet. He lashed out at fear-mongering Republicans who were "shifting the boast of the full dinner pail made in 1928 to the threat of the continued empty dinner pail in 1932."[18] The turnout for FDR's appearance in Pittsburgh was a black eye for the Republicans, who had controlled city and county government since the Civil War. "Franklin D. Roosevelt crashed a home run last night at Forbes Field which soared over the fence and landed in the G.O.P.'s own backyard," wrote one reporter.[19]

Pennsylvania had been a bastion for the GOP since 1865. Sen. Boise Penrose, who died in 1921, was the last singular political boss in the state. After his death, political power was shared by William Vare, the boss of the Philadelphia machine; Joseph Grundy, president of the Pennsylvania Manufacturer's Association; and William Larimor Mellon in Pittsburgh.[20] Democratic Senator Joe Guffey in 1932 told his party if it wanted to break the Republican grip on the state, they had to elect FDR president.

David Lawrence, a Catholic who became the future mayor of Pittsburgh and governor of Pennsylvania, also was drawn to the social gospel contained in the papal encyclicals. He saw first-hand the effect that poverty, dilapidated housing, lack of health care, unemployment and a polluted environment had on Pittsburgh residents. Cox spoke on FDR's behalf in Catholic wards while Ellenbogen spoke to Jewish voters. Robert Vann, the publisher of the influential *Pittsburgh Courier*, helped lead black voters from the ranks of the GOP to the Democratic Party.

Pittsburgh and Allegheny County remained in dire economic straits. The Reconstruction Finance Corporation loaned Pennsylvania $7.5 million in aid with a promise for an additional $5 million after Gov. Gifford Pinchot had requested $45 million. The government said it would provide free milk to 50,000 undernourished school children in Pittsburgh and Allegheny County. The Allegheny County Relief Association pleaded for $2.5 million in contributions to fund relief.[21]

The turning point for the Hoover campaign in Pennsylvania came when he toured the Monongahela Valley by train. Hoover viewed the lifeless mills and the column of smokestacks no longer belching fire and smoke from steelmaking. No longer did the hum of industrial machinery echo through the valley.[22] Still, large crowds greeted Hoover as he traveled through western Pennsylvania.[23] He promised "no one shall be hungry or cold" in the upcoming winter.[24] But as election day drew closer, Allegheny County Republicans canceled their traditional "pep rally" before the election as Roosevelt predicted a landslide victory. The Great Depression was the backdrop of the 1932 election with an unemployment rate of nearly 24 percent. Hoover, with a history of failed promises, and FDR, who had been reelected governor of New York by a landslide, faced each in November. Roosevelt picked House Speaker John Nance Garner of Texas as his running mate to solidify the southern, conservative wing of the Democratic Party. FDR ended up carrying 41 states. Although Hoover carried Pennsylvania, FDR carried Pittsburgh and Allegheny County.[25]

Roosevelt's victory gave Lawrence, the new patronage boss, control over 57,000 jobs in western Pennsylvania. Along with $70 million in federal funds through the Works Progress Administration for construction of highways, water lines, playgrounds and parks, Lawrence was able to build a Democratic machine.[26] Hoover carried Pennsylvania by a 5.5 percent margin, but Pittsburgh and Allegheny County went for Roosevelt. He carried the city by 27,000 votes, winning 26 of the 32 wards. He carried the county by 37,000 votes.[27]

Roosevelt's election and his creation of the Works Progress Administration and a promise to create three million jobs buoyed the nation that better economic times were ahead. In Pittsburgh, business leaders held a premature celebration. More than 100,000 people staged a mock funeral parade with floats and 30 bands, saying goodbye to "old man hard times." Beulah Corey was named "Miss Better Times," riding astride a horse through downtown to the cheers of the crowd.[28]

After Roosevelt's election, Cox kept a low profile but said he was not getting out of politics. "People ask me why I don't stay on the pulpit and quit messing in business and political affairs. I am and always will be the shepherd of a flock and when I see my flock slowly being devoured by the wolves of Wall Street, I fight them. They hear only the voice of Wall Street and not the voice of the people."[29]

He continued to serve St. Patrick's and helping feed the poor. He became involved in local politics, supporting candidates for mayor, and sought a political job as a tax assessor with the city. The people of Pittsburgh had not heard the last from Father Cox. The rest of his life would be a carnival sideshow.

In 1936, Cox tried to muster support for another march on Washington n support of the Townsend Plan, the brainchild of Dr. Francis Townsend of Long Beach, California, who believed the best way to stimulate the economy was by instituting a pension for the retired and elderly.

Backers wanted voters to influence their local congressmen to vote for the plan, but a stubborn Cox insisted on going to Washington himself. "It won't do anybody any harm for us to tell the president and Congress what people are thinking back home," said Cox.[30] "We don't want to embarrass the Townsend people in Washington but we haven't asked them for an indorsement [sic] of our trip."[31]

The poverty rate among the elderly was over fifty percent, so the plan called for people over 60 to receive $200 a month pension funded by a $2 billion government bond issue. Townsend's thinking behind the plan was that a huge amount of money infused into the nation's money supply would stimulate purchasing power and create more jobs. The only catch was the money had to be spent quickly. Townsend calculated that a tax on an estimated $935 billion in gross business revenue would produce between $20 billion and $24 billion a year.[32]

Cox's latest "march" turned out to be nothing more than a bus trip.[33] Only 40 people accompanied him to Washington, where he met briefly with Dr. Townsend. The group drove eight hours in a bus over the same ice- and snow-covered roads that Cox had crossed four years earlier. Roosevelt agreed to see Cox, but the priest was unable to persuade the president to support the plan. As a consolation prize, FDR gave Cox a piece of sandstone from the White House, which was undergoing renovation, to place in the new church Cox was building.[34]

Cox returned home. The following year, a fire destroyed his beloved church. Cox was about to write a final chapter to his controversial life that would tarnish his reputation as a humanitarian.

17

Up in Smoke

A five-alarm fire on March 21, 1935, swept through St. Patrick's Church in the Strip District, leaving only the altar and a crucifix standing amid the smoldering ruins.[1] The church once served as a place of worship for Pittsburgh's Catholic aristocracy before becoming a workingman's parish.[2] Men in top hats and tails, and women wearing billowy dresses that swept along the floor, attended Mass at St. Patrick's until working families from the Strip and nearby Lawrenceville began attending services there.[3]

St. Patrick's had been founded more than three decades before the Catholic Diocese of Pittsburgh was established. The church began as a chapel on a 60-by-64-foot lot on land donated by Col. James O'Hara, who served in the Revolutionary War and as mayor of Pittsburgh in 1803.[4] The church's first pastor, William Francis Xavier O'Brien, walked for several months from Baltimore before reaching Pittsburgh in 1808.[5] Bishop Michael Eagan of Philadelphia dedicated the church two years later. The first church was located at the intersection of Liberty and Washington Streets. The second was built along 14th Street before Father Cox built the present building in the Strip District.

When the fire broke out in 1935, police officer William Joyce and a pedestrian, William Heck, rushed into the blazing structure to search for victims. One of Cox's assistant pastors ran into the flaming sacristy and rescued the Blessed Sacrament. Several homeless people were trapped on the upper floors of the rectory. Cox's father lived in the building but managed to escape along with eight homeless men living in the basement. Cox's housekeeper, Charlotte Rieger, was trapped on the third floor but escaped by jumping into a net held by firemen.[6] One of the walls collapsed just as firefighters leaned a ladder against it.

The cost of building a new church was estimated at $200,000, but

Cox immediately pledged to replace the historic church. "There must be a St. Patrick's Church in Pittsburgh. There has always been one but where and when it will be erected I can't tell," Cox said.[7]

Once the diocese approved construction, Cox purchased 350 pounds of Italian marble for the floor from Henry Phipps, a business partner of Andrew Carnegie, that Phipps used to build his natatorium.[8] Cox paid $400 for the marble and had men living in the shantytown haul the stone on trucks to the building site. Then he embarked on a 13,000-mile journey to the Middle East to find materials to use in the construction.

Cox sailed on the SS *Byron*, and while he was on his way to Greece, one of the sailors died of a heart attack. He described the man's burial at sea and took up a collection of $185 for the man's wife and four children in Athens.[9] The sailor's body, wrapped in a white sheet, was carried onto the deck and a piece of board with a lighted candle was placed on his chest. Fellow sailors followed a Greek custom by kissing the deceased on the forehead as the captain read a prayer. A fifty-pound weight was tied to the man's feet as his body was dropped into the water. The ship's horn sounded as the man's body crashed into the waves.[10]

Cox traveled to Cairo, Egypt, and then to Palestine before reaching Jerusalem, where he visited the home of Joseph of Arimathea and celebrated Mass at a nearby French monastery. He visited King David's Well and the Mount of Olives, where Jesus ascended into heaven, and the Church of the Nativity, where Christ was born.[11] Cox spent time at the Via Dolorosa, Golgotha, and the Valley of Kidron, and saw the tree where Judas Iscariot hanged himself after betraying Jesus.[12] In Jerusalem, Cox bought a mother-of-pearl crucifix that stood four feet high.[13] The pearl, he claimed, came from the Sea of Galilee. The wooden cross was made from trees cut in the Garden of Gethsemane and contained carvings of the 12 apostles surrounding the pearl inlay. A carving of Christ on the cross was made from ivory.[14]

Cox brought back 700 stones taken from Calvary, the Garden of Gethsemane and the Holy Sepulcher. Each stone was wrapped in paper and Cox marked where it was found. He also received the piece of sandstone from the White House as a gift from President Roosevelt.[15] In a note to Cox FDR wrote: "For the new church of Father Cox. The piece of stone from the north wall of the White House removed during repairs of October 1935. Franklin D. Roosevelt."[16]

He built a replica of the Holy Stairs patterned after the Scala Sancta in Rome. The Scala Sancta are said to be the stairs that Jesus ascended in the palace of Pontius Pilate in Jerusalem where Pilate washed his hands to absolve himself of Jesus' fate. The stairs are considered so sacred in the eyes of the Catholic Church that the 28 steps can only be climbed on one's knees. At each step, the penitent says a private prayer.[17]

Cox hosted tours of the French shrine at Lourdes and wanted to build a replica of the shrine outside the new church because he claimed holy water from Lourdes restored his failing eyesight.[18] To raise money for the construction, he held the Garden Stakes Lottery as a fundraiser. Contestants paid one dollar and submitted three names for the shrine and a chance at winning the $10,000 grand prize. Police had been investigating Cox's gambling ventures and suspected he had rigged six other lotteries so he could keep the lion's share of the take by not having to pay real winners.

The "winners" were picked at random from phone books from 27 states, Canada, Puerto Rico and Washington, D.C., or were relatives of the promoters, or didn't exist.[19] They were selected by a group of shady promoters who pocketed most of the prize money.[20] The investigation revealed that Cox may have fixed other lotteries to raise money for his charitable work.[21]

Dr. Henry F. Walker of Pasadena, California, won the grand prize. He was the physician of one of the promoters.[22] Another "winner" said she allowed her name to be used as a contestant as a favor to an uncle who was one of the promoters.[23] A $500 "winner" was the daughter-in-law of one of the promoters and used her maiden name on the ticket. Another had the same address as the boarding house where another of the promoters lived.[24] Cox had publicly pledged that the contest would be run honestly: "Be assured that this contest will be conducted under my personal supervision in a manner guaranteeing complete fairness and affording each and every person who competes the opportunity of receiving unbiased consideration from those whom I have personally selected for their ability, intelligence and integrity to serve as my judges."[25]

An indictment charged that most of the money was divided among the promoters and Cox for their personal use.[26] During their investigation, postal inspectors found thousands of dollars in cash that was supposed to go to the winners.[27] The indictment alleged Cox was using the postal system to become one of the country's biggest lottery operators.[28] They also discovered that Cox held 11 other lotteries and two raffles that raised questions among federal investigators about their honesty.[29] The headquarters for the contests was in a schoolroom next to St. Patrick's.[30]

Cox was shocked by the indictment. In 1930, Cox had been named one of Pittsburgh's ten outstanding citizens by the Pittsburgh Advertising Club and the *Pittsburgh Press*. Cox bested such notable Pittsburghers as

Treasury Secretary Andrew Mellon; Edgar Kaufmann, the department store owner; Howard Heinz, president of the H.J. Heinz Company; as well as the presidents of the University of Pittsburgh and Carnegie Tech, Pittsburgh Mayor Charles Kline, several corporate officials, and other clergymen.[31] The following year he had been voted the most popular radio personality in the city.[32] "It was the biggest surprise in the world to me. I was surprised to see the article in the paper, worse than the original shock."[33] U.S. Attorney Charles Uhl said he would prosecute Cox "to the limit. If these charges are true, they will prove that there was no intention of awarding prizes legitimately."[34]

Cox was defiant saying, the government would have to call out the army to stop him. He also claimed to have contacted Postmaster James Farley, who gave his blessing for the contest.[35] "We were told to go ahead," Cox claimed. "In fact, they cooperated with us. If they show us something is wrong, we'll stop it but they'll have to show us something is wrong. We have an obligation to the people who entered."[36] Testimony by the government would prove that wasn't true.

Cox was a snake-oil salesman who concocted various schemes to raise cash. When a miner in 1935 claimed a miraculous image of Christ appeared out of the soot from his chimney, Cox had the chimney dismantled and shipped to St. Patrick's, where he charged the curious a quarter to view the image.[37]

The Great Depression spawned widespread gambling and get-rich-quick schemes that preyed on cash-strapped victims. Lotteries have long been part of the social fabric of Pittsburgh. They were used by churches, colleges and government to raise money, but soon attracted swindlers and con men.[38] The First Presbyterian Church of Pittsburgh held the "Pittsburgh Lottery" in 1807 to pay for construction of a church, but the contest was mired in scandal. "No correct account of the amount of tickets sold was ever rendered ... that lottery business ended in complete failure," wrote a church elder.[39]

Pennsylvania authorized the Union Canal Company to hold a lottery in 1833 to raise $400,000 to build a canal along the Susquehanna River. The canal lottery distributed $33 million in prizes between 1811 and 1833, but only $225,000 went toward construction[40] because of the "sticky fingers" of ticket brokers.[41]

In the 1930s, an estimated 5,000 people were selling lottery tickets in Pittsburgh. The winning numbers were based on the daily results published by the New York Clearing House Association, which settled financial deals between banks. The association stopped publishing the results in 1930 because lottery promoters were trying to bribe association employees for the numbers in advance of their release.[42]

Pennsylvania banned lotteries in 1860, but authorities seldom enforced the law until the early 20th century.[43] When a Catholic church in Pittsburgh in 1912 held a raffle for a car, authorities issued arrest warrants for Fred Clarke, manager of the Pittsburgh Pirates, and star pitcher Marty O'Toole, who sponsored the contest.[44]

No one was immune from prosecution. U.S. Senator James Davis of Pennsylvania was indicted by a federal grand jury in 1932 for using lotteries to promote fundraisers for the Loyal Order of Moose, of which he was director general. The Moose awarded cash prizes based on the numbers on attendance tickets to fundraisers and charity balls.[45] The government charged that Davis was the "power behind the throne" of the Moose and steered more than $172,000 into personal bank accounts.[46] Davis was acquitted.

Bingo was banned for a time, even though the game was invented in Pittsburgh in 1935 by Hugh J. Ward, who staged games at carnivals and fairs in Pittsburgh and western Pennsylvania.[47] The Pittsburgh Catholic Diocese banned bingo at 444 churches in 10 counties in the late 1930s after the Allegheny County District Attorney said bingo was a "lucrative racket of professional promoters and gamblers."[48]

Cox held lotteries on horse races and baseball games even though the federal government considered this form of betting illegal.[49] Lotteries in Pittsburgh and Allegheny County were big business, raking in an estimated $30 million annually, which far surpassed the amounts raised for relief. In 1930, bettors hit for $500,000 on number 805, putting lottery operators in the North Side, South Side, Hill District and East and West Ends out of business.[50]

Cox first came under police scrutiny in 1934 when a man selling tickets for the Father Cox Relief Fund was arrested with 500,000 tickets for horse races, an automobile raffle and baseball pools.[51] Questions about the honesty of Cox's previous contests was raised in 1932 when he staged a sweepstakes contest in the Grand National Steeplechase. Irene Davis of Pittsburgh was notified she was one of the winners even though neither she nor her husband had purchased a ticket and the horse chosen in her name was a scratch. "I know enough about horses to know that the horse has to win or come in second to get anything," she said.[52]

The most surprising revelation that came out of the investigation was that Cox operated a night spot near Pittsburgh that was raided by police. Coxtown had become the Calmwood Swimming Association, a gambling joint and nightclub that sold liquor and held dances four nights a week. The raid was part of a federal investigation into allegations that Cox was using the mail to conduct gambling.[53] Later that year, police raided a gambling den in the Strip District, seizing records linking Cox to gambling and other lotteries whose outcomes were questionable, making him "one of the country's biggest operators of such enterprises."[54]

Cox was warned that his lottery was illegal and in a July 1, 1937, letter to Cox from a government attorney, he was told using the mails to solicit donations from contestants was mail fraud. He blamed the government investigation for scaring away potential players. "A lot of subscriptions would have arrived during the final days if the government hadn't stepped in. As it was, many persons were frightened by the government's action and changed their plans to participate," he said.[55]

Thomas Harkins, the chief promoter, proclaimed his innocence to reporters who waited for him outside his attorney's office in Pittsburgh. He claimed he didn't know the names of any relatives who were among the winners. "Let me alone," he told reporters. "I have something to work out that may put me in the clear. I have nothing to hide. I have nothing to run away from. There are others in this case. There's a lot to come out on this, a lot that only myself and the Postal Inspectors know."[56]

18

The Trial

The trial of *U.S. v. James Renshaw Cox* was held in the spring of 1938 in Pittsburgh's federal courthouse before Judge Frederic Palen Schoonmaker. Prosecutor John D. Ray outlined his case to the jury.[1] Promoters Arthur Wicks and Bernard Clifford testified for the government that Cox personally controlled the money and wrote the rules for the contest. Wicks told the jury Cox learned the promoters could not raise the $25,000 needed to pay off the winners and began scheming to find a way out of their predicament.

Wicks testified that he chose the winning name, "Wayfarer's Halo Garden," after considering "Wayfarer's Garden" and "Wayfarer's Rest." Wicks testified that Clifford traveled to Florida to borrow $10,000 from a man he knew in Miami. Clifford was carrying two postdated checks that Cox signed in exchange for the loan. The trip was unsuccessful because the man refused to loan the money.

Before the defense attorneys presented their case, they asked Schoonmaker to issue a direct verdict of acquittal, arguing the government had failed to prove the mails were used to defraud contestants. "For a man to take part in a conspiracy, he first must know it exists," argued Cox's attorney, Oliver K. Eaton. Schoonmaker denied the motion.[2]

Eaton began his defense of Father Cox by telling the jury that Cox was not seeking personal enrichment and had been duped by shady promoters. "His interest was for charity.... What he did was allow his name to be used in the enterprise he believed to be perfectly legal."[3] Eaton called then-Congressman Henry Ellenbogen, who testified that he visited the U.S. Department of Justice and met Post Office officials after Cox expressed concern over management of the contest. Ellenbogen said he told the promoters that no prizes would be awarded until he learned the government's legal position on the lottery. He suggested that the prize

Garden outside St. Patrick's Church (author's photograph).

money should be placed in an escrow account in Cox's name pending a government ruling.

Cox testified for a day and a half in his own defense, telling the jury that he now realized the contest was rigged but denied knowing that at the time. Wicks said that he gave Cox a receipt for $25,000 that proved Cox paid them that amount and that the money was to be used to pay the winners. "But I refused to accept it," Cox said. "I took the receipt and tore it up because it was no good."[4]

During contentious cross examination by Ray, Cox became so agitated that Eaton warned his client to stop being argumentative. "Don't argue, Father. Just answer the questions."[5]

Cox admitted he knew the amount of revenue the promoters hoped to raise fell short of the goal. "There were two ways to raise money and pay the prizes or to fix the prizes to make them look as if they were paid?" Ray asked.[6] "It is now obvious to you that the contest was fixed," said Ray.

"Yes, and that was wrong," Cox answered.[7]

Asked about a December 1937 meeting at the William Penn Hotel in Pittsburgh where it was decided that the winners would be paid little or nothing of the prize money, Cox said "I learned about that in court."[8]

Ray then asked Cox if he had changed the contest's rules. "I made no changes. I had nothing to do with the prospectus. They brought it to me already made up," Cox answered.[9]

"Did you have anything to do with the printing?"

"No," replied Cox.[10]

Three days before Christmas in 1937, Cox testified he met with Wicks and Harkins in his office. The two promoters presented Cox with checks with sufficient amounts to pay the prize money. "The checks were wrapped in deposit slips," Cox said. "When I opened them, I found the checks were signed by a Mr. Sol Bloom, Wicks and Harkins. They said don't put them through. Hold them."[11]

"And what about your money?" Ray asked.

"I told them I would hold it until they showed me the checks were good," Cox said.[12]

On Christmas Eve, another meeting was held. Cox explained the men wanted him to return the checks. "They said it would be evidence of good faith. And also they wanted me to give them $5,122 so we can show our friends. I said take your checks and receipts."

"Mr. Wicks testified you prepared the receipt," said Ray.

"I did not," Cox replied.[13]

Cox said he was angry when he learned the promoters had distributed the prize money without telling him. He learned of the payouts by accident when he went to breakfast at a hotel and an employee told Cox he had won $10. "He was very happy," Cox said. "I did not see the win sheets until the third or fourth of January. I always believed it was legal and still believe it was legal."

"You know no one had money in escrow?" Ray asked.

"I believed J.C. Pierman."[14]

Ray continued hammering away at Cox. "Why didn't you see that it [money] was put up?

"Because they were promoters and they were just using my name," Cox said.

"You put your signature on that?" Ray noted.[15]

"Yes," replied Cox.

"There was never anything in your mind that anything was dishonest at headquarters?"

"No, sir," Cox answered.

"Did you look at the books?"

"No, sir," replied Cox.

"Your attention on December 23 was to go ahead?" Ray asked.

"Yes," replied Cox. "The contest was in my name and I knew if the awards were not paid, there would be trouble."[16]

Ray's closing summation took two hours. He told the jury that the government had "amply and beyond a reasonable doubt" proved its charges. "Father Cox either told the truth in the literature of the contest or he was in on the fix. He either misrepresented what he was going to do, and if he did he knew about the fix. Either way he perpetrated a fraud,"[17] Ray concluded.

Eaton concluded his case by calling 14 character witnesses that included attorneys, physicians, a city councilman and a police detective.[18] Eaton told the jurors that Cox was "the greatest humanitarian who has ever lived in the Pittsburgh district" and was a victim of the unscrupulous promoters. "These smart fellows from Cleveland thought they put one over on Father Cox. The whole affair was a slippery scheme to hook Father Cox."[19]

Schoonmaker instructed the jury to carefully consider the testimony of the two main government witnesses, Wicks and Clifford, who pleaded guilty. "Such testimony may be of a character to convince you," the judge said. He also told jurors to weigh the testimony of Cox's character witnesses because their testimony might create reasonable doubt in their minds as to the priest's guilt.[20]

Cox waited in the hallway, surrounded by his elderly father and supporters, reading his prayer book while the jury deliberated for 26 hours without sleep.[21] The jury room was 25 by 16 feet and had two windows. Jurors sat at chairs and deliberated over two oak tables. By the time the deliberations were finished, the floor was littered with cigarette butts and scraps of paper used as ballots. Court officers could hear the jurors laughing and crying during the deliberations. The panel was deadlocked. There were four holdouts against convicting the priest. One juror remained steadfast against a conviction, saying he never would vote to convict Cox.

The jury's forewoman, Marie Doering, read a note to the judge telling him the panel was at an impasse on Cox. "Our convictions on four of the five defendants are set and we feel that further balloting will result in no further verdicts," she said. Schoonmaker told the jurors to go back and try one final time to reach a verdict. "The court is of the opinion that the jury should deliberate further. While undoubtedly the verdict should represent the opinion of all jurors, there is no reason why opinions cannot be changed in conferences in the jury room. I would like you to reach a conclusion as to the one remaining defendant and I am going to ask you to return and deliberate further for a short time."[22]

"All the jurors felt there was no evidence proving that the contest was a lottery," said another juror. "We all felt that as long as the government did not say outright that it was a lottery, we weren't competent to define a lottery ourselves."[23]

Eight jurors believed the contest was a fraud. Four jurors agreed the contest was rigged but that Cox had nothing to do with the fix.[24] While the jurors decided his fate, Cox waited for the verdict in the courtroom, his right arm stretched across the back of a bench. The jurors entered the courtroom with exhausted looks on their faces. Forewoman Marie Doering handed the judge a note reading they had voted 35 times. "We, the jury, after balloting all through the night and this morning wish to report we have arrived at verdicts on four of the five defendants and are unable to reach on the fifth. Our convictions are set and we feel that further balloting will result in no further verdicts."[25]

Schoonmaker ordered the jurors to try once more to reach a verdict. After further unsuccessful deliberations, the judge declared a mistrial. "It was 8–4, 8–4, 8–4 so finally, as we'd get ready to ballot, someone would start singing, 'Hi ho, hi ho, it's off to vote we go.' But the votes never changed. We had a regular songfest," said a juror.[26] The jurors were drained emotionally. "I hope I never have to serve on another jury," said one. "I was never so disgusted in all my life."

Harkins was convicted on one count of operating a lottery but acquitted on fraud charges. Attorney Max Schoonmaker, the son of the judge who had defended Harkins, bowed his head on the counsel table and wept openly.[27]

Cox smiled slightly as the verdict was read. He shook hands with supporters as he walked to the elevators. Eaton said his client had been vindicated. For once in his life, Cox was silent. "I have nothing to say," he told reporters.[28]

Newspapers that had lauded Cox over the years for his charitable work now viewed him in a different light.

19

"A Hitler Hatchet Man"

Father Cox was humbled by the verdict and soundly criticized by Pittsburgh newspapers for duping contestants who thought they were contributing money to a worthy cause. His reputation as a humanitarian and "shepherd of the poor" was tainted by charges he had pocketed most of the prize money. There was more bad news for Cox in 1939. Coxtown, the experimental community that he developed during the height of the Depression, and later transformed into a nightclub, was sold after Cox defaulted on a $13,000 mortgage.[1]

Cox soon was back in the headlines after he spoke to a group of Rotarians in the basement of a Methodist church in a Pittsburgh suburb and denounced fellow priest, the Rev. Charles Coughlin of Detroit, as a shill for Adolf Hitler, igniting a fierce debate among Catholics in the Pittsburgh Diocese that was heard all the way in Rome.[2]

Coughlin was an anti–Semite who accepted money from the Nazis and tried to justify the Nazi rampage of *Kristallnacht* by blaming the Jews for the German response to the assassination of a German diplomat in France by a Jew. Cox told his audience that Coughlin was nothing more than a bigot wearing a clerical collar. On the night of November 10, 1938, the Nazis unleashed a reign of terror across Germany that resulted in the deaths of 39 Jews, the destruction of 257 synagogues and the arrests of 30,000 Jews who were sent to concentration camps.

Rampaging Germans, fueled by the government, destroyed Jewish-owned businesses. The broken glass of store windows littering the streets led to the name "the night of the broken glass." Ten days later, Coughlin went on the air and blamed the Jews and their "radical tendencies" for the German response. The government said the incident was a populist uprising, but the outburst was fueled by the Nazis.[3] Coughlin became the "new hero of Nazi Germany."[4] Although Cox's answer to

Coughlin was not heavily covered by Pittsburgh newspapers, its impact was immediate.

> As a Catholic priest, I am grieved and humiliated that another Catholic is the vanguard of this Bigot Brigade. He is profaning his pulpit by preaching the pagan doctrine of anti–Semitism. For my part, I choose today to cry out against this sorry spectacle of the Detroit priest, ordained to teach the love of God, encouraged each Sunday over a radio hookup in parroting poisonous Nazi propaganda and huckerstering the heresies of Hitler. A Catholic priest has become a Storm Trooper! Coughlin has become a Hitler hatchet man![5]

The *Pittsburgh Criterion* ran Cox's picture on page one of its June 9 edition, praising him for his stand and castigating Coughlin:

> Father Cox is not the national figure you are. Not by any means. For he is not the entrepreneur, the conniver, the publicity-seeker that you have so deftly proved to be. But today he stands distinguished as the first officer of your church to condemn you publicly in terms which no other clergyman of Catholic faith has either had the courage or patience to use. He used no soft language. He did not make his point by indirection. He employed no euphemisms, for he did not feel you should be spared. He, in effect, defrocked you and exposed your ugly nakedness as one of the greatest menaces to peace and brotherhood that has arisen in this generation.[6]

The Canadian-born priest was a little-known pastor of the Church of the Little Flower in Royal Oak, Michigan, until he built a nationwide audience following during the Great Depression with a Sunday afternoon radio program, *The Hour of Power*, which had an estimated audience of 30 million listeners.[7] Coughlin began his broadcast career in 1926, but by the 1930s, his sermons had shifted from theology to economic and political issues and the Jews.

He became a national figure by tapping into FDR's rising popularity and the New Deal. "President Roosevelt is not going to make a mistake for God Almighty is guiding him," Coughlin once proclaimed.[8] Coughlin soured on Roosevelt by 1936 and became one of the president's most vocal critics and one of the nation's leading anti–Semites.[9] He accused FDR of being in league with the Jews. "We consider you [FDR] a traitor to the American interests, a tool of international bankers and a menace to Christian civilization. We will not be duped to fight with atheistic Russia. Until 1937, we were staunch Democrats. You made us good American Republicans."[10]

The Bishop of Detroit, Michael Gallagher, Coughlin's superior, ordered him to apologize. Coughlin backtracked. "I'm not saying Mr. Roosevelt is a communist," he said. "I never said it and never will. I do say he had adopted communist activities, and I just didn't get up here and say that he did; I have proven it.[11] He continued, "I have never heard anyone call Mr. Roosevelt a Communist. I must confess I have said he was 'communistic.' It's up to me to prove he was communistic or else get out of the picture. Does he hold a doctrine and theories that are held by the communists? My answer is absolutely yes."[12]

Coughlin was known as the "mad monk of Royal Oak." His "silver tongue" and "golden voice" drew listeners, Catholic and non–Catholic, to his message that the Jews had too much influence in the media, government and banking in the United States.[13]

His popularity coincided with the rise of anti–Semitic groups such as the Black Legion, the Silver Shirts and the Knights of the White Camellia, which used a swastika as their symbol. Many Americans adopted Coughlin's views that Jews were responsible for the nation's economic turmoil.[14]

Cox told his Rotary Club audience he was embarrassed that a fellow priest could harbor so much hatred toward another culture. Cox called the charges leveled against Jews by Coughlin "silly, ridiculous and baseless." He pleaded with Coughlin to "cease this bigotry" and saw Coughlin "as a priest wearing the robes of a Klansman."[15]

Coughlin had spoken in Pittsburgh three years earlier and denied he harbored any hatred toward Jews. "They tell me that on such and such occasion I have berated the Jew and I have stirred up anti–Semitic feeling against the Jew. May God strike me dead the day I do that thing," he told his audience.[16]

> At no time have I ever raised my voice or lifted my pen against the Jewish people as a whole. At all times I have pleaded for cooperation of religious Jews to stem the red tide of Communism. It is true I have regarded Nazism and still regard it as a defense mechanism against Communism. It is true many Jews were among those responsible for furthering Communism in Germany and burying that country to such a despondent state that Nazism became a reality. Must we conclude that the only reason for this attack against me is to shield from observation those who directly or indirectly support Communism abroad and at home?[17]

Cox compared Coughlin's accusations of a world Jewish conspiracy to the prejudice experienced by Catholics when extremist groups accused the Pope of trying to take over the White House when Al Smith ran for president in 1928 as the first Catholic nominee.[18] "If Father Coughlin is right then the Ku Klux Klan is right and if the Ku Klux Klan is right about the Jews, it is also right about the Catholics and colored people and Father Coughlin condemns himself and all that he represents," said Cox.[19]

Coughlin once was the darling of Pittsburgh Catholics, who rose to his defense when CBS canceled his radio program because of his support for the New Deal and criticism of America's "money barons."[20] The diocesan newspaper, the *Pittsburgh Catholic*, wrote: "They realized that in Father Coughlin they had met their most bitter adversary. They recognized in him a mental giant, and, furthermore, they knew he was armed with the philosophic and theologic teachings of the Catholic Church that, down through the ages, has been a constant defender of the poor man and the down-trodden laborer."[21]

As the Depression worsened and unemployment increased, anti–Semitism flourished. Right-wing groups united because of opposition to Communism and the New Deal, which the right viewed as benefiting the left in American politics.[22] Coughlin fanned this hatred through the Union of Social Justice and Pittsburgh members of the America First Committee, of which aviator Charles Lindbergh was the most prominent member. The organization opened an office on a busy street in downtown Pittsburgh and claimed to have 200 members.[23] Coughlin had endorsed the committee in *Social Justice*, a vitriolic newspaper he controlled.

"While as Catholics we cannot do anything to stop Father Coughlin, you may rest assured that all Catholic people and priests are not in sympathy with him. In my humble opinion, his attacks upon the Jews are abhorrent to everyone who believes in the Fatherhood of God and this Brotherhood of Man," said Cox.[24]

A Pittsburgh editorial writer questioned Coughlin's credibility, calling him the "great vowel roller. The only reason the world doesn't rock and shiver whenever he goes on the air is that he is so lamentably shy on accuracy." The writer hoped Coughlin would "withdraw from all radio activities in the best interests of the people."[25]

Coughlin and Cox were not always at odds. Cox had previously led bus trips to Detroit to listen to Coughlin preach.[26] Coughlin financially supported Cox's 1932 hunger march on Washington. Coughlin became one of the most influential men in America through his nationwide radio program, his newspaper, and his affiliation with the Christian Front, an anti–Semitic organization that organized boycotts of Jewish-owned businesses and equated Jews and communists.

He used code words, such as "international bankers," to accuse Jews of controlling the world's economy, which he claimed led to the Depression. After Germany annexed Czechoslovakia, Coughlin wrote that Hitler was unstoppable until the wrongs against Germany were corrected. He viewed the German government as a defense against the spread of communism.

Coughlin compared Jews to the money changers in the Temple, as referred to in the Gospels, and held them responsible for the banking crisis. Coughlin initially leveled his attacks on banks and big business.[27] He masked his references to Jewish bankers and financiers by employing phrases such as "entangling alliance," "money trust," and "international money plutocracy."[28]

He claimed that Nazi Germany was a victim of an international power struggle instigated by Jews intent on "the liquidation of Americanism at home.[29] "When we get through with the Jews in America, they'll think the treatment they received in Germany was nothing," Coughlin said to a cheering crowd in the Bronx.[30]

Coughlin was a theological lightning rod among Catholics because of his controversial views on social justice that were based on reforming the nation's monetary policy. He began mixing his sermons on economic philosophy with virulent anti–Semitic remarks, leading his critics to call him a Nazi stooge.

Coughlin viewed himself, not as anti–Semitic, but anti-communist. He saw the persecution of the Jews in Nazi Germany as an attack against communism, which he believed was a greater threat than Nazism.[31] He believed that Jews were responsible for the Russian Revolution of 1917 because so many of Lenin's supporters were Jews.[32]

Cox was unable to fathom how Coughlin could hate Jews but claim to love Christ. "I cannot understand how Christians can hate anyone, above all Jews," he said. "Christ was a Jew, and likewise, His immaculate mother, whom we revere so high, was a Jewess. So were the apostles and all [sic] the writers of the New Testament or Bible."[33]

Cox stood in opposition with ministers and rabbis in 1927 when the City of Pittsburgh announced plans to spend public money to pay for a visit to Pittsburgh by Queen Marie of Romania, whose government mistreated its Jewish citizens. Two years later, he spoke at a rally at Soldiers and Sailors Memorial Hall protesting Arab persecution of Jews in Palestine.[34] Cox was aided by Jewish merchants in the Strip District, who later provided him with money and food for his 1932 march on Washington, D.C.

Coughlin and Cox were men of the cloth but cut from different fabric. Both were opponents of capitalism and big business, advocates for the poor, and critics of Hoover's indifference to the economic suffering of Americans.[35] They relied on radio to get their message to the public. They were egoists who enjoyed seeing their names in the headlines.

Both priests built their reputations through radio. Both men were orators who understood the power of words. Both used their radio ministries as an extension of the pulpit. Both were staunch anticommunists who mixed religion, economics and politics in their sermons. Both supported the bonus payment to World War veterans. Both had followings among Depression-weary Catholics, formed political parties that adopted a Nazi-like salute, and challenged the Democrats and Republicans for the presidency.

Both were ruined by scandal. Cox escaped prison for mail fraud while Coughlin faced pressure from the government and church for his activities. Coughlin accepted money from Nazi Germany but failed to register as a foreign agent. A series of shady business deals also came under scrutiny. It was his connection to *Social Justice* that caused a grand jury to investigate him for sedition because of the newspaper's outspoken support for Nazis and Fascists. The government revoked *Social Justice*'s mailing privileges in 1942, and Coughlin folded the publication under a church threat that he would be suspended as a priest.

Coughlin became the voice for Protestants and urban Catholics who opposed the New Deal. Cox, who grew up in poverty, appealed to the unemployed because of his work in feeding the poor and homeless. Cox saw Coughlin's rejection of the New Deal as a rejection of the papal encyclicals, which Cox viewed as a blueprint for improving the lives of workers.

Cox accused Coughlin of misrepresenting the evidence that he claimed to have amassed of a Jewish plot to control the world's wealth. "Father Coughlin has produced forged documents, misquotations and deliberate misrepresentations as evidence of his accusations against the Jews. Only a Communist or Nazi Court would permit such so-called evidence as he used to bolster his alibis for retailing alien propaganda."[36]

He pointed out there was only one Jewish member of Roosevelt's cabinet and on the U.S. Supreme Court. "[Jews] are civic minded. They are patriotic. They are loyal to the land of their adoption," Cox said.[37]

The Jews didn't control the wealth or political power of the United States, he continued. Much of the nation's wealth, Cox said, was held by a few families.

I can assure you that the Mellons, Morgans, Rockefellers, and the Fords can buy all the Jews in the United States. I protest against this infamous doctrine of radicalism. I denounce racial prejudice. Above all, I cry out against anti–Semitism. It is immoral. It is un–Christian. It is un–American. Christ was a Jew and we, his followers must defend His people.[38] Father Coughlin, I adjure you in the name of bigotry. A bigot wearing the robe of Klansman is infamous, a bigot wearing the robe of a priest is despicable. You do not speak for the Catholic clergy. You do not speak for the millions of Catholic laity who wish to live in peace and harmony with their fellow citizens. As a student of economics or a political orator you would be ignored. Unfortunately, you speak as an individual Catholic priest and as such you command attention and that is the shame and danger.[39]

Cox's remarks were published in pamphlet form by the Pittsburgh *Jewish American Outlook* and distributed nationwide, which furthered widened the gap between Catholics who supported Coughlin and those who opposed him. The reaction following Cox's speech was so strong that it prompted one Pittsburgh newspaper to ban all letters concerning Cox and Coughlin because they contained "religious, racial and personal slurs of such a nature we cannot publish them."

> We endeavor to give as much latitude as possible to letter writers but there are limits of propriety which must be observed. Therefore, letters on the Cox-Coughlin subject are not being published. It is a tragic fact that so much of the bitter controversy centers around two men who are priests. We took that position because many of the letters received were so venomous in tone, so full of religious and racial prejudice, and so bitter in personalities that it seemed impossible to present them without arousing a dangerous and unworthy controversy. This is an era of bitter feelings—of racial prejudices, political hatreds and clashing ideologies, it is neither good journalism nor good Americanism to assist in or provoke such feelings—and though we again announce that letters which will promote racial and religious controversies cannot be printed.[40]

The paper said Coughlin was "a dangerous and demagogic man who was leading this country into paths of discord and hatred." The newspaper had no praise for Cox, stating he "is not a fit pot to call a kettle black,"[41] referring to Cox's involvement in illegal gambling and a fraud-ridden contest and subsequent trial "in which he gained the doubtful vindication even though a majority voting for conviction."[42]

Among the letters that were published, several writers praised Coughlin for his candor in criticizing Jews. "We have one of the honest men who is not afraid to tell the truth," wrote one man. Another denied that Coughlin was a Fascist, Nazi or anti–Semite. "He is a true American telling the lower classes of American people what we can expect to get out of the Government and President down in Washington—nothing but poverty and enslavement. Father Cox, in my estimation, has felt the sting for his outrageous speech against Father Coughlin from the people of Pittsburgh."[43]

L.C. Pritchard was critical of *Pittsburgh Press* editors for not running a Coughlin speech on the front page. "Knot only R yoo a heel n liar, yoo R a cheet to. Why don't you print Fr. Conklin's hole speech on frunt page ware evry won kin reed it without lookin inside yur danged sheet."[44]

Coughlin accused Cox of being part of a Jewish plot to smear his name and reputation, charging Cox with taking payoffs "for the work of the Jew." Even the Vatican came to Coughlin's aid. The Apostolic Delegate to the United States, Amleto Giovanni Cicognani, demanded that Bishop Boyle censure Cox. Boyle refused.[45] A Coughlin supporter accused Cox of being a communist. "Are you afraid the communists are going to get the upper hand here that if you side with them and consciously or unconsciously do their bidding you will be spared the persecution which will follow?"[46]

Church officials warned Catholics that anyone who supported Coughlin was not a true Catholic. Father Charles Owen Rice went on radio and warned Catholic supporters of Coughlin they were committing mortal sin by accepting his beliefs.[47] The Catholic Diocese of Pittsburgh took great pains to distance itself from Coughlin and his newspaper, *Social Justice*, which had reprinted the fictitious 19th century tale, *Elders of the Protocol of Zion*, that purported to be minutes of a meeting of Zionist leaders hatching plans for world domination.

The editor of the *Pittsburgh Catholic* said the material in *Social Justice* was nothing more than Nazi propaganda.[48] "The fact that *Social Justice* sees fit at a time when national unity is essential to promote disunity; that it obviously seeks to promote intolerance of certain racial and religious groups."[49]

Coughlin had a strong following in Pennsylvania, especially among Catholic blue-collar workers. Christian Front membership included poor Irish and German Catholics who also blamed Jewish bankers for the country's economic collapse.[50] Members of the right-wing Christian Front in Pittsburgh numbered about 200. Coughlin's supporters met at Pittsburgh hotels, but after these meetings, they often vandalized city shops owned by Jews and beat their owners. The movement in Pittsburgh and Philadelphia was thought to be behind attacks on synagogues.[51]

The Catholic Church in the United States denounced racism and condemned individuals for stoking anti–Semitic beliefs. Without mentioning Coughlin by name, Catholics, Protestants and Jews issued a warning in 1939 against "hatreds deliberately fomented against cultural groups by unscrupulous or misled individuals."[52]

Coughlin's Union of Social Justice was viewed as an American form of Fascism.[53] Coughlin was linked to the America First Committee, which many Americans also equated with Fascism.[54]

The American Jewish Committee began investigating Coughlin's statements and accused him of conducting an anti–Semitic campaign that went against the teaching of the Catholic Church. That may have been the turning point in Coughlin's career. Coughlin's statement led to protests of Nazi-related organizations and boycotts of German-made products sold in Pittsburgh. Nazi propaganda leaflets printed in Germany began circulating in Pittsburgh, referring to Coughlin as the "courageous 'radio priest'" and urging people to read his book, *Am I an Anti-Semite?* The book, it was claimed, "irrefutably demonstrates ... the ultimate connection between international.... Jewry and Bolshevism and its tangible menace to American democracy."[55]

The church made it clear that Coughlin did not speak for Catholics. Cardinal George Mundelein of Chicago said while Coughlin had a right to his opinion, "he is not authorized to speak for the Catholic Church, nor does he represent the doctrine or sentiments of the church."[56]

Cox said it was Coughlin—and fascism—that threatened American democracy, not Jews.

> You forget the teachings of Christ—tolerance and brotherhood. You are in effect anti–Catholic as well as anti–Semitic. The real menace to America today is the attempt of the Coughlin kind of propagandist who wants to establish a fascist form of government by labeling it Americanism and coupling it with the prejudice and intolerance of the new streamlined Ku Klux Klan program. We should all join in making Democracy the best defense against all isms.[57]

Roosevelt began pressuring the Vatican to silence Coughlin. A federal grand jury investigated him for taking money from the Nazis and failing to register as a foreign agent. The church threatened him with suspension from the priesthood unless he severed his ties to *Social Justice* and halted his radio broadcasts. Coughlin began 25 years of enforced silence that ended in 1966. He outlived Father Cox by 28 years, dying on October 27, 1979, at the age of 88.

20

Final Days

When World War II began, Cox tried to join priests from the Pittsburgh Catholic Diocese who were enlisting in the Army and Navy, but he was rejected because of his age and high blood pressure. At five-feet, seven inches tall and weighing 245 pounds, he had suffered three minor strokes and his health was precarious at best.[1]

He was hospitalized for five days in 1933 after suffering his first stroke, and doctors said he was "far from a well man." His physicians advised the priest to "get more rest and less worry."[2] Newspapers kept readers updated on his recovery.

Cox asked his old friend, Henry Ellenbogen, to help him obtain a commission in the Army so he could serve in Europe. Cox cited his prior military service and frequent trips to Europe as evidence of his ability to serve again in the military.[3] Ellenbogen contacted military officials in Washington on Cox's behalf, but the Army wasn't interested in the overweight Cox.

Cox's sole contribution to the war effort was a song. He wrote the music and lyrics in 1942 for "It's Taps for the Japs," blasting the Japanese for attacking Pearl Harbor. The tune was sung by Johnny Mitchell, a former organist at St. Patrick's Church, and was performed by bandleader Mickey Ross who led the WJAS radio orchestra in Pittsburgh.[4]

> There's a day ev'ry Yankee will remember,
> While all was clear and calm.
> At Pearl Harbor in December,
> came Japan to wreck and bomb!
> From Manila to Alaska all this nation must defend.
> Rise up, all ye Americans!
> Fight bravely to the end!
>
> [chorus]
> Now it's taps for the Japs

When they're caught in the traps
They prepared for the U.S.A.
For they spied, while we tried
To decide, help and guide,
All the world in a peaceful way.
On that fateful Sunday morning,
We were attacked without a warning.
Now it's taps for the Japs
And they're bound to collapse,
Since they fired on the U.S.A.

On V-E Day, Pittsburgh erupted into spontaneous celebrations. People held block parties in their neighborhoods while parades were held downtown. Schools emptied and employees left their jobs to join the celebrations. Gov. Edward Martin ordered all bars in Pennsylvania closed as a precaution. Cox told worshipers at an ecumenical prayer service at city hall to "bend your knees in prayer but do not bend your elbows in drink and riotous conduct."[5]

Cox interjected himself into controversies that questioned his judgment. He went to bat for a former police chief who killed two men he thought were car thieves. Cox sponsored a parole application for William Duerr, the former police chief of Kennedy Township, after he had only served eight months of a prison term of two years less a day for his manslaughter conviction. Police had set a trap for car thieves, but the two unsuspecting men stumbled into the ambush and mistakenly were killed. The sentence kept Duerr within the jurisdiction of Allegheny County rather than the state, which meant he could be freed at any time. Judge Henry Ellenbogen heard the case and granted Duerr parole on Christmas Eve, but city newspapers never explained the relationship between Cox and Ellenbogen, his longtime friend.[6]

In 1943, Cox married 17-year-old Truna Fontana to Roxie Long, 47, at St. Patrick's Church in the Strip District. Long was a habitual criminal whom newspapers dubbed the most arrested man in Pittsburgh and Allegheny County, with an arrest record dating to 1917.[7] Long, whose real name was Rocco Di Pippa, was a bootlegger, con man, thief, truck hijacker, robber, forger and escape artist. Fontana's parents told police their daughter had been kidnapped until she showed up with her new husband.

Cox's health problems increased as he grew older. He was plagued by a knee injury while serving in France in World War I. He developed chronic arthritis after he accidentally fell over a suitcase.[8] He was receiving $30 a month disability from the Veterans Administration for the undocumented knee injury. Cox was lucky to be receiving anything. The law

Cover of sheet music for Cox's composition "It's Taps for the Japs," his contribution to the war effort during World War II, 1942 (Dr. and Mrs. Mason, Father James Renshaw Cox Collection, Saint Patrick–Saint Stanislaus Kostka Parish, Pittsburgh, Pennsylvania).

required that a disability must be incurred on active service in the line of duty. Physicians who examined Cox never filed a written medical report on the injury. His pension was reduced, so Cox appealed.[9]

The reduction in his pension benefit was the result of the Economy Act imposed by FDR in 1933. The law cut the pay of government employees, the military and veterans benefits by 15 percent and overall government spending by 25 percent. It resulted in $1 billion in savings that Roosevelt used to fund the New Deal.

Ellenbogen again interceded on Cox's behalf with the appeals board. He recounted to the three-man board Cox's exploits of the 1932 hunger march, his tireless humanitarian efforts, and the $200,000 debt he had incurred feeding the poor. He also pointed out that Cox had campaigned for President Roosevelt, helping him win western Pennsylvania in 1932, hoping that mention might sway the appeals board. Pittsburgh Mayor David Lawrence and Pennsylvania Sen. Joe Guffey "are very much interested in the outcome of the case," Ellenbogen said.[10] "He was a great champion of labor in the early days of the Roosevelt Administration and had a lot to do with turning western Pennsylvania and perhaps a larger territory into the Roosevelt column.... I am only presenting you the facts about his life to indicate to you that I would not be here today if I did not sincerely and with a full heart believe in the justice of his claim."[11]

Ellenbogen produced a medical report from Cox's personal physician that Cox's knee hurt so badly that he was unable to fully genuflect while celebrating Mass. "This state of affairs causes him considerable embarrassment, as he is the focus of attention when celebrating Mass," the doctor wrote.[12]

Cox grew bitter. He claimed there were two physicians on duty at the hospital in France when he was injured, but the Army couldn't find any records proving that doctors treated Cox. "Why should I be forced to pay for the mistake of a hospital administration of which I was part?" Cox wrote. "Certainly, it was not my business to check up whether the doctors who attended me put it on file."[13] His bitterness increased. Cox charged that his treatment by the Veterans Administration was due to prejudice "because of his militant stand on behalf of the underprivileged."[14]

Ellenbogen questioned the board how Cox could be rated at a certain level of disability in one year and less in another. He said if anything, Cox's condition had worsened. Ellenbogen told the appeals board that Cox believed "a great injustice has been done and has convinced himself and us and many others that it ought to be righted before he passes away because he is coming along in years."[15] "It is a bitterness of a cripple, you might say that carries his disability with him, is always aware of it in daily life as well as in the performance of his ministerial functions."[16]

The problem, Ellenbogen continued, "was not only the knee, but the whole person; it is the whole body of the claimant that is affected. I have no interest, except that I want to see that justice is done to a great citizen of Western Pennsylvania. Father Cox is really a great man and dearly beloved by all who know him." The appeals board refused to modify Cox's disability ruling. While doctors found a slight swelling in the joint of the right knee, "there is no evidence of bone injury forming in the knee joint."[17] "There is no official record of any injury to or treatment for the right knee during military service and at the time of this officer's discharge he certified that he had no wound, injury or disease incurred in military service of the United States or otherwise."[18]

Gen. Omar Bradley, then head of the Veterans Administration, wrote Guffey in 1946 that since no record of any injury was found, Cox was considered physically sound when he was discharged. "It is found that modification of the decision rendered from June 19, 1941, is not indicated," Bradley wrote.[19] Ellenbogen asked Senator Guffey to break the news to Cox. "I will put it to him as gently as I can. I know he will not like it, but I will do what I can," Guffey said.

When Cox turned 60, Ellenbogen appealed to Cox's friends and supporters to help the priest pay his debts. For a $10 contribution, they would receive an autographed photo. "After years of pay, pay, pay, Father Cox has come to a place where a few thousand dollars would enable him to clear up all his outstanding debts," Ellenbogen wrote.[20]

Holy Week began on March 19, 1951, with heavy rain on Palm Sunday. Then temperatures dropped, turning Pittsburgh streets into ice rinks. The next day, an inch of snow fell on the city despite predictions of a much heavier snowfall.[21] Cox was working on his latest sermon while getting ready for bed. He was feeling faint and called for Father Walter Karaveckas, his assistant, who was in another room.

Cox asked his housekeeper, Mary Spehar, to remove his shoes. As Cox walked to the bathroom, he collapsed.[22] Father Karaveckas administered the Last Rites of the Catholic Church. An ambulance arrived and took Cox to Mercy Hospital, where he was placed in an oxygen tent. Cox had suffered three strokes before and his blood pressure and weight had been a problem all his life. He died at 1:29 a.m. as his brother, Dr. Earl Cox, and sister, Mrs. Dennis Dwyer, stood by his bedside.[23]

In Cox's two-paragraph will, he left $500 each to his sister and brother and the same amount to a religious charity.[24] One city newspaper bannered the news of his death across the top of page one.[25] An editorial writer described Cox as "a man of militant faith."[26]

> Father Cox's zealous regard for the poor and those down on their luck merited him a reputation far beyond the borders of this city.... In the life of this city over a harsh era that now seems happily gone he was a force for social good. The colorful priest will be remembered in these parts for his works of mercy during the black days of the Great Depression. Without government aid, with funds drawn solely from his own appeals, he fed and provided clothes for thousands of men in the early Thirties who shuffled in daily bread lines to his churchyard.[27]

More than 10,000 people paid their last respects to Cox on Easter Sunday in 1951.[28] His funeral was held on a sunny but cold and windy day when he was remembered as a man "marked by an all-consuming love of the poor" and "a filial devotion to the Blessed Mother," said Bishop John Dearden, who celebrated the Mass. "He loved the poor, the neglected, the

More than 10,000 people paid their respects to Father Cox after he died in 1951. People stood outside the church during the funeral Mass (James R. Cox Papers, 1923–1950, AIS.1969.05, Archives & Special Collections, University of Pittsburgh Library System).

discouraged. With kindness so great as to defy the spirit, he received them, administered to them and gave himself up unto them. To the sick he brought radio messages of faith, hope and love of God, Dearden eulogized.[29]

Cox had been at St. Patrick's for 28 years. He was 37 when he was named pastor, the youngest priest at the oldest parish in the diocese. He said he never wanted to lead any other church. "I'll die here at St. Patrick's," he said. "I want nothing more."[30] Cox once told a friend, "I pray that when my time runs out, I will be taken while at work for the Lord."[31]

His prayers were answered.

Appendix:
The World According
to Father Cox

Interview with Father James R. Cox, pastor of Old St. Patrick's Church at Pittsburgh, Pa. No date.
Source: James R. Cox Papers, 1923–1950, AIS.1969.05, Archives & Special Collections, University of Pittsburgh Library System.

Despite claiming to be a patriot who loved to wrap himself in the flag, Cox proposed a military coup to install a dictator to replace the president.

A supreme dictatorship by the Army and Navy was proposed today as the "way to put this country back on its feet" by Father James R. Cox, the Pittsburgh priest who led an army of 25,000 "blue shirt" jobless men on Washington back in January 1932.

Deliver to one man the powers of dictatorship backed by the Army and Navy, and in 12 or 15 years this country will be fit to live in. President Roosevelt is the man for the job. He is honest, fearless and just and a man with ideas. At present, he is sadly handicapped by our vicious party system which in the years since our glorious democracy was first established has so warped our government that today it can be called only an oxcart excuse for government.

Are we not now under a dictatorship? Are we not now under the heel of a rubber-stamp Congress which imposes upon us the dictatorship of party rule? Are we not now the helpless victims of an oxcart government, conceived in the horse and buggy era which strips our purses bare in the form of unjustified and cruelly exorbitant taxes?

Why must the taxpayers be made to pay for a House of Representatives which does nothing but follow out the orders of the party and a Senate which gets paid taxpayers' money for doing nothing, and that badly?

Why must the people pay and pay for 48 puerile governors in 48 unnecessary states? Why must they take food out of their mouths to pay the salaries of so-called assemblies in 48 cut-up sections of the country. The governors do nothing that a $150-a-week clerk couldn't do. The assemblies don't do anything that the Army and Navy couldn't do and do better, more efficiently.

Here's my plan to put a stop to all this waste. Name a dictator first. Give him complete control for 12 or 15 years. Let him actually assume the traditional power of the President as Commander-in-chief or the armed forces of the nation. But don't ham-string him with a Supreme Court.

The Supreme Court, that has always been 100 percent upon the bulwark of American liberty, has become the laughing stock of the world because of its inept continuance of opposition to popular will.

This all sounds like Fascism but it's more than Fascism; it's the only way to bring sense out of chaos. Today we are absolutely bankrupt and mismanaged, not because our President is not doing his best for all the people, but the system prevents him from saving the tax revenues from being filched and wasted by the multiplication of useless officials in federal, state and municipal employ. Perhaps this waste of public funds is necessary to insure reelection under our party system. Under a dictatorship, no.

James R. Cox Papers

Do Not Play on Air Casette 9
Source: James R. Cox Papers, 1923–1950, AIS.1969.05, Archives & Special Collections, University of Pittsburgh Library System.

Some of Cox's sermons were too controversial to be broadcast. His frank discussion on sex and birth control to his radio listeners was too much for WJAS in Pittsburgh and refused to broadcast the sermon.

Recently, a meeting was held by the hierarchy of the Catholic Church in Washington, D.C. During that meeting they denounced the present methods of birth control as race suicide. And they said this country might be left without enough manpower for national defense by the end of the century as the result of dissemination of birth control information to servicemen. Opening a three-day family life conference sponsored by the National Catholic Welfare Council, Bishop Joseph P. Hurley of St. Augustine, Florida, said ten million future American fathers were being given birth control information in the army on the vastest scale known to history. Assuming that the present manpower shortage was due to birth controllers of two decades ago, Bishop Hurley said if present anti-family practices continue to be taught to ten million potentially American fathers if is entirely possible that we will not have sufficient manpower to defend ourselves by the end of this century. And the reason we have been forced to call upon men with families who should remain at home and assist in the production of younger soldiers' needs, the reason we had to call them to the colors in this World War Number two is because of the preaching of these birth controllers for the past 25 years. Now it is my notion that if we say these people are teaching wrong methods, then it is our business to teach the right methods. We say that no contraceptive should ever be used for the prevention of children. We say the home in which a child is born, in the womb of the mother is such a beautiful home made by God that nothing should be used in the way of instruments which would destroy that home made by God any more than we would go into a beautiful home where a family lives and destroy it by fire and water or flooding it by the wrong kind gas. We say that if God made that home where children ought to be born, then that home should not be hurt, mutilated or injured by the use of any unnatural or any kind of contraceptive other than the contraceptive that nature has provided. That man should increase and multiply, that there is a place for each and every one of us. He said the relations between men and women should not only bring children into the world but should be for their mutual comfort. But he said in bringing children into the world the health of the woman must be consulted. And the ability of the man to support those children should be looked into. That's the reason in the Catholic Church we admit and approve of the ... legitimate system of birth control. That is the subject we can explain to you in a very simple way. There are only about 8 days in a month that children will come into the world in the relations between a husband and wife ... asks the husband and wife to abstain from relations during these eight days of danger. Now this sound like that maybe should be reserved for a private office but my dear friends they're not reserving the information about the wrong kind of birth control to offices. They're telling it over the back fences. They're talking about it at parties. Everybody knows about it. We sit back and do not want to tell what it should tell because we're afraid they may think we're not as modest as we should be. If someone knows everything and they're not using that knowledge in the best interests of society, then we ought to tell them what is the best methods. We ought to flood the mail with pamphlets. We ought to fill the newspapers with the good news

about our way of doing the thing. We should have lobbyists in the legislatures to tell them the right system when they're passing laws. We should
have pro-baby clinics beside their anti-baby clinics. We ought to borrow
their literature and make a few corrections and send it back to them our
way. We're not fighting with anybody. We're just telling the right way and
they're giving the wrong way and robbing us of manpower that will ruin
us in the next one hundred or two hundred years. They're trying to
frighten the poor into having few babies. We will try to inspire them to
have more and also to provide conditions that will make it possible for
them to have more as far as it concerns the women's health and the husband's ability to make money. They talk about depopulating the slums.
We will talk about repopulating Park Avenue. They complain of babies in
poor environments. We will complain of fine environments without
babies. They worry about mothers with too many children. We will fret
about mothers with no children. Talk about flats crowded with babies.
Will talk about penthouses inhabited by servants and dogs. They are troubled about teeming tenements. We will be troubled by teeming towers.
They are troubled about children without medical attention. We're concerned about doctors with no patients except little poodles. When they
tell us we're not feeding our children properly we will ask how they know
because they've never fed any. When they complain about our boys and
girls being denied higher education, we will defy them to educate their
dogs. When they croak that maybe our sons will go to war, we will reply
that even war is better than the peace of non-existence. It's better to be
able to go to war than never to have existed at all. We will tell them dying
bravely in battle is better than to not to have lived at all. They have been
saying they want to improve the race. Now is their chance. We're ready
to show them how. When they argue children need better heredity, we
will reply with simply dignity. Very well Park Avenue, you have the heredity
now give us these fine babies. The time has passed when they can frighten
and deceive us. They told us if we had large families, we must do without
luxuries like automobiles. Now see what has happened. Their automobiles are immobilized for lack of gasoline and the decencies they tried to
destroy are being defended on a dozen fronts by the sons of the poor born
in spite of them. Without these sons of the poor, there would be no eleven
million men now engaged in the defense of democracy and humanity.
When our sons come back, as most of them surely will through the mercy
and grace of God, they will say to these people you wanted children of the
poor to only have things only you could buy. Very well, either pay for those
things for the children of others or give them to children of your own....

You are not dead yet but you are dying for fear of living. You're afraid to let people come into the world and you're dying and you're ruining your race for your aristocracy and you're ruining America because you do not want what God intended to come into the world to live. Open your eyes and look around you. There are joys which you have never dreamed. There are happinesses we know that you will never know. People who have brought children into the world have known ennobling sorrows of fatherhood and motherhood and the joys compared to. They are less than nothing. There are no joys in nightclubs, in gatherings, in weekend parties that even began to compare to looking into the eyes of that innocent babe because in the eyes of these babes you can see your God and you can feel the embrace of the Almighty in their arms because God breathes the immortal soul into that little bit of clay that you bring into the world ... those who you bring into the world will live with you in the measure of God.... Why should we be wiser than God? ... I say to you follow God's natural system....

Hitler's Hatchet Man by the Rev. James R. Cox, St. Patrick's Catholic Church

Source: "Coughlin Hit by Father Cox as Nazi Parrot," Pittsburgh Press, June 5, 1939; James R. Cox Papers, 1923–1950, AIS.1969.05, Archives & Special Collections, University of Pittsburgh Library System.

Cox had developed personal relationships with a number of Jewish residents in Pittsburgh. So when Father Charles Coughlin blamed Jews for the nation's economic problems and began serving as a mouthpiece for Adolf Hitler, Cox publicly denounced his fellow cleric.

Many, many times I have been asked: "Why is Father Coughlin permitted to make his radio speeches in spite of protests from all sides? The Catholic Church does not interfere with the ideas and principles of her children so long as they are not opposed to her teachings in matters of faith and morals. The attitude of the Church is like that of the United States Government which guarantees to every citizen the right to life, liberty and the pursuit of happiness and guarantees free speech, free press and free assemblage. It is only the preaching or the attempt to overthrow our government by force that will bring action on the part of our authorities against any person or group.

The right of free speech in the United States of America is regarded so sacred that a priest born under another flag is permitted to call the President of the United States "a liar" and is not jailed or taken off the air or silenced by the Church and State. President Roosevelt may have changed his attitude on an issue which probably a change of conditions made necessary. Father Coughlin, if my memory serves me right, promised at one time that unless his Lemke Party received nine million votes for President, he would cease to broadcast. Father Coughlin is still on the air.

While as Catholics we cannot do anything to stop Father Coughlin, you may rest assured that all Catholic people and priests are not in accord or sympathy with him. In my humble opinion, his attacks upon the Jews are abhorrent to everyone who believes in the Fatherhood of God and the Brotherhood of Man. To my way of thinking, it is very bad taste for a priest, a man of God, who preaches love of God and love of neighbor to either directly or indirectly foster hate on the basis of race, color or religion.

If Father Coughlin is right then the Ku Klux Klan is right about the Jews, it is also right about the Catholics and colored people and Father Coughlin thereby condemns himself and all that he represents. Father Coughlin in one breath accuses Jews of being Communists and in the next of being international bankers. Some may be one or the other but how can international bankers be Communists?

You cannot compare the civil war in Spain with the persecution of the Jews throughout the world. Spaniards were fighting Spaniards and it was their country, their people and their concern. German or Italian troops who hated Jews fought on the side of Franco but the Jews did not kill or persecute anyone in that struggle. The Jews are a minority in every part of the world, wanderers on the face of the earth, helpless many times and hated—they have no country, no flag-nobody to send protests for them, except friends under every flag in the part of the world who pity God's chosen people, persecuted because they try to overcome almost insurmountable obstacles and achieve something. God help them for they are still His people. Jews succeed by hard work. Remember also they have the blessing of God because they are still His Chosen people.

If Father Coughlin were not a priest and chose to attack Catholics on the strength of the bogus Knights of Columbus Oath, God help us Catholics. Yet Father Coughlin has produced forged documents, misquotations and deliberate misrepresentations as evidence of his accusations against Jews. Only a Communist or Nazi Court would permit such so-called evidence as he used to bolster his alibis for retelling alien propaganda. Nothing he ever spoke or printed justified his easy generalizations and his wicked innuendoes.

The charges made against Jews by Father Coughlin are paradoxical. For instance: that most of the Jews are communists; that the Jews are responsible for the Russian Revolution and the subsequent establishment of Soviet Russia; that the Jews are internationalists; that the Jews are international bankers; that the Jews influence unduly and thereby control the present administration; that the Jews control newspapers, the radio and theaters; that the Jews want a world war.

I will not defend the Jews against these silly, ridiculous and baseless charges. The Jews do not need my defense. Rather I would point out to my brother priest that these inflammatory charges that he and other potential fire-brands are making today against the Jews had their counterpart in the wake of prejudice against the Catholics about ten years ago when intolerant groups whispered that the pope was coming to take over the white House and the control of America, and, strange to say, millions of good folks believed this.

I would remind my brother priest that the simple child-like mentalities of certain groups who can be swayed tomorrow against Catholics and he, above all, as a Catholic Priest should be the last man to encourage rabble-rousing mob vengeance and mass hysteria. Rather he should appeal for peace and order, for good-will and for cooperation and neighborliness among all of the religious groups in America.

He must not forget that we are guaranteed in this country complete religious freedom of conscience. A man may worship God as he sees fit; if there be among us any who do not believe in God and are willing to accept the consequence of that unbelief, under our American system of religious freedom—they have that right. In our country, a man has as much right to be an agnostic, an infidel, a doubter, a Mohammedan, a heathen, a Protestant or a Jew as Father Coughlin and I have to be Catholics.

Under our American system of political freedom, a man has a right to be a Socialist, a radical, a Republican or a Democrat, yes, and even a Communist if he wishes to be, so long as and until the Supreme Court of the United States declares that Communist Party is not a lawful of constitutional party. But how can Jews be both Communists and International bankers at the same time? If there are any Jewish bankers, there are a hundred times more Irish Bankers, German Bankers, Polish Bankers, Italian Bankers. Since when it is a violation of our Constitution and our Bill of Rights to be a banker?

If there are any Jews who own newspapers, there are a hundred times more Irish, Scottish and what-not newspaper owners. The Hearst, Scripps-Howard and Patterson-McCormick newspapers, the largest and most influential in America are not owned by Jews. The Jews do not control the wealth. I assure that the Mellons, Morgans, Rockefellers, and the Fords can buy and sell all the Jews in the United Sattes [*sic*].

The Jews do not dominate the Government of the Nation, state or city. There is only one Jew in the President's cabinet. There is only one Jew on the Supreme Court. There are those, including Coughlin, who are claiming that the Jews dominate President Roosevelt—the President who has been the greatest human being to grace the White House, and who has rendered service to all classes of people without regard to race, color or creed. What a preposterous accusation.

The Jews are good citizens. They help to build up communities in which they live. Their home life is the most exemplary of all people. They take care of their aged parents. They educate their children. They cooperate in all philanthropic and charitable endeavors. They are patriotic. They are loyal to the land of their adoption. We have in Pittsburgh the Falk Clinic or the poor, made possible by a Jew.

If we paint the whole Jewish situation with the paint of the so-called bad Jew, how can be Catholics hope to escape the tar and feathers of the doings of Al Capone and Jimmy Hines or the mistakes of some of the clergy? Who am I or Father Coughlin to sit in judgment? Judge who is a good Jew and who is a bad Jew? Judge not that ye be not judged. It gathers in this group and that group striking down the innocent along with the guilty. The Jews today, the Catholics tomorrow, and the Negro always.

As a loyal American citizen, I believe it to be my duty to protest against the actions of any man, priest or layman who invades the United States of America with pernicious Nazi propaganda to accomplish his ambition to make or break the president. Father Coughlin, I adjure you in the name of God cease this bigotry! A bigot wearing the robes of a Klansman is infamous—a bigot wearing the robes of a priest is despicable. You do not speak for the Catholic Church. You do not speak for the Catholic clergy. You do not speak for millions of Catholic laity who wish to live in peace and harmony with their fellow citizens. As a student of economics, or as a political orator, you would be ignored. Unfortunately, you speak as an individual Catholic priest and as such you command attention, and that is the shame and danger.

You forget the teachings of Christ—of tolerance and brotherhood. You are in effect anti–Catholic, as well as anti–Semitic. The danger to American democracy does not come from Communism, but from Fascism—and you know it. Communism is too abhorrent to the American mind to be accept by Americans reared in the traditions of religious liberty. The real menace to America today is the attempt of the Coughlin kind of alien propagandist who wants to establish a fascist form of government by labeling it Americanism and coupling with it the prejudices and intolerance of the new, streamlined Ku Klux Klan program. We should all join in making democracy work better—as the best defense against all isms.

It is false Americanism which discriminates against his fellow citizens. It is false patriotism which persecutes on account of accident of birth or choice of faith. To my mind soldiers are the real Americans—the real patriots. They do not preach bigotry and hatred. Brotherhood was gained on our battlefields. Democracy was achieved where soldiers encamped. Tolerance was found in the trenches. Catholics, Protestants and Jews fought and won the American Revolution. They invented in our factories, they will make it work in a big way under Democracy—the form of free government which made America great and which, with God's help, will be greater.

An American should know no distinction of race, color or religion. The United States of America has been made under the Fatherhood of God and the Brotherhood of Man. While assisting at the bedside of hundreds of American boys who had been wounded in action in France during the World War and who were about to give up their lies, I would end my ministrations by saying: Buddy is there anything more I can do for you? They would look up and say: Padre, if I die, take me back to God's country and tell my mother I am proud and happy to give my life for Old Glory!—real American sentiments and Patriotism. All of us should pledge America a sincere and enthusiastic allegiance to your flag and my flag.

> Your flag and my flag and how it flies today;
> In your land and my land, and half a world away!
> Rose-red and blood-red the stripes forever gleam.
> Snow-white and soul-white the good forefathers dream;
> Sky-blue and true-blue, with stars to gleam at night-
> The gloried guidon of the day, shelter through the night.

Scandalous Attire
Source: Sept. 9, 1926, *Pittsburgh Post.*

His prudish nature surfaced in one sermon in which he criticized women for their immodest dress.

In olden days courting was done with no light but the grate. Girls dressed modestly then. The young men callers liked to entertain in darkened parlors. Now it is different. They want the full light so that they can see everything the girls show. Courtships that should not last longer than one year are now prolonged indefinitely and are interspersed with cabarets, trips to road houses, jazz dances and auto petting parties in every city park. All this has brought about a grave situation demanding the serious attention of parents and superiors.

Atlantic City
Source: "Nude Beauty Contests by '35 Are Forecast by Father Cox," *Pittsburgh Gazette Times*, Sept. 9, 1926

Cox bemoaned the annual beauty pagent claiming that each year the contestants wore less and less. He predicted that women would eventually appear naked at the bathing beauty contest.

The bathing beauty contests and the pageants at Atlantic City are the adoration of the nude in a barbarous state of present day society. Rome in its worst days was an example of modesty in comparison with the present day monkey shines.

Trial Marriages
Source: "Scrap Over Batting Averages Enough for Divorce, Pastor Says, Scorns Trial Marriages," *Pittsburgh Gazette Times*, April 1, 1926

The Catholic Church opposed divorce and Cox wanted government to ban divorce arguing a spouse did not need a good reason to end a marriage.

Trial marriages which are becoming the custom today because of divorce, are not progressive, but are a return to barbarism.... Divorces now a days may be obtained because of a disagreement over a necktie or an argument over the batting average of a favorite baseball player. Homes cannot be built and cannot endure on such a foundation as this, and a nation cannot endure unless is preserves the sacredness and stability of the home as we are not doing in America.... Christ gave the best law ever made for conjugal happiness which makes in the best interests of the many even though a few may suffer when He said: What God hath joined together let no man put asunder.

Modern Life
Source: *Gazette Times*, April 1, 1926

Cox opposed jazz music and black bottom dancing as the devil's music.

Modern life may be summed up as jazz, jazz, jazz which is the most perfect example of discord in a discordant age. We can well understand why moderns like jazz when we learn their philosophy of life, their religion, their ideals are but jazz, just a discord that cries to heaven for vengeance because it breaks every law on the plea that it is in fashion.

Scarlet Women
Source: "Father Cox Scores Methods Used in Curbing Activity of Scarlet Women," *Pittsburgh Press*, Oct. 25, 1926

Cox defended prostitutes who were arrested for plying their trade but questioned why men weren't charged for using their services.

It has been an axiom that women everywhere are as virtuous as men permit them to be. Therefore, if Pittsburgh is such a cesspool of vice, if the city is loaded with scarlet women, where are the scarlet men who have made women what they are? Where are the men who are so liberal in keeping them in luxury and sin? Since these men must exist or the women would find no business, what are we going to do with the scarlet men arrested or imprisoned the same as women. Many places of business would be closed and the ranks of the professional men in the city might be sadly depleted for a while and even the wheels of justice might be missing from the judgment seats. As a matter of fact, the control of vice in Pittsburgh is better than in almost any large city in the world.

Jobless Resolution
Source: "Cox Resolution Warns of Danger of Revolt in Nation If Relief Fails," *Pittsburgh Press*, Jan. 7, 1932. (Read into the *Congressional Record*.)

Cox presented President Hoover with a resolution calling for ways of ending the nation's suffering. Some of his proposals were included in Roosevelt's New Deal legislation.

Whereas, in this land of ours, the United States of America, the soil is rich, the earth is bursting with abundance, the bins are filled with grain, the storehouses are laden with goods, the shelves are overflowing with merchandise, the vaults are stacked with bars of gold, and the very channels of trade are choked with undisputed surpluses of the products of the mills and mines and farm.

Now, therefore, be it resolved by the army of the jobless marching under the leadership of the Rev. Cox:

First, that Congress appropriate $5,000,000,000 to be raised by the issue and sale of bonds and to be expended for the creation of work in public construction, including highways, public buildings, hospitals in rural areas, reforestation, flood control, and water and power conservation.

Second—that Congress immediately appropriate to the several states and municipalities according to their needs and number of unemployed, sufficient sums of money to be distributed, through agencies now functioning for the purpose of providing food, clothing and shelter to the needy and hungry who are out of work.

Third—that the money for these appropriations be raised by the increase up to 60 percent per annum, of the surtaxes on large incomes, effective on incomes earned in 1932; by the immediate raising of federal inheritance taxes on large estates up to 70 percent; and by the levying of a large gift tax to prevent the evasion of the inheritance taxes, an evil so flagrantly practiced now.

Chapter Notes

Preface

1. "Priest to Run for President If Pleas for U.S. Aid Fails," *Pittsburgh Sun-Telegraph*, Jan. 17, 1932.

2. "Journey Home Is Started by Cox and Army," *Pittsburgh Post-Gazette*, January 8, 1932. While Cox was meeting with Hoover, Congress was reviewing the president's proposed $2 billion spending plan to help states through the Reconstruction Finance Corporation.

3. "Nine Children Face Hunger After Father Disappears," *Pittsburgh Press*, Feb. 5, 1930.

4. T.H. Watkins, *The Hungry Years: A Narrative History of the Great Depression in America* (New York: Henry Holt, 1999), 55.

5. Clothes Room Journal, Dec. 10, 1930–Jan. 4, 1934, James A. Cox Papers, 1923–1950, AIS.1969.05, Box 2, Folder 5, Archives of Industrial Society, University of Pittsburgh.

6. *Ibid.*

7. "Father Cox's Own Story," *Pittsburgh Press*, Jan. 10, 1932.

8. *Ibid.*

9. The Black Shirts represented Italian fascists. The Silver Shirts, formally known as the Silver Legion of America, were founded by William Dudley Pelley, an anti-Semite and admirer of Hitler. The Brown Shirts were known as the "Friends of New Germany" and were patterned after the *Sturmabteilung*, the paramilitary wing of the Nazi Party. The Khaki Shirts were created by Art Smith from the ranks of World War I veterans who were part of the Bonus Expeditionary Force.

10. "Father Cox Urges Troops Be Sent into Louisiana," *Pittsburgh Post-Gazette*, March 16, 1935.

11. "Italy Enthused Over War in Africa, Says Father Cox," *Pittsburgh Post-Gazette*, Aug. 21, 1935.

12. The Khaki Shirts were led in 1933 by Art Smith, an anti-Communist and anti-Semite. Smith and his followers planned to seize a National Guard Armory in Philadelphia, march on Washington, install FDR as dictator, and then begin killing Jews. Philip Jenkins, *Hoods and Shirts* (Chapel Hill: University of North Carolina Press, 1997), 103.

13. "Cox Asks Vets to Join His Party," *Pittsburgh Post-Gazette*, Aug. 5, 1932.

14. "Says People Don't Want Dictator in U.S.," *Pittsburgh Press*, Aug. 3, 1935.

15. *Ibid.*

16. *Ibid.*

17. "Interview with Father James R. Cox, Pastor at Old St. Patrick's Church at Pittsburgh, Pa." James R. Cox Papers, 1923–1950, AIS.1969.05, Archives Service Center, University of Pittsburgh, no date, Box 1, Folder 2.

18. "Lawmakers Hit by Father Cox," *Pittsburgh Post-Gazette*, Feb. 24, 1932.

19. Thomas H. Coode, and John D. Petrarulo, "The Odyssey of Pittsburgh's Father James Cox," *Western Pennsylvania Historical Magazine* 55, no. 3 (July 1972): 238.

20. "Crowds Throng Home Here to See Miracle," *Pittsburgh Press*, Sept. 22, 1927; "Father Cox: Bread Lines & Garden Stakes Makes News," *Bulletin Index*, Dec. 7, 1937.

21. http://www.saintsinthestrip.org/5_3_0.html.

22. John Ray Ewers, "Father Cox's Blue Shirts," *The Christian Century*, June 22, 1932, 797.

23. Mark Barrett, "A Shepherd of the Jobless," *First Things*, Dec. 23, 2012.

24. "Father Cox Flies Home, Said Mass High in Zep," *Pittsburgh Sun-Telegraph*, April 10, 1936.

25. "Flying Pastor Tells of Being Lost," *Pittsburgh Sun-Telegraph*, March 20, 1929; Father Cox Papers, box 6, Folder 3.

26. *Ibid.*

27. "Scores Urge Father Cox to Try Rome Hop," *Pittsburgh Post-Gazette*, Dec. 16, 1927.

28. "New York to Rome Flight Project by Father Cox," *Pittsburgh Post-Gazette*, Dec. 15, 1927; "Girl Not to Make Sea Hop with Local Priest," *Pittsburgh Press*, Dec. 19, 1927.

29. "New Plans Eliminate Girl in Pittsburgh-Rome Hop," *Pittsburgh Post-Gazette*, Dec. 19, 1927.

Introduction

1. Jerry Vondas, "Father Cox Still Marches in Memory," *Pittsburgh Press*, Feb. 27, 1983.

2. Gussie Shore interview by Harold Kimball and Ann Faigen, May 8, 1986, National Council of Jewish Women, *Pittsburgh and Beyond: The Experience of the Jewish Community*, Tape 1, Side 1. Archives Service Center, University of Pittsburgh.

3. "Storm Catches Rear Guard of Father Cox's Marchers," *Pittsburgh Post-Gazette*, Jan. 6, 1932.

4. John D. Petrarulo, "A Short Biography of Father James R. Cox of Pittsburgh" (master's thesis, California State College, 1972), 6.

5. Rev. James R. Cox, "Father Cox Reveals Drama of March to Washington," *Pittsburgh Press*, Jan. 17, 1932.

6. *Ibid.*

7. "Padre Cox' Army Tells Harding of Help for Jobless," *Pittsburgh Post*, Feb. 3, 1922.

8. *Ibid.*

9. *Ibid.*

Chapter 1

1. Keith A. Zahniser, *Steel City Gospel: Protestant Laity and Reform in Progressive Era Pittsburgh* (New York: Routledge, 2005), 22.

2. Anthony Penna, "Changing Images of Twentieth Century Pittsburgh," *Pennsylvania History* 40, no. 1 (January 1976): 49.

3. Rollin Smith, "Pittsburgh Millionaires and Their Organs," *Annual Organ Atlas*, 2010, 70.

4. Zahniser, 22.

5. *Ibid.*

6. *Ibid.*, 35.

7. Kenneth Heineman, *A Catholic New Deal. Religion and Reform in Depression Pittsburgh* (University Park: Pennsylvania State University Press, 1999), 91.

8. Paul Underwood Kellogg, *The Pittsburgh Civic Frontage* (New York: Russell Sage Foundation, 1914).

9. Michael P. Weber, *Don't Call Me Boss: David L. Lawrence, Pittsburgh's Renaissance Mayor* (University of Pittsburgh Press, 1988), 3.

10. Charles McCollester, *City at the Point* (Homestead: Battle of Homestead Foundation, 1924), 124; Francis Ellington Leupp, *George Westinghouse: His Life and Achievements* (Boston: Little, Brown, 1918), 139.

11. Edward White, ed., *Pittsburgh the Powerful: An Interpretation of the Commercial, Financial and Industrial Strength of a Great City* (Pittsburgh: Industry Publishing, 1907), 22.

12. "The East End Electrical Road," *Pittsburgh Press*, March 2, 1888.

13. Joel A. Tarr, "Infrastructure and City-Building in the Nineteenth and Twentieth Centuries," in *City at the Point*, ed. Samuel P. Hays (University of Pittsburgh Press, 1989), 230.

14. *Ibid.*

15. *Ibid.*, 88.

16. Rev. Edward M. McKeever, "Earlier Lawrenceville," *Western Pennsylvania Historical Magazine* 5 (January 1922): 283.

17. Victor A. Walsh, "Across 'The Big Wather': The Irish-Catholic Community of Mid-Nineteenth Century Pittsburgh," *Western Pennsylvania History Magazine* 66, no. 1 (January 1983); Tom Fontaine, "Though scattered all over, Irish are region's 2nd-largest nationality," *Pittsburgh Tribune-Review*, March 15, 2014.

18. Coode and Petrarulo, 218; U.S. Census 1900, familysearch.org/pal:/mm9.1.1/MS1G-3WT.

19. "The Coxes Were Methodist: Son—A Priest—Wants Hoover's Job," *Bulletin Index*, Sept. 1, 1932.

20. Raymond Talley, "Childhood Poverty Explains Father Cox's Zeal for Jobless, Mother Reveals," *Pittsburgh Press*, June 20, 1932.

21. Personal Diary of Father Cox, James R. Cox Papers.

22. Diana Nelson Jones, "Historic Status Sought for Lawrenceville Academy," *Pittsburgh Post-Gazette*, Oct. 2, 2008.

23. Talley.

24. *Ibid.*

25. "Death Recalls 'I Remember,'" Cox Papers, Fox 2 folder 1; "The 1907 Crisis in Historical Perspective." Fas.harvard.edu/~histecon/crisis-next/1907/. The financial crisis was triggered by an attempt to corner the market on stock of the United Copper Company. The panic began in New York City when the New York Stock Exchange fell fifty percent from the previous year, triggering bank failures and business bankruptcies.

26. "Padre Cox's Army Tells Harding of Help for Jobless," *Pittsburgh Post*, Feb. 3, 1922.

27. *Ibid.*

28. "Aged Mother Lauds Work of Her Son," *Gettysburg Times*, Jan. 7, 1932.

29. Personal Diary of Father Cox, James R. Cox Papers.

30. *Ibid.*

31. *Ibid.*

32. Lincoln Steffens, "Pittsburg: A City Ashamed; the Story of a Citizens' Party That Broke Through One Ring into Another," *McClure's Magazine*, May 1903, clpgh.org/exhibitssteffens.html.

33. "Flinn as Political Boss and Legislator Worked for Himself," *Gazette Times* (Pittsburgh), April 4, 1912.

34. "Millions of Dollars of Public Money Went into Flinn Coffers," *Gazette Times*, April 5, 1912. Booth-Flinn continued to thrive decades after Flinn's death. The company built the Liberty Tubes and Westinghouse Bridge in Pittsburgh, the Holland Tunnels in New York City, and had a hand in the construction of the Chesapeake Bay Bridge in Maryland. The firm was sold in 1950 to satisfy a $3 million estate tax debt. "Booth and Flinn Firm to Be Sold to Satisfy $3,000,000 Estate Tax," *Pittsburgh Post-Gazette*, Aug. 17, 1950.

35. John Bodnar, Roger Simon and Michael P. Weber, *Lives of Their Own: Blacks, Italians and Poles in Pittsburgh, 1900–1960* (Urbana: University of Illinois Press, 1982), 23.

36. *Ibid.*

37. Smith, 70.

38. Andrew Canadine, *Mellon: An American Life* (New York: Random House, 2006), 104.

39. *Lives of Their Own*, 22.

40. Kellogg, 634.

41. Joel A. Tarr, and Terry F. Yosie, "Critical Decisions in Pittsburgh Water and Wastewater Treatment," in Joel A. Tarr, ed., *Devastation and Renewal: An Environmental History of Pittsburgh and Its Region* (University of Pittsburgh Press, 2003), 70.

42. Frank E. Wing, "Thirty-Five Years of Typhoid: The Fever's Economic Cost to Pittsburg and the Long Fight for Pure Water," *Charities and Commons* (Feb. 6, 1909): 63.

43. *Ibid.*, 90.

44. Kellogg, 88.

45. *Ibid.*, 3.

46. Thomas L. Lattimore, "Pittsburgh as a Foster Mother," in *The Pittsburgh District: Civic Frontage* (New York: Survey Associates, 1914), 337.

47. *Ibid.*

48. Edward K. Muller, "Ash Pile or Steel City?" *Pittsburgh History* (Summer 1991): 58.

49. *Ibid.*, 54, 70.

50. Joel A. Tarr, "Framing the City at the Point. The Development of Pittsburgh's Infrastructure in the 19th Century," in *City at the Point*, ed. Hays, 230.

51. *Ibid.*, 503.

52. *Ibid.*

53. Zahniser, 22.

Chapter 2

1. "Westmoreland Miners' Strike," by James Coles, Ralph Cordier Collection, Specialized Collections, Indiana University of Pennsylvania.

2. *Catholic Pittsburgh's 100 Years*, Catholic Historical Society of Western Pennsylvania (Chicago: Loyola University Press, 1942), 150.

3. Cox letter to mother, Nov. 4, 1910, Dr. and Mrs. Mason, Father James Renshaw Cox Collection, Saint Patrick–Saint Stanislaus Kostka Parish, Pittsburgh, PA.

4. Cox was probably referring to glasses with tinted lenses, much like sunglasses. He never explained what his eye problems were.

5. "Priest to Head Party of 200 Pittsburghers to Film Shrine," *Pittsburgh Post*, Oct. 20, 1926.

6. Rev. James Cox, "Impressive Ceremonies at Lourdes Stir Pilgrims," *Pittsburgh Post-Gazette*, July 23, 1932.

7. Rev. James Cox, "Pilgrimage to Lourdes Described by Father Cox," *Pittsburgh Post-Gazette*, July 19, 1932.

8. Catalogue of the Officers, Faculty and Students of St. Vincent College and Seminary, Saint Vincent Archabbey Print, 1910, 9, 11, 19.

9. Charles A. Boyle, *The Black Hussars* (Bellevue, WA: Mabo Publishing, 1999), 15.

10. Daniel Moore, "The Boom and Bust of Pennsylvania Coal Towns," *Pittsburgh Post-Gazette*, March 17, 2016.

11. Gertrude Gordon, "Desolation and Misery Caused by Strike," *Pittsburgh Press*, Sept. 7, 1910.

12. Richard Lloyd Jones, "Pennsylvania's Russia," *Colliers*, 1911, 22.

13. Judith McDonough, "Worker Solidarity, Judicial Oppression and Police Repression in the Westmoreland County, Pennsylvania Coal Miners' Strike,1910–1911," *Pennsylvania History* 64 (1997): 385.

14. *Ibid.*, 390.

15. Harvey D. Smith, "Morrison and Feehan Visit Miners' Camp," *Pittsburgh Press*, Sept. 7, 1910.

16. "Murder of Twenty in Strike Charged," *New York Times*, June 1, 1911.

17. Report on the Miners' Strike in Bituminous Coal Field in Westmoreland County, Pa., 1910–1911, 62d Congress, 2d Session, U.S. House of Representatives, 89.

18. Report on the Miners' Strike, 33.

19. Gertrude Gordon, "Operators' Tyranny

Has Thrown Pall of Sadness Over Latrobe District," *Pittsburg Press*, Sept. 6, 1910.

20. Gertrude Gordon, "Public Sympathy and Help Pouring in for the Strikers," *Pittsburg Press*, Sept. 10, 1910.

21. *Ibid.*

22. "Tragedy and Loss in Country's Longest Strike," *New York Times*, April 30, 1911.

23. Jones, 23.

24. *Ibid.*

25. "Ready to Petition Congress," *Pittsburgh Post*, April 22, 1911.

26. "Women and Girls Are Sent to Jail in Strike Region," *Pittsburgh Press*, June 1, 1911.

27. Mary Harris, *Autobiography of Mother Jones* (Chicago: Charles H. Kerr, 1925), 147.

28. *Ibid.*

29. Gertrude Gordon, "Strikers Live on Berries," *Pittsburgh Press*.

30. Albert Fried, ed., *Communism in America: A History in Documents* (New York: Columbia University Press, 1997), 125.

31. "Businessmen of Pittsburgh Take a Hand," *Pittsburgh Press*, Sept. 13, 1910.

32. McDonough, 340.

33. Harvey D. Smith, "Coal Barons' Oppression Felt Keenly in County Seat," *Pittsburgh Press*, Sept. 6, 1910.

34. Saintcecelia.net/history.html.

35. Report on the Miners' Strike, 80.

36. Jones, 22.

37. "Miners Relief Fund to Be Used at Once," *Pittsburgh Press*, Dec. 19, 1927.

38. John K. Morrow "Says Pinchot Broke Faith with Miners," *Pittsburgh Post-Gazette*, March 11, 1931

39. *Ibid.*

Chapter 3

1. "Church Feast Observed by Catholics," *Gazette Times*, July 14, 1913.

2. Thomas F. Coakley, D.D., *Description of Epiphany Church*, Pittsburgh 1919. The Sanctus is part of the Mass ritual and includes verses from Isaiah 6:3; Daniel 7:10; and Mt., 21:9. "Holy, holy, holy, Lord God of hosts, heaven and earth are full of Thy Glory. Hosanna in the highest. Blessed is he who comes in the name of the Lord. Hosanna in the highest."

3. "Will Appear in Amateur Production," *Pittsburgh Sunday Post*, Jan. 14, 1912.

4. "Father Cox Lauds Diligence of Greb in Radio Sermon," *Gazette Times*, Oct. 26, 1926.

5. "Cox Lauds Diligence of Greb." Greb, known as the "Pittsburgh Windmill," was the light heavyweight champion of the world from 1922 to 1923.

6. "Lyceum Athletics Picks Up in a Big Way," *Pittsburgh Press*, March 21, 1915.

7. M.R. Goldman, MD, "The Hill District as I Knew It," *Western Pennsylvania Historical Magazine* 51, no. 3 (July 1968): 279.

8. *Ibid.*, 280.

9. Sister Sally Witt, "Hell Was Not Made for Us: Father James R. Cox and the Catholic Church of Pittsburgh in the 1940s" (master's thesis, Duquesne University, 1989), 19.

10. James A. Cox Papers, "State Guard," cassette 16, June 11, 1945.

11. *Ibid.*, "Do Not Play on Air," cassette 9, no date.

12. "Timeless Priest, with Yen for Peanuts and Good Deeds, Finds Himself Famous," *Pittsburgh Press*, Jan. 8, 1932.

13. Witt, "Hell Was Not Made for Us."

14. William G. Lytle Jr., "90,000 Get Blessed at Eucharistic Rally," *Pittsburgh Press*, Oct. 13, 1930; "Over 100,000 Take Part in Eucharistic Day Rally," *Pittsburgh Catholic*, Oct. 16, 1930.

15. "10,000 in Streets to Do Homage to Eucharist," *Pittsburgh Press*, Oct. 13, 1930.

16. *Rerum Novarum*, w2.vatican.va/content/leo-xiii/en/encyclicals/documents/hf_l-xiii_enc_15051891_rerum-novarum.html.

17. *Ibid.*

18. *Quadragesimo Anno*, http://w2.vatican.va/content/pius-xi/en/encyclicals/documents/hf_p-xi_enc_19310515_quadragesimo-anno.html.

19. Richard J. Altenbaugh, "The Children of the Instrument of a Militant Labor Progressive: Brookwood Labor College and the American Labor College Movement of the 1920s and 1930s," *History of Education Quarterly* 23, no. 4 (Winter 2000): 397.

20. Timothy Kelly, "Pittsburgh Catholicism," *U.S. Catholic Historian* 18, no. 4 (Fall 2000): 65.

21. Leo XIII, *Rerum Novarum*, May 15, 1891.

22. Pius XI, *Quadragesimo Anno*, May 15, 1931.

23. Raphael Huber, "The Present Crisis," in *Our Bishops Speak*, Raphael Huber, ed. (Milwaukee: Bruce Publishing, 1952), 372.

24. John A. Ryan, and Joseph Husslein, *The Church and Labor* (New York: Macmillan, 1920), 13.

25. *Ibid.*

26. Ryan and Husslein, 13.

27. Huber, 273.

28. *Ibid.*

29. *Ibid.*, 14.

30. Dietz was an early supporter of the America Federation of Labor. Hensler, Rice and O'Toole were co-founders of the Catholic Radical Alliance. Kazinsky was active during the nationwide 1919 steel strike.

31. Kenneth Heineman, "Iron City Trinity: The Triumphs and Trial of Catholic Social

Activism in Pittsburgh," *U.S. Catholic Historian*, no. 22 (Spring 2004): 123.

32. Robert Garland, "The Scotch-Irish in Western Pennsylvania," *Western Pennsylvania History Magazine* 6, no. 2 (April 1923). In addition to commerce, the Scotch-Irish also were involved in the founding of the University of Pittsburgh and Washington Academy, which later became Washington & Jefferson College, 73. The Mellon, Oliver and Jones families, at one time, were the three largest landowners in Pittsburgh, 78. "It will be generally admitted that the people of this race have contributed in a large measure to the building of Pittsburgh the great Industrial Empire of Western Pennsylvania of which Pittsburgh is the center," 81.

33. Huber, 273.

34. "Priest Warns of Fascism Peril in U.S." *Pittsburgh Post-Gazette*, July 6, 1939.

Chapter 4

1. "Introduction of War Time Diary of Rev. James R. Cox," *Grotto News*, undated, Dr. and Mrs. Mason, Father James Renshaw Cox Collection, Saint Patrick–Saint Stanislaus Kostka Parish, Pittsburgh, Pa., 15.

2. *Ibid.*

3. "Appointed Chaplain," *Pittsburgh Catholic*, May 26, 1917.

4. John Franklin Miner, Jr., *The General Committee on Army and Navy Chaplains During World War I*, 1966, 2.

5. *Ibid.*

6. "A History of Base Hospital No. 27," U.S. Army Office of Medical History, history. amedd.army/mil/booksdoc/html.

7. Georgia Powers, "Pitt Hospital Corp Leaves for War Medicine Training in Army Camp," *Pittsburg Press*, July 12, 1917.

8. James Cox to Earl Cox, Oct. 29, 1917, Dr. and Mrs. Mason, Father James Renshaw Cox Collection.

9. "Chaplain J.R. Cox," Pittsburgh Catholic, Dec. 27, 1917.

10. "Somewhere in France," The Pittsburgh Catholic, Nov. 29, 1917.

11. "Introduction of the War Time Diary of Rev. James R. Cox," 15, Dr. and Mrs. Mason, Father James Renshaw Cox Collection.

12. H. Winnett Orr, MD, *An Orthopedic Surgeon's Story of the Great War* (Norfolk, NE: Huse Publishing, 1921), 55.

13. Max E. Hannum, "Base Hospital No. 27," *Pittsburgh Press*, May 25, 1919. The unit arrived with 500 beds, but eventually increased the number to nearly 5,000. Doctors treated 19,000 soldiers during the war. Out of that number, 227 died. Elizabeth Williams, *Pittsburgh in World War I: Arsenal of Democracy* (Charleston: History Press, 2013), 96. In 1948, Cox returned to Angers during a pilgrimage to Lourdes and was named Canon of the Cathedral of Angers. "Father Cox Made Canon in France," *Pittsburgh Press*, Nov. 17, 1918.

14. James Cox to Julia Cox, March 27, 1918, Dr. and Mrs. Mason, Father James Renshaw Cox Collection.

15. James R. Cox to Julia Cox, Sept. 26, 1918, Dr. and Mrs. Mason, Father James Renshaw Cox Collection.

16. James Cox to Julia Cox, Feb. 2, 1918, Dr. and Mrs. Mason, Father James Renshaw Cox Collection.

17. James R. Cox to Earl Cox, Oct. 29, 1917, Dr. and Mrs. Mason, Father James Renshaw Cox Collection.

18. "Chaplain Tells of Pitt Unit Overseas," *Pittsburgh Press*, April 14, 1919.

19. James Cox to Julia Cox, Sept. 5, 1918, Dr. and Mrs. Mason, Father James Renshaw Cox Collection.

20. Madame Poplar to Julia Cox, July 19, 1918, Dr. and Mrs. Mason, Father James Renshaw Cox Collection.

21. *Ibid.*

22. "Chaplain Tells of Pitt Unit Overseas," *Gazette Times*, April 4, 1919.

23. C.M. Daley, "Praises Work of Rev. James R. Cox," *Pittsburgh Press*, Feb. 10, 1938.

24. "Priest Was Man of Action, Prayer," *Pittsburgh Press*, March 20, 1951.

25. *Ibid.*

26. James R. Cox to Julia Cox, Nov. 2, 1917. Dr. and Mrs. Mason, Father James Renshaw Cox Collection.

27. "Father James R. Cox," *Pittsburgh Catholic*, Aug. 1, 1919.

28. Veterans Administration Appeal Board, C-390, 653, Henry Ellenbogen Papers, Senator John Heinz History Center, Box 30, File 6.

29. "Aged Mother Lauds Work of Her Son," *Gettysburg Times*, Jan. 7, 1932.

30. "Father Cox to Observe Anniversary Tuesday," *Pittsburgh Post-Gazette*, Sept. 3, 1927.

31. Walsh, 154, 157.

32. "Newsy Notes of Parish Affairs," *Pittsburgh Catholic*, Nov. 15, 1923.

33. "St. Patrick's to Observe Centenary," *Pittsburgh Press*, April 23, 1911.

34. *Ibid.*

35. Saintsinthestrip.org.

36. *Ibid.*

37. Rich Sebak, "Going Underground in the Strip," *Pittsburgh Magazine*, Feb. 19, 2010; Barry Paris, "St. Patrick's Church: Year 175," *Pittsburgh Post-Gazette*, March 17, 1983.

38. The Strip: a socio-economic religious

survey of a typical section of Pittsburg, made by the Christian Social Services Union, Methodist Episcopal Church Union and other cooperating agencies, July–September 1915, 10.

39. *Ibid.*

40. *Ibid.*, 36.

41. "Priest Scores Police in Strip for Violations," *Pittsburgh Press*, Oct. 17, 1928.

42. "State Politics Called Rotten, Full of Fraud," *Pittsburgh Post-Gazette*, Feb. 1, 1930.

43. Liggett Brands "Vice of City as Worst in Land," *Pittsburgh Press*, July 10, 1930.

44. *Ibid.*

45. *Ibid.*

46. "Priest Scores Police in Strip for Violence," *Pittsburgh Press*, Oct. 17, 1928.

47. Julien Comte, "The Next Page: The Lessons of Prohibition," *Pittsburgh Post-Gazette*, Feb. 3, 2008.

48. "Unsolved Gang Murders Total 100 in 3 Years," *Pittsburgh Press*, July 30, 1932.

49. "Heavily Armed Cops Sent to Patrol Strip," *Pittsburgh Post-Gazette*, Sept. 10, 1927.

50. Loomis Mayfield, "Voting Fraud in Earl Twentieth-Century Pittsburgh," *The Journal of Interdisciplinary History* 24, no. 1 (Summer 1993): 68.

Chapter 5

1. "Fr. Coakley First Priest on Radio," *Pittsburgh Catholic*, Nov. 6, 1930; "Religious and Charitable," *Pittsburgh Press*, Nov. 16, 1921.

2. "First Religious Service Broadcast 31 Years Ago," *Pittsburgh Press*, Jan. 5, 1952.

3. Daniel J. Heisey, *St. Vincent Seminary from Its Origins to the Present* (Latrobe: St. Vincent Archabbey Publications, 2006), 76, 77.

4. "High Mass for Father Cox to Be Celebrated Monday," *Pittsburgh Post-Gazette*, March 21, 1951.

5. "Father Cox of Pittsburgh," *Look Magazine*, Dec. 31, 1940; Cox Papers, box 2, folder 1.

6. "Boggs & Buhl Install Radio Department," *Gazette Times*, Dec. 11, 1921.

7. "Walsh Scorned by Pastor for Failing to Curb Vice and Crime," *Pittsburgh Daily Post*, Oct. 11, 1926.

8. "Father Cox's Plea for Mayor Herron Surprises Him," *Pittsburgh Press*, Sept. 3, 1033; "Scully Challenges Rev. Cox's Claim," *Pittsburgh Press*, Nov. 2, 1930; "Father Cox Booms Judge Ellenbogen," *Pittsburgh Press*, Jan. 6, 1938. When Cox changed political parties from Democrat to Republican in 1935, he urged his radio listeners to do the same. "Father Cox Quits Democratic Party," *Pittsburgh Post-Gazette*, Aug. 23, 1935.

9. Len Barcousky, "History Books 33 Years in the Making," *Pittsburgh Post-Gazette*, May 29, 2008.

10. "Dictator McNair Urged by Priest," *Pittsburgh Press*, Aug. 10, 1934. Cox quit the job two days later. He said he took the post because he "needed the money. Anyone who thinks a political job is easy should visit the assessor's office. I never worked so hard in my life." "Father Cox Resigns Office with City for Second Time," *Pittsburgh Press*, Nov. 11, 1934. Cox's appointment drew criticism from editorial writers who said Cox "runs the mayor a close race for headline hunting." Kermit McFarland, "Playing Politics with Taxation," *Pittsburgh Press*, Aug. 19, 1934.

11. "Priest Backs Candidacy of Mayor Herron," *Pittsburgh Post-Gazette*, June 20, 1933.

12. "Father Cox Asking Aid in Clearing Relief Deficit," *Pittsburgh Post-Gazette*, June 20, 1933.

13. "United Action Urged by Cox," *Pittsburgh Post-Gazette*, May 30, 1932; "Borough Denies Cox Corruption Charge," *Pittsburgh Press*, June 1, 1932.

14. "Father Cox Asks Votes for G.O.P.," *Pittsburgh Post-Gazette*, Oct. 12, 1935.

15. "Bribe Charges by Father Cox Meet Denials," *Pittsburgh Post-Gazette*, Nov. 3, 1930. Pinchot was elected governor in 1930 in a close race over John Hemphill. Pinchot received nearly 51 percent of the vote while Hemphill received nearly 48 percent.

16. www.radiostratosphere.com.

17. "Slow, Certain Gain in Trade Is Predicted," *Pittsburgh Post-Gazette*, Sept. 15, 1930. The sale of radios was spurred by the development of the heterodyne receiver by Edwin Armstrong in World War I. The receiver allowed listeners to listen clearly to a single station without overlap from other frequencies. Armstrong sold the patent to Westinghouse for $335,000. Westinghouse, in turn, sold it to RCA, which began producing the popular Radiola AR 218 in 1924. Susan L. Cook and Karen Krupar, "Defining the Twentieth Century and Impacting the Twenty-first; Semantic Habits Created through Radio," *Etc: A Review of General Semantics*, no. 4 (October 2010): 417.

18. "Remembering Fr. James Cox," *Pittsburgh Catholic*, Dec. 15, 1989, in *Fighter with a Heart: The Writings of Charles Owen Rice*, ed. Charles McCollester (University of Pittsburgh Press, 1996), 20. On Jan. 2, 1921, KDKA broadcast the first religious service in Pittsburgh from the Calvary Episcopal Church. The Rev. John W. Sproul broadcast religious services from the "Glory barn" in the South Side. Sproul had his own radio station,

WMBJ, and claimed to have converted over 1,000 people at his services. "Sproul Opens Final Drive in City," *Pittsburgh Press*, March 3, 1929.

19. John D. Petrarulo, "A Short Biography of Father James R. Cox" (master's thesis, California State College, 1972).

20. Heineman, 26.

21. "Do Not Play on Air," Tape 9, Cox papers.

22. *Ibid.*

23. *Ibid.*

24. *Ibid.*

25. "Birth Control Protest Made," *Pittsburgh Post-Gazette*, Nov. 7, 1929.

26. James R. Cox Papers, Tape 9.

27. "Birth Control Lecture Set by Priest," undated, James R. Cox papers, Box 2, Folder 7.

28. *Ibid.*

29. *Ibid.*

30. *Ibid.*

31. *Ibid.*

32. *Ibid.*

33. Norman St. John Stevas, "A Roman Catholic View of Population Control," *Law and Contemporary Problems* 25, no. 3 (1960): 446. In 1930, Knaus and Ogino published the results of their research. In 1951, Pope Pius XII approved the rhythm method.

34. *Ibid.*, 449.

35. *Ibid.*

36. Witt, 8.

37. *Ibid.*, 18.

38. "Error in Sacco Case, Says Cox," *Pittsburgh Post-Gazette*, Aug. 29, 1927.

39. "Walsh Scorned by Pastor for Failing to Curb Vice and Crime," *Pittsburgh Daily Post*, Oct. 11, 1926.

40. Mrs. Garland to Cox, undated, Dr. and Mrs. Mason, Father James Renshaw Cox Collection.

41. "Drinking, Flappers, Sheik Are Topics of Father Cox," *Pittsburgh Post-Gazette*, March 20, 1930.

42. *Ibid.*

43. "Priest Exposes Vile Conditions in Atlantic City," *Pittsburgh Press*, Sept. 9, 1926.

44. "Nude Beauty Contests by '35 Are Forecast by Father Cox," *Pittsburgh Press*, Sept. 9, 1926.

45. *Ibid.*

46. "Father Cox Sees Legs, Garters and Lingerie as Courtship's Doom," *Pittsburgh Post*, Feb. 25, 1926, James Cox papers, Box 1, Folder 5.

47. *Ibid.*

48. *Ibid.*

49. "Father Cox Blames Church for Vice Here, Thinks Blue Laws 'Silly fuss,'" *Gazette Times*, Oct. 11, 1926; "Urges Broader View of Sabbath," *Pittsburgh Post-Gazette*, Aug. 29, 1927.

50. "Scrap Over Batting Average Enough for Divorce Pastor says, Scorns Trial Marriages," *Gazette Times*, April 1, 1926.

51. "Father Cox Defends Dancing," *Pittsburgh Post-Gazette*, May 2, 1927.

52. "Father Cox Sees Legs." The "Black Bottom" featured a man and woman slapping their backsides while jumping forward and backward while stomping their feet and gyrating their hips.

53. "Father Cox Raps Flapper Types," *Pittsburgh Post-Gazette*, Sept. 21, 1925.

54. "Sins of Man Blacker Than Women's Says Pastor; Skeleton as Illustration," *Pittsburgh Post-Gazette*, March 13, 1927.

55. *Ibid.*

56. Rev. James R. Cox, "Rev. Cox Points Moral in New Talkie at Penn," *Pittsburgh Press*, June 12, 1931.

57. *Ibid.*

58. "Father Cox Urges Giving Women Right to Vote," *Pittsburgh Press*, July 1, 1915.

59. "Father Cox Scores Methods Used in Curbing Activity of 'Scarlet Women' in City," *Gazette Times*, Oct. 26, 1926.

60. *Ibid.*

61. *Wage-Earning Pittsburgh* (New York: Russell Sage Foundation, 1914), 73.

62. "Father Cox Scores Methods."

63. "Her Films Are Boycotted by Hibernians," *Pittsburgh Post-Gazette*, April 27, 1948.

64. Coode and Petrarulo, 234.

65. *Ibid.*

Chapter 6

1. "Father Cox Assails 'Racketeers' of Labor," *Pittsburgh Sun Telegraph*, no date; Judge Henry Ellenbogen Papers, H. John Heinz History Center, box 30, folder 7.

2. "Evans Insists City Can't Pay More Firemen," *Pittsburgh Press*, May 12, 1942.

3. *Ibid.*

4. "The Coxes Were Methodist."

5. "32 Taxi Drivers Face Traffic Court Here," *Pittsburgh Press*, Oct. 3, 1930.

6. "Battle Marks Taxi Strikers Mass Meeting," *Pittsburgh Post-Gazette*, March 24, 1930.

7. *Ibid.*

8. "Pitched Battles Fought in Streets of East End; Taxi Set on Fire," *Pittsburgh Post-Gazette*, Feb. 14, 1930.

9. "Riots, Bloodshed Mark Cab Strike; Eight Arrested," *Pittsburgh Post-Gazette*, Jan. 30, 1930.

10. "Girl Decoy Lures Cab into Ambush; Driver Is Beaten," *Pittsburgh Post-Gazette*, March 3, 1930.

11. "Cab Drivers Reject Strike Peace Move," *Pittsburgh Post-Gazette*, Jan. 27, 1930.

12. "Promise Taxi Service Today," *Pittsburgh Post-Gazette*, Jan. 20, 1930.

13. "Mayor Calls Parley to End Taxi Row Here," *Pittsburgh Press*, July 23, 1930.

14. "Gas Bombers Rout 500 at Strike Meeting," *Pittsburgh Press*, Sept. 30, 1930.

15. *Ibid.*

16. *Ibid.*

17. "Midnight Peace Meeting in Parish House Succeeds," *Pittsburgh Press*, Feb. 27, 1930.

18. "Priest Urges Pastors Aid Cab Strike," *Pittsburgh Post-Gazette*, Feb. 18, 1930.

19. *Ibid.*

20. "Cab Heads Answer Priest on Strike Statements," *Pittsburgh Press*, Feb. 19, 1930.

21. *Ibid.*

22. *Ibid.*

23. "The Coxes Were Methodist."

24. "Labor Strife Is Deplored by Priests Here," *Pittsburgh Post-Gazette*, June 28, 1937.

25. *Ibid.*

26. *Ibid.*

27. "A.F. of L. Wins Heinz Election," *Pittsburgh Press*, June 9, 1937.

28. "Attack on Unions Answered."

29. "Lewis and CIO Running America, Says Father Cox," *Pittsburgh Post-Gazette*, Oct. 26, 1937.

30. "The Dynamite of the Encyclicals," KDKA, Pittsburgh, May 15, 1937, Charles Owen Rice Papers, Box 3, Archives of Industrial Society, University of Pittsburgh.

31. "Attacks on Unions Answered."

32. T. William Bolt, "Pittsburgh's Labor Priests in the 1930s," unpublished manuscript, Charles Owen Rice Papers, Box 2, folder 32, Archives of Industrial Society, University of Pittsburgh.

33. "Cox Again Assails Labor Chief; Fagan Rallies to Green Defense," *Pittsburgh Press*, Feb. 20, 1932.

34. *Ibid.*

35. *Ibid.*

36. *Ibid.*

37. *Ibid.*

38. *Ibid.*

39. "Blue Shirt Army Started by Cox," *Pittsburgh Press*, Feb. 20, 1932.

40. Patrick J. McGreevy, *Rev. Charles Owen Rice: Apostle of Contradiction* (Pittsburgh: Duquesne University Press, 1989), 17.

41. *Ibid.*

42. "The Dynamite of the Encyclicals."

43. *Ibid.*

44. "The Critic," Winter 1987, in McCollester, ed., *Fighter with a Heart*. The CIO recruited Communists to help organize unions because of their experience in mass organizing. After the CIO achieved their goal, communists were purged from its ranks.

45. Kenneth J. Heineman, "A Catholic New Deal: Religion and Labor in 1930s Pittsburgh," *Pennsylvania Magazine of History and Biography* 118, no. 4, 1994, 371.

46. *Ibid.*

47. *Ibid.*, 364.

Chapter 7

1. Richard Oulahan, "Hoover's Inauguration Today Draws 100,000 to Capital in Gala Dress; Coolidge Acclaimed on the Streets," *New York Times*, March 4, 1929.

2. Inaugural Address of Herbert Hoover, AVALON PROJECT, Documents in Law, History and Diplomacy, Avalon.law.yale.edu/20th_century/hoover.asp.

3. Bruce Rae, "Hoover Inaugurated Before Throng in Rain; Pledges Effort to Enforce Law, Parting with Coolidge Is Climax of Day's Ceremony," *New York Times*, March 5, 1929.

4. "Hoover Asks Obedience to Dry Law," *Pittsburgh Press*, March 4, 1929.

5. Paul Bloch, "President Hoover," *Pittsburgh Post-Gazette*, March 4, 1929.

6. *Ibid.*

7. "Mellon Report Shows Surplus of $185,000,000," *Pittsburgh Post-Gazette*, July 1, 1929; "Billion Is Cut from Federal Debt in 1929," *Pittsburgh Post-Gazette*, Jan. 1, 1930.

8. "Tons of Delicacies in Food Show Exhibit," *Pittsburgh Press*, Feb. 19, 1929.

9. Fred H. Kury, "Throngs View Late Models at Auto Show," *Pittsburgh Press*, Jan. 20, 1929.

10. "Recreation Almost Untouched by Depression," *Pittsburgh Post-Gazette*, Aug. 13, 1931.

11. "Atmosphere Here Brings Complaint from Jean Harlow," *Pittsburgh Post-Gazette*, Dec. 28, 1931.

12. Paul Johns, *A History of the American People* (New York: HarperCollins, 1997), 733.

13. *Ibid.*, 734, 742.

14. *Ibid.*, 739.

15. Amity Shlaes, *The Forgotten Man: A New History of the Great Depression* (New York: Harper Perennial, 2008), 90–91.

16. "Huge Crowds See Parade, Pageant of Light Jubilee," *Pittsburgh Post-Gazette*, Oct. 24, 1929.

17. "Selling Panic Wrecks Stock Exchange; New York Frenzied," *Pittsburgh Press*, Oct. 24, 1929.

18. *Ibid.*, 3.

19. W.W. Forster, "Billions Lost in Market," *Pittsburgh Press*, Oct. 28, 1929.

20. W.W. Forster, "Huge Losses in Wall Street; Sales Set All-Time Record," *Pittsburgh Press*, Oct. 29, 1929.

21. Elmer C. Walzer, "Bankers Confident of Stock Rise," *Pittsburgh Press*, Oct. 30, 1929; "Bull Market Gives Traders Huge Profits," *Pittsburgh Press*, Dec. 31, 1929; "Stock Prices Slump 4 Billions," *Pittsburgh Press*, May 3, 1930.

22. *Ibid.*, 235.

23. "A Storm Unforeseen, Always About to Pass," *New York Times*, Oct. 28, 2008.

24. George Swetnam, "Flashback: Father Cox," *Pittsburgh Press*, Oct. 28, 1973. Crouse had been a middleweight boxer from Pittsburgh. He had a record of 60–10–4 with 46 knockouts. In 1913, he served three months in a chain gang in Panama for hitting a police officer who tried to arrest him while breaking up a fight. "May Try to Free Crouse," *Pittsburgh Press*, Aug. 22, 1913. Crouse was a dapper dresser who always wore a boutonniere in the breast pocket of his suit. In later life, he dressed shabbily, worked on occasion, and survived on handouts from friends. He continued to attend Sunday Mass every week. He died of a heart attack in the hotel room where he lived. Myron Cope, "Former Boxer Buck Crouse Found Dead in Northside Hotel Room," *Pittsburgh Post-Gazette*, June 21, 1956.

25. *Ibid.*

26. *Ibid.*

27. *Ibid.*

28. "Father Cox Appeals for Relief Funds; The Press Gives $100, Urges Public Aid," *Pittsburgh Press*, April 23, 1930.

29. "Charity Racket Involves Cleric," *Pittsburgh Press*, June 24, 1932.

30. "3,500 Needy Receive Free Food Each Day," *Pittsburgh Press*, April 23, 1932.

31. "Dozen Derelicts Receive Treat at Old St. Patrick's," *Pittsburgh Post-Gazette*, Dec. 26, 1930.

32. James W. Howell, Philip Mutthower, and Francis D. Tyson, Activities from February 1931 to February 1933, Allegheny County Relief Association.

33. "Plea Made for Children," *Pittsburgh Post-Gazette*, Oct. 25, 1932.

34. "Farmers Give Loads of Food in Needy Town," *Pittsburgh Post-Gazette*, Feb. 3, 1932.

35. "Many Suffer in Cold Wave," *Pittsburgh Post-Gazette*, 11, 31, 1930.

36. "Little Relief from Bitter Cold Is Seen," *Pittsburgh Post-Gazette*, March 4, 1930.

37. Harvey O'Connor, *Mellon's Millions: The Biography of a Fortune. The Life of Andrew W. Mellon* (New York: John Day Company, 1933).

38. O'Connor.

39. "Relief Chiefs Seek New Funds," *Pittsburgh Press*, March 1, 1932; "160,000 in County Face Starvation," *Pittsburgh Press*, March 20, 1932.

40. "Pastors Indict Starvation in Land of Plenty," *Pittsburgh Press*, Sept. 7, 1931.

41. Lynne Conner, *Pittsburgh in Stages: Two Hundred Years of Theater* (University of Pittsburgh Press, 2007), 112.

42. Boyle was born Oct. 8, 1873 in Johnstown, Pennsylvania. His parents had emigrated from Ireland. Boyle was ordained at St. Vincent's July 2, 1898, and was assigned to a parish just outside Pittsburgh. In 1889, while he was a seminarian, the dam at the South Fork Fishing and Hunting Club near Johnstown ruptured, sending water cascading toward the city. Boyle walked 35 miles home to Johnstown to learn that his father, four brothers and three sisters had perished. Only his mother and one brother survived. *Catholic Pittsburgh's One Hundred Years*, 75.

43. "Welfare Drive Spurred by Bishop Boyle," *Pittsburgh Post-Gazette*, Nov. 7, 1933.

44. Raphael Huber, ed., *Statement by the Bishops of the Administrative Committee of the National Catholic Welfare Conference on the Present Crisis* (Milwaukee: Bruce Publishing, 1933), 274.

45. "Many Meals Served by Carnegie Priests," *Pittsburgh Catholic*, May 19, 1932; "4,114 Fed in Week by Catholic Priest," *Pittsburgh Catholic*; "Many Non-Catholic Tots Fed by Priests," *Pittsburgh Catholic*, Oct. 6, 1932.

46. "Catholic Charities Spent $787,792 Here in Relief for Year," *Pittsburgh Catholic*, May 4, 1933.

47. "To Open Campaign for Welfare Fund," *Pittsburgh Catholic*, Nov. 5, 1931; "New Appeal Made for Clothing Drive for Poor of Diocese," *Pittsburgh Catholic*, Nov. 26, 1931.

48. "2,500 Fed in Pittsburgh," *New York Times*, March 19, 1930.

49. *Ibid.*

50. Richard Lowitt and Maruine Beasley, eds., *One Third of a Nation: Lorena Hickok Reports on the Great Depression* (Urbana: University of Illinois Press, 1981), 11.

51. Michael Fullilove, *Rendezvous with Destiny. How Franklin Roosevelt and Five Extraordinary Men Took America into the War and into the World* (New York: Penguin Press, 2013), 107.

52. *Ibid.*, 12.

53. "Fur to Fly in Relief Fight, Cox Says," *Pittsburgh Sun Telegraph*, Jan. 28, 1932.

54. "Priest to Run for President if U.S. Aid Fails," *Pittsburgh Sun-Telegraph*, Jan. 17, 1932.

55. "1931 to Constitute Year of Readjustment," "Local Leaders Are Expanding in Confidence," "Business to Reap Profits from 1930 Sobering Process," "More Enduring Progress Seen," "Many Reasons Why Business Will Recover," "Full Progress of Recovery to Be Evident,"

"Trade Upturn Seen for 1931," "Near End Seen for Liquidation," *Pittsburgh Post-Gazette*, Jan. 2, 1930.

56. "Future for Workers Bright Declares Secretary Davis," *Pittsburgh Post-Gazette*, Sept. 3, 1929.

57. "Secretary Davis' Vision," *Pittsburgh Post-Gazette*, Sept. 3, 1929.

Chapter 8

1. "Vet Dies as Bonus Check Arrives," *Pittsburgh Post-Gazette*, April 3, 1931.

2. *Ibid.*

3. *Ibid.*

4. "Rockne Funeral to Be Broadcast on Radio Chain," *Pittsburgh Post-Gazette*, April 3, 1931.

5. Gilbert Love, "Dining Car Shades Drawn in Mill Towns," *Pittsburgh Press*, Nov. 2, 1936.

6. "Mayor Replies to Letter on Slum Reform," *Pittsburgh Post-Gazette*, Sept. 19, 1933.

7. "Rocks on Roof Anchor Huts to Earth in Depression Colony," *Pittsburgh Press*, Feb. 5, 1933.

8. "Father Cox Takes Office as Mayor of Shantytown," *Pittsburgh Press*, Sept. 30, 1931. In 1935, the city of Pittsburgh set fire to the shantytown. The homeless men living there were moved to an abandoned school in another part of the city. City council was appalled by the filth the men created in their new digs. A reporter described the living conditions "as filth so revolting as to be indescribable." The journalist described the men as "weak-faced old men cooking mulligan stew over a coal stove." W.C. Farson, "City Has Picturesque 'Hobo Jungle,'" *Pittsburgh Post-Gazette*, Sept. 23, 1935; "Jobless Get School House," *Pittsburgh Press*, Feb. 20, 1934.

9. *Ibid.* Cox kept detailed records of every item he distributed in a clothes room journal from Dec. 10, 1930, through December 1934. He listed the name of every individual who came to the church, followed by a breakdown by month and year of each article of clothing that was distributed. Page after page lists the number of socks, suits, pants, vests, hats, shirts, dress coats and underwear handed out. There also is a list of the number of meals served and food baskets given to families. Cox also kept track of the number of haircuts and food purchases. Clothes Room Journal, Box 2, Papers of Father James R. Cox.

10. Charles P. Johnson, "Shantytown Digs in for the Winter," *Pittsburgh Press*, Nov. 8, 1931.

11. *Ibid.*

12. *Ibid.*

13. *Ibid.*

14. "Church to Give Beds for 300," *Pittsburgh Press*, Nov. 30, 1930.

15. "Mayor Replies to Letter on Slum Reform," *Pittsburgh Post-Gazette*, Sept. 19, 1933.

16. "Police Declare War on Bums," *Pittsburgh Press*, Aug. 8, 1933. In 1934, Pittsburgh firemen set the shantytown ablaze. "Shantytown Goes Up in Flames as Firemen Stand Guard," *Pittsburgh Press*, June 16, 1934.

17. "Father Cox Pauses in Hop Plans to Feast Newsboys," *Pittsburgh Press*, Jan. 3, 1928.

18. "Hoover Told Business Is Normal Again," *Pittsburgh Post-Gazette*, Jan. 24, 1930.

19. *Ibid.*

20. "Mills Report Hoover Drive Helped Trade," *Pittsburgh Post-Gazette*, Jan. 4, 1930.

21. Raymond Z. Henle, "24 Millionaires Have $5,000,000 Incomes Taxed," *Pittsburgh Post-Gazette*, Feb. 3, 1930.

22. "Hobo Colony Gets Food from Pastor," *Pittsburgh Press*, Dec. 2, 1930.

23. "Soup Lines Here in This Man's Town," *Pittsburgh Press*, Oct. 17, 1982.

24. William Faust, "Reporter in Soup Line Finds Hungry Men Patiently Waiting for Serving of Bread, Bowl of Vegetables," *Pittsburgh Press*, March 18, 1930.

25. "Report Disclaims Need of Bread Line," *Pittsburgh Press*, May 19, 1930.

26. "Relief Chief Denies Saying All O.K. Here," *Pittsburgh Post-Gazette*, Jan. 23, 1932.

27. *Ibid.*

28. "1931 to Be Year of Readjustment," *Pittsburgh Post-Gazette*, Jan. 2, 1931.

29. Kenneth J. Heinemann, "A Tale of Two Cites: Pittsburgh, Philadelphia and the Elusive Quest for a New Deal Majority," *Pennsylvania Magazine of History and Biography* 132, no. 4 (October 2008): 314.

30. James N.J. Henwood, "Politics and Unemployment Relief, Pennsylvania, 1931–1939" (Ph.D. diss., University of Pennsylvania, 1975), 2–3.

31. "Special Session Call Gives Plan to Help Jobless," *Pittsburgh Post-Gazette*, Nov. 2, 1931.

32. Henwood, 6.

33. "Hoover Vetoes Extra Session to Plan Relief," Pittsburgh Press, Nov. 9, 1930.

34. *Ibid.*

35. Melvin Dubofsky, and Warren Van Tine, *John L. Lewis: A Biography* (Urbana: University of Illinois Press, 1986), 113.

36. *Ibid.*, 100.

37. *Ibid.*, 113.

38. "Miners March on Triangle; Rally in Park," *Pittsburgh Post-Gazette*, July 1, 1931.

39. "36-Hour Prayer Meeting Closes," *Pittsburgh Press*, Jan. 16, 1932.

40. "Catholics Here in Prayer to End World Depression," *Pittsburgh Post-Gazette*,

Chapter 9

undated, Dr. and Mrs. Mason, Father James Renshaw Cox Collection.

41. "Mother Offers Boy in Payment for Debts," *Pittsburgh Press*, Dec. 3, 1931.

42. "Five Boys Killed by Fumes in Picking Coal in Old Mine," *Pittsburgh Post-Gazette*, Dec. 30, 1930.

43. "Board Up Pits on Southside," *Pittsburgh Post-Gazette*, Oct. 1, 1932.

44. "500 Men Working for Free Coal for Winter," *Pittsburgh Post-Gazette*, Oct. 1, 1932.

45. "Hays Jobless Dig Plenty of Winter Coal," *Pittsburgh Post-Gazette*, Nov. 1, 1932.

46. Ann Belser, "Reminders of the Great Depression," *Pittsburgh Post-Gazette*, Oct. 27, 2008.

47. "Insurance Policy of Man Who Ended Life Lapsed," *Pittsburgh Press*, Nov. 11, 1930.

48. "South Side's Best Ditch Digger Jobless, Ends Life," *Pittsburgh Press*, July 16, 1931.

49. "Man, Who Aided Needy in Strip, Dies in Poverty," *Pittsburgh Press*, Feb. 4, 1934.

50. "Nine Children Face Hunger After Father Disappears," *Pittsburgh Press*, Feb. 5, 1930.

51. "Jobless Man Killed as He Steals Food," *Pittsburgh Press*, Jan. 12, 1932.

52. "Artist Kane Dies 'Broke' Despite Fame," *Pittsburgh Post-Gazette*, Aug. 11, 1934. Kane had worked as a house painter. When he was 68, he became famous as a primitive artist, selling his works to some of Pittsburgh wealthy families. He died of tuberculosis at age 78. After his death, a daughter filed his will, which revealed he had personal property worth at least $4,000. "Pittsburgh Artist Left Small Estate," *Pittsburgh Press*, Aug. 20, 1934.

53. "Bandit Stages Bread Robbery," *Pittsburgh Post-Gazette*, Jan. 8, 1932.

54. "Fr. Delaney Protests to Mayor Against Eviction of Destitute," *Pittsburgh Catholic*, April 13, 1933.

55. "Despair Portrayed in Miner's Plight," *New York Times*, July 12, 1931.

56. "Hungry Children Fed by Raphael House," *Pittsburgh Catholic*, Jan. 14, 1932.

57. "160,000 in County Face Starvation as Relief Funds Are Exhausted," *Pittsburgh Press*, March 20, 1032.

58. "Depression Children Happy Despite Lack of Care," *Pittsburgh Press*, Feb. 12, 1935.

59. "Survey Shows Children Hard Hit by Depression," *Pittsburgh Press*, May 26, 1934.

60. Bruce M. Stave, *The New Deal and the Last Hurrah: Pittsburgh Machine Politics* (University of Pittsburgh Press, 2009), 112.

61. Thomas H. Coode, and John F. Baum, *People, Poverty, and Politics: Pennsylvania During the Great Depression* (Lewisburg: Bucknell University Press, 1981), 225.

62. *Ibid.*, 27.

63. Beers, 72.

Chapter 9

1. Rev. James R. Cox, "Father Cox Reveals Drama of March to Washington," *Pittsburgh Press*, Jan. 17, 1932.

2. "Red Thursday Parades to Be Staged Here," *Pittsburgh Post-Gazette*, March 5, 1930; "Reds Refused Permit, Will Defy Police," *Pittsburgh Post-Gazette*, March 6, 1930; "Red Parade Here Turns into Fiasco," *Pittsburgh Post-Gazette*, March 7, 1930.

3. "More Aid Asked by Unemployed," *Pittsburgh Press*, July 27, 1933.

4. "Mayor Again Refuses to Act in Children's Shoe Crisis," *Pittsburgh Press*, Oct. 31, 1935.

5. Jack Johnstone, "The Work of Our Party in Pittsburgh," *The Communist*, April 1934, 346.

6. "Radicals Hold Rally in Park," *Pittsburgh Press*, May 1, 1930.

7. "Governor Appeals to People in Fight to Save Relief Plan," *Pittsburgh Press*, Dec. 3, 1931. The General Assembly had proposed $20 million for relief, but Pinchot wanted $35 million that would be funded by a two-cent increase in the gasoline tax. The oil companies lobbied hard and blocked the proposed tax hike.

8. "Jobless Start Capital March by Auto Truck," *Pittsburgh Press*, April 18, 1931.

9. "Capital Eyes Red Marchers," *Pittsburgh Post-Gazette*, Nov. 30, 1931.

10. Mark McColloch, Richard Oestreicher and Joel Sabadasz, "Unemployed Organizing in the 1930s," Allegheny County Labor Council, aflcio.org.

11. "Hunger Marchers Arrive in City," *Pittsburgh Press*, Dec. 4, 1931; "Evict 'Hunger' Marchers Here," *Pittsburgh Press*, Dec. 5, 1931.

12. "Red Parade Here Turns into Fiasco," *Pittsburgh Post-Gazette*, March 7, 1930.

13. "Jobless Start Capital March by Auto Truck," *Pittsburgh Press*, April 13, 1931.

14. Ray E. Knestrick, "Hunger March," *The New Republic* 67, no. 868 (July 22, 1931): 263.

15. *Ibid.*

16. Henwood, 135.

17. "Verona Councilmen Fear Riot, Bar Chambers Door," *Pittsburgh Press*, Oct. 27, 1931.

18. "Unemployed Parade Converges Upon Washington," *Pittsburgh Post-Gazette*, Dec. 7, 1931. In addition to Jacob Coxey, Rosalie Jones in 1913 led 8,000 women known as the "Army of the Hudson" to Washington, demanding the right to vote on the eve of Woodrow Wilson's inauguration. Jones wore a cloak and carried a staff. She forbade her followers from accepting handouts from bystanders. In

some areas, she was harassed and spat on by jeering crowds of boys. Diana Rice, "Armies that Hiked to Impress Congress," *New York Times*, June 12, 1932.

19. John Dos Passos, "Red Day on Capitol Hill," *The New Republic* 69, no. 890 (Dec. 23, 1931): 153.

20. "Hunger Marchers Foiled by Capital Police," *Pittsburgh Press*, Dec. 8, 1931.

21. *Ibid.*

22. "Idle March on Harrisburg," *New York Times*, April 19, 1931.

23. Rev. James R. Cox, "Father Cox Reveals Drama of March to Washington," *Pittsburgh Press*, Jan. 17, 1932.

24. *Ibid.*

25. "Father Cox Fears Revolution If Government Doesn't Change," *Greensburg (Pennsylvania) Daily Tribune*, Jan. 7, 1932.

26. "'Shantytown's' Priest Plans 'Jobs March,'" *Pittsburgh Press*, Dec. 11, 1931.

27. "Father Cox Reveals Drama of March to Washington."

28. Petrarulo, 37.

29. *Ibid.*

30. "Unemployed Army Goes to Capital Today," *Pittsburgh Post-Gazette*, Jan. 5, 1932.

Chapter 10

1. "Storm Catches Rear Guard of Father Cox's Marchers," *Pittsburgh Post-Gazette*, Jan. 6, 1932.

2. Petrarulo, 6.

3. "Father Cox's March Plans Complete," *Pittsburgh Post-Gazette*, Jan. 4, 1932.

4. *Ibid.*

5. Rev. James R. Cox, "Father Cox Reveals Drama of March to Washington," *Pittsburgh Press*, Jan. 17, 1932.

6. *Ibid.*

7. "Route of Jobless March to Washington," *Pittsburgh Press*, Jan. 5, 1932.

8. *Ibid.*

9. Personal Notes on Father Cox's 1932 March, Elmer Cope Papers, Box 8, Ohio Historical Society.

10. *Ibid.*

11. There would be other marches on Harrisburg and Washington following Cox's trek, but none would receive the warm welcome that greeted Cox and his followers. Various groups stormed Harrisburg demanding aid for the unemployed, but the public and politicians were growing tired of the rhetoric that accompanied the marches. "The only significance of these marches is the use made of them by politicians for their own ends. Beyond that they have no real importance except in pointless political phenomena."

12. "Father Cox Reveals Drama to Washington."

13. "Cold Showers Drench City," *Pittsburgh Post-Gazette*, Jan. 45, 1932.

14. Kurt F. Stone, *The Jews of Capitol Hill: A Compendium of Jewish Congressional Members* (Lanham, MD: Scarecrow Press, 2011), 141.

15. *Ibid.*

16. "Storm Catches Rear Guard."

17. V.D. Sedlak, "Jobless Marcher Tells His Story of Pilgrimage," *Pittsburgh Press*, Jan. 13, 1932.

18. *Ibid.*

19. Fred Remington, "News Bulletins Problems for TV," *Pittsburgh Press*, Nov. 13, 1955.

20. "Father Cox's Army Starts for Capital," *New York Times*, Jan. 6, 1932.

21. McCloskey had a tumultuous political career as mayor, city councilman, county commissioner and chairman of the Pennsylvania Boxing Commission.

22. Curtis Miner, *Forging a New Deal: Johnstown and the Great Depression, 1929–1941* (Johnstown: Benshoff Printing, 1993), 11.

23. "Father, Son Both in Fight," no date, no publication, Eddie McCloskey Collection, Johnstown Area Heritage Association.

24. William Harris Glosser, Jr., et al., FBI Report 25-8728, Nov. 23, 1943, FOIA No. 376125, File No. 25-151788, Eddie McCloskey Collection.

25. *Ibid.*

26. Randy Whittle, *Johnstown, Pennsylvania: A History, 1895–1936* (Charleston, SC: History Press, 2005), 206.

27. "Unemployed Army Goes to Capital Today," *Pittsburgh Post-Gazette*, Jan. 5, 1932.

28. "Cox's Hikers Fed by Ex-War Nurse," *Pittsburgh Post-Gazette*, Jan. 13, 1932.

29. Robert Taylor, "Cox's Jobless Army Camping in Huntingdon," *Pittsburgh Post-Gazette*, Jan. 6, 1932.

30. Vondas, "Father Cox Still Marches in Memory."

31. "Career of This West Natrona Clergyman Has Been Exciting and Interesting," *Pittsburgh Press*, May 24, 1941.

32. Heineman, 26.

33. "Father Cox Reveals Drama of March to Washington."

34. Coode and Petrarulo, 221.

35. *Ibid.*

36. "Governor Feeds Jobless Marchers in Harrisburg," *Pittsburgh Press*, Jan. 6, 1932.

37. *Ibid.*; David Jones, "Jobless Parade in Harrisburg; Food Supplied by Gov. Pinchot," *Pittsburgh Post-Gazette*, Jan. 6, 1932.

38. Robert Taylor, "Greeted by Pinchot," *Pittsburgh Post-Gazette*, Jan. 7, 1932.

39. *Ibid.*

40. *Ibid.*

41. *Ibid.*

42. William J. Lytle Jr., "15,000 Stand in Rain, Hear March Lauded," *Pittsburgh Press*, Jan. 6, 1932.

43. *Ibid.*

44. "Pinchot Cheers Trek on Capitol," *New York Sun*, Jan. 6, 1932, Cox Papers.

45. Lytle.

46. "Father Cox Reveals Drama of March to Washington."

47. "Father Cox's Own Story."

Chapter 11

1. "Father Cox Marches in Memory."

2. "Father Cox's Own Story," *Pittsburgh Press*, Jan. 10, 1932.

3. "Musician in Cox Army Collapses, $1,050 in Pockets," *Pittsburgh Press*, Jan. 8, 1932.

4. "Cox's Army of Idle Arrives at Capital," *New York Times*, Jan. 7, 1932.

5. Robert Taylor, "Cox Leads Jobless Army into Washington," *Pittsburgh Post-Gazette*, Jan. 7, 1932.

6. *Ibid.*

7. "Here's Food Supplied to Jobless Marchers," *Pittsburgh Press*, Jan. 7, 1932.

8. "Sidelights on Father Cox's Jobless Army of 14,000," *Pittsburgh Sun-Telegraph*, Jan. 7, 1932.

9. *Ibid.*

10. "Father Cox's Own Story."

11. Robert Taylor, "Cox's Army Starts for Home After Making Plea for Aid," *Pittsburgh Post-Gazette*, Jan. 8, 1932.

12. "Sidelights on Father Cox's Jobless Army," Pittsburgh Press, Dr. and Mrs. Mason, Father James Renshaw Cox Collection.

13. Cox's parade was illegal under a seldom-enforced law banning demonstrations at the capitol. In 1882, Congress enacted a law banning the use of banners, parades, processions, flags and speeches on the Capitol steps.

14. "Jobless Marchers Appeal to Hoover," *New York Times*, Jan. 8, 1932.

15. Heineman, *A Catholic New Deal*, 24.

16. *Ibid.*, 23.

17. "Father Cox: Breadlines & Garden Stakes Makes News," *Bulletin Index*, Dec. 9, 1937.

18. William G. Lytle Jr., "President Hears Cox Plea," *Pittsburgh Press*, Jan. 7, 1932.

19. "President Smiles as Jobless Appeal," *Pittsburgh Press*, Jan. 7, 1932.

20. "Jobless Marchers Appeal to Hoover," *New York Times*, Jan. 8, 1932.

21. *Ibid.*

22. *Ibid.*

23. *Ibid.*

24. Editorial, *Pittsburgh Courier*, Jan. 9, 1932.

25. "Father Cox's Petition to President, Congress," *Pittsburgh Press*, Jan. 8, 1932.

26. *Ibid.*

27. "Jobless Marchers Appeal to Hoover."

28. Raymond Z. Henle, "Mellon Aids Cox Marchers Left Behind," *Pittsburgh Post-Gazette*, Jan. 9, 1932.

29. *Ibid.*

30. "Relief Trucks Begin Picking Up Stragglers on Long Hike," *Pittsburgh Post-Gazette*, Jan. 7, 1932.

31. *Ibid.*

32. William G. Lytle Jr. "Weary Marchers Parade Downtown at End of Journey," *Pittsburgh Press*, Jan. 8, 1932.

33. "Cox's Army Back, Exhausted After March to Capital," *Pittsburgh Post-Gazette*, Jan. 9, 1932.

34. William G. Lytle Jr., "Return from Hunger March," *Pittsburgh Press*, Jan. 8, 1932.

35. *Ibid.*

36. *Ibid.*

37. William Lytle, Jr., "City Cheers Jobless Army," *Pittsburgh Press*, Jan. 8, 1932.

38. "Radio Carries Speech by Cox," *Pittsburgh Post-Gazette*, Jan. 8, 1932.

39. "Cox's March," *Pittsburgh Press*, Jan. 8, 1932.

40. *Ibid.*

41. Charles H. Joseph, "Father Cox's Army," *Jewish Criterion* 79, no. 11 (July 9, 1932).

42. A.C. Burke, "Condemns Cox March as Useless," *Pittsburgh Press*, Jan. 28, 1932.

43. Stephen Mizerak, "A Truck Driver Defends Father Cox Against His Critics," *Pittsburgh Press*, Jan. 28, 1932.

44. Roy Greene, "Says Hoover Is Not Statesman," *Pittsburgh Press*, Feb. 13, 1932.

45. "The Jobless March," *Pittsburgh Catholic*, Jan. 14, 1932.

46. "What Other Catholic Editors Say About Father's Cox's Jobless March," *Pittsburgh Catholic*, Jan. 21, 1932.

47. *Ibid.*

48. "Welfare Fund Asks Millions More for Needy," *Pittsburgh Post-Gazette*, Jan. 8, 1932.

49. "Father Cox Awakened Congress in Job Hike, Says Visiting Priest," *Pittsburgh Press*, Jan. 11, 1932.

50. Ewers, 795.

51. *Ibid.*

52. "Cox's Army Back."

53. Lytle, "City Cheers Jobless Army."

54. Robert Taylor, "Cox's Army Starts Home After Making Plea for Aid," *Pittsburgh Press*, Jan. 8, 1932.

55. "Cox in Denial Hoover Enemy Backed March," *Pittsburgh Post-Gazette*, Jan. 16, 1932.

56. "Mellon Supplies Train Fares for Cox Marchers," *New York Herald Tribune*, Jan. 9, 1932, Cox papers, Box 1, Folder 7; Raymond Henle, "Mellon Aids Cox Marchers Left Behind," *Pittsburgh Post-Gazette*, Jan. 9, 1932. Congressmen Edmund F. Erk of the city's north side, and Patrick J. Sullivan of Homestead, paid the train fares for 16 stranded marchers. "Crowds Jam St. Patrick's to Hear Cox," *Pittsburgh Post-Gazette*, Jan. 11, 1932.

57. *Pittsburgh Catholic*, Jan. 21, 1932.

58. "Father Cox," *The Militant* 5, no. 5 (Jan. 30, 1932): 4.

59. "Hoover Makes New Plea for Rigid Economy," *Pittsburgh Post-Gazette*, Jan. 9, 1932.

60. *Ibid.* The publicity from the march brought Cox publicity of a different sort. Elizabeth Dilling, an anticommunist activist and writer who published *Red Network*, included Cox on a list of radicals as "people to be watched." The list included Eleanor Roosevelt, writer Theodore Drieser, Monsignor John Ryan, and Supreme Court Justice Louis Brandeis. Cox welcomed the distinction. "If they are going to call me a radical because I wish to make progress according to the right principles, then they can call me what they wish," he said. "Pittsburghers Called Radical—They Like It," *Pittsburgh Press*, May 8, 1936.

Chapter 12

1. David Greenberg, *Calvin Coolidge* (New York: Henry Holt, 2006), 78–79.

2. "Father Cox Demands U.S. Pay Veterans in Full," *Pittsburgh Press*, Jan. 23, 1932.

3. "Veterans March in Capital to Press Bonus Demands," *Pittsburgh Post-Gazette*, June 7, 1932.

4. Raymond Henle, "Father Cox Places Bonus Demand Before President," *Pittsburgh Post-Gazette*, June 10, 1932.

5. "Cox Asks Vets to Join His Party," *Pittsburgh Post-Gazette*, Aug. 5, 1932.

6. "Father Cox Brands Waters Politics Charge as False," *Pittsburgh Press*, March 2, 1933.

7. *Ibid.*

8. *Ibid.*

9. *Ibid.*

10. "Father Cox Places Bonus Demand Before President."

11. *Ibid.*

12. *Ibid.*

13. *Ibid.*

14. *Ibid.*

15. "Veterans Besiege Sharpsburg," *Pittsburgh Press*, June 6, 1932.

16. *Ibid.*

17. J. Edgar Hoover to Attorney General, Sept. 7, 1932, "Bonus March," Bureau of Investigation.

18. *Ibid.*

19. Rich Gigler, "He Was a 'Soldier' in the Bonus Army," *Pittsburgh Press*, James Cox papers, Box 2, Folder 2.

20. Robert Taylor, "Last of Bonus Army Disbands," *Pittsburgh Press*, Aug. 7, 1932.

21. "Butler Insists State Will Go to Roosevelt," *Pittsburgh Press*, Oct. 23, 1932.

22. Taylor, "Last of Bonus Army Disbands."

23. "Cox Pilgrims Begin Trip to Europe Today," *Pittsburgh Post-Gazette*, June 10, 1932.

Chapter 13

1. "Cox Plans to Make Run for President," *Pittsburgh Press*, Jan. 17, 1932.

2. "Jobless Party Plan Started by Cox," *Pittsburgh Press*, Jan. 10, 1932.

3. "Third Party Rumblings," *Pittsburgh Catholic*, Jan. 14, 1932.

4. "Thousands Marching to Cox Rally," *Pittsburgh Press*, Jan. 16, 1932.

5. "Priest Invites Wealthy to Local Job Rally," *Pittsburgh Sun-Telegraph*, Jan. 15, 1932.

6. "Jobless Party Will Run Cox for President," *Pittsburgh Sun-Telegraph*, Jan. 17, 1932.

7. "Thousands Marching to Cox Rally."

8. "60,000 Families Seeking Aid; 500 Pleas Are Made Every Day," *Pittsburgh Press*, Feb. 2, 1932.

9. "160,000 in County Face Starvation as Relief Funds Are Exhausted," *Pittsburgh Press*, March 20, 1932.

10. "Proposed City Relief Bonds Run into Snag," *Pittsburgh Post-Gazette*, June 21, 1932.

11. "Relief Bonds Sale Refused by Poor Board," *Pittsburgh Press*, Dec. 29, 1932.

12. "Father Cox Wires Hoover a Warning," *New York Times*, July 29, 1932.

13. "Interview with Father James R. Cox, pastor of Old St. Patrick's Church at Pittsburgh, Pa.," Father Cox Papers.

14. *Ibid.*

15. "Grafters Must Go, Says Leader, Father Cox," *The Standard*, Montreal, Canada, June 11, 1932.

16. *Ibid.*

17. *Ibid.*

18. "Father Cox Sure He'll Be Elected," *Pittsburgh Press*, June 30, 1932.

19. Rev. James Cox, "Eucharistic Meet Viewed by Father Cox from Plane," *Pittsburgh Post-Gazette*, July 13, 1932.

20. "Father Cox Launches Presidential Drive," *New York Times*, July 27, 1932.

21. "Candidate Cox," *Time* 20, no. 3 (August 1932).

22. "Father Cox Returns, Ready for Vote Drive," *Pittsburgh Press*, July 27, 1932. Section 285.3 of the *Codex Iuris Canonici* bans priests from running for elective office. Most of the clerics who served in Congress over the past 225 years were Protestant. The Rev. Robert Drinan was a congressman from 1970 to 1980. The Rev. Robert J. Corwell served from 1975 to 1977. "History of Clergy in Congress," pewforum.org/2015/01/05/history-of-clergy-in-congress.

23. Ewers, 797.

24. "Father Cox Returns, Ready for Vote Drive," *Pittsburgh Press*, July 27, 1932.

25. *Ibid*. Sailing back to the United States, Cox claimed he had "rubbed shoulders" with Treasury Secretary Andrew Mellon on the trip to Europe. Although they sailed on the same ship, the two men never saw each other.

26. *Ibid*.

27. *Ibid*.

28. "Party Discord Flatly Denied by Cox," *Pittsburgh Post-Gazette*, July 27, 1932.

29. "Jobless File Name as National Party," *New York Times*, Feb. 28, 1932. Cox seemed oblivious to the fact that Smith had lost his bid for the presidency because of his religion.

Chapter 14

1. "Axes Ring Out Near Coxtown," *Pittsburgh Press*, June 5, 1932.

2. *Ibid*.

3. "Cox Opens Campaign with Sunday Speech," *Pittsburgh Press*, Aug. 26, 1932.

4. "Cox Cheered by Followers at Coxtown," *Pittsburgh Post-Gazette*, Aug. 29, 1932.

5. *Ibid*.

6. Patricia Bartos, "Relics of Radio Priest and Labor Activist Presented to Pittsburgh Diocese by Relatives," *Pittsburgh Catholic*, March 12, 2008.

7. "Cox and Jobless Go to Convention," *Pittsburgh Press*, Aug. 14, 1932.

8. Robert Taylor, "Father Cox's Jobless Army Crossing Ohio," *Pittsburgh Press*, Aug. 15, 1932.

9. "Cox and Jobless Go to Convention."

10. "Cox Expects Million Attend Meet," *Pittsburgh Post-Gazette*, March 29, 1932.

11. "Drive to Bar Meet Charges by Father Cox," *Pittsburgh Post-Gazette*, Aug. 11, 1932.

12. "Father Cox Nominated for President with Mason Running Mate," *St. Louis Globe*, Aug. 16, 1932.

13. *Ibid*.

14. *Ibid*.

15. *Ibid*.

16. Robert Taylor, "Cox and 'Coin' Both Will Run for President," *Pittsburgh Press*, Aug. 17, 1932.

17. "Cox and 'Coin' Both Will Run for President."

18. *Ibid*.

19. Robert Taylor, "Bitterly Opposed Factions Nominate Cox and 'Coin' Harvey for President," *Pittsburgh Press*, Aug. 17, 1932.

20. Frank Butler, "Jobless Party Nominates Cox for Presidency, Ends Convention," *Pittsburgh Post-Gazette*, Aug. 18, 1932.

21. "Cox and 'Coin' Both Will Run for President."

22. James O'Neal, "Messiah vs. Messiah vs. Messiah," *The American Mercury*, Oct. 1932, 180.

23. *Ibid*.

24. Martin Payer, "The Convention of Father Cox's Quasi-Fascist Jobless Party," *The Militant* 35, no. 131 (Aug. 27, 1932).

25. "Cox Unmoved by Harvey Bolt," *Pittsburgh Sun Telegraph*, no date, Dr. and Mrs. Mason, Father James Renshaw Cox Collection.

26. "Bitterly Opposed Factions Nominate Cox and 'Coin' Harvey for President."

27. Frank Butler, "Local Backers of Father Cox on Trek East," *Pittsburgh Post-Gazette*, Aug. 19, 1932.

28. Heineman, *A Catholic New Deal*, 28.

29. Mark Shields, "Father Cox Jobless March Haunts Leaders of the Major Parties," *Pittsburgh Sun-Telegraph*, Jan. 26, 1932.

Chapter 15

1. Mark Sullivan, "The Man Who Would Be Shepherd-in-Chief," *Our Sunday Visitor*, June 29, 2008.

2. "Broke Cox Comes Home," *Pittsburgh Press*, Sept. 25, 1932.

3. Krupnick died in 1956 after he was hit by a milk truck. He was 56. "Driver Cleared in Traffic Deaths," *Pittsburgh Press*, Oct. 11, 1956.

4. James R. Akerman, ed., *Cartographies of Travel and Navigation* (Chicago: University of Chicago Press, 2006), 185.

5. Andrew J. Krupnick, Father Cox's Campaign for the Presidency of the United States (in 1932; a diary), Father Cox Papers, 1923–1951, Archives of Industrial Society, University of Pittsburgh, 11.

6. *Ibid*. By comparison, the Democrats spent more than $2.2 million electing FDR in 1932 while the GOP spent a total of $2.9 million in a losing effort. Louise Overacker, "American Government and Political Campaign Funds in a Depression Year," *American*

Political Science Review 27, no. 5 (October 1933): 773. The American Presidency Project, presidency.ucsb.edu/data/financing.php.

7. "Father Cox Stranded in West," no date, no name, James Cox papers.

8. *Ibid.*

9. *Ibid.*

10. "Cox Campaigns in Nearby Ohio," *Pittsburgh Post-Gazette*, Aug. 30, 1932.

11. "Cox Appeals for Votes in Nearby Ohio," *Pittsburgh Post-Gazette*, Aug. 30, 1932.

12. Krupnick, 2.

13. *Ibid.*, 11.

14. *Ibid.* 7. Wooster is the home of Wooster College, which was founded by the Presbyterian Church in 1866. Until 1969, it was owned by the Presbyterian Synod of Ohio. wooster.edu.

15. *Ibid.*, 8.

16. *Ibid.*

17. *Ibid.*

18. "Ohio Officials Battle Over Cox Visit," *Pittsburgh Sun-Telegraph*, Sept. 30, 1932, Dr. and Mrs. Mason, Father James Renshaw Cox Collection.

19. *Ibid.*, 12.

20. *Ibid.*, 13.

21. *Ibid.*, 17.

22. *Ibid.*, 14.

23. Krupnick diary, 14.

24. *Ibid.*, 15.

25. "Cox in Farm Strike Area," *Pittsburgh Sun Telegraph*, undated, Father James Renshaw Cox Collection.

26. "Ban Cox in Iowa Town," no publication, no date, Dr. and Mrs. Mason.

27. Krupnick diary, 24.

28. *Ibid.*, 25.

29. *Ibid.*, 26.

30. *Ibid.*

31. *Ibid.*, 24.

32. *Ibid.*

33. *Ibid.*

34. *Ibid.*, 29.

35. *Ibid.*

36. *Ibid.*, 34.

37. "City Banquet Honors Cox, Tisdal," *Elk City Morning Times*, Sept. 20, 1932.

38. Krupnick, 37.

39. *Ibid.*, 38.

40. Donald W. Whisenhunt, *Utopian Movements and Ideas of the Great Depression. Dreamers, Believers and Madmen* (Lanham, MD: Lexington Books, 2013), 77.

41. *Ibid.*, 78.

42. *Ibid.*, 99.

43. *Ibid.*, 41.

44. *Ibid.*, 45.

45. *Ibid.*, 46.

46. "Broke Cox Comes Home," *Pittsburgh Press*, Sept. 25, 1932.

47. "Father Cox in Oakland," *Berkeley Daily Gazette*, Oct. 1, 1932.

48. Whisenhunt, 64.

49. Krupnick diary, 50.

50. *Ibid.*, 44.

51. *Ibid.*

52. Krupnick, 44.

53. *Ibid.*

54. "Women Gives Financial Aid to Cox Party," *Pittsburgh Post-Gazette*, Sept. 26, 1932.

55. *Ibid.*, 59.

56. "Cox Will Fly Home Today to Seek Cash," *Pittsburgh Press*, Sept. 22, 1932.

57. "Women Gives Financial Aid to Cox Party."

Chapter 16

1. "Cox Quits Race, Aids Roosevelt," *Pittsburgh Press*, Oct. 18, 1932.

2. "Father Cox Quits Stump," *New York Times*, Oct. 13, 1932.

3. "Cox Quits Race, Aids Roosevelt."

4. "Woman Gives Financial Aid to Cox Party," *Pittsburgh Post-Gazette*, Sept. 26, 1932.

5. "Father Cox Quits Stump: Jobless Party Candidate Out of Funds, but 'Still in the Race,'" *New York Times*, Oct. 13, 1932; "Roosevelt Gets Aid of Rev. Cox," *Spokane Daily Chronicle*, Oct. 18, 1932; "Endorsing Roosevelt, Cox Quits as Nominee," *Tuscaloosa News*, Oct. 18, 1932; and *Williamsport Gazette and Bulletin*, Oct. 19, 1932.

6. Leo Sack, "Norman Thomas Says Father Cox Offered to Make Trade for Support of Socialists," *Pittsburgh Press*, Oct. 22, 1932.

7. *Ibid.*

8. "Cox Renews His Attacks Upon Socialist Candidate," *Pittsburgh Post-Gazette*, Oct. 25, 1932.

9. "Cox Drops Out of Race; Will Aid Roosevelt," *Pittsburgh Post-Gazette*, Oct. 19, 1932.

10. John B. Townley, "Huge Crowds Cheer Roosevelt," *Pittsburgh Press*, Oct. 19, 1932.

11. "Highlights of Politics," *Pittsburgh Press*, Oct. 18, 1932.

12. "Cox Quits Race, Aids Roosevelt."

13. *Ibid.*

14. Heineman, 30.

15. *Ibid.*

16. "Roosevelt Opposes Bonus Payment Until Treasury Has Surplus of Cash," *Pittsburgh Post-Gazette*, Oct. 20, 1932.

17. "Roosevelt and Knox Near City," *Pittsburgh Press*, Oct. 19, 1932.

18. John T. Woolley and Gerhard Peters, The American Presidency Project (online), Santa Barbara, Calif., www.presidency.ucsb.edu/ws/?p10=88339.

19. Kaspar Monahan, "Franklin D. Roosevelt Hits Home Run in G.O.P.'s Own Backyard," *Pittsburgh Press*, Oct. 20, 1932.

20. Stave, 25.

21. "U.S. to Lend State $5 Million More," *Pittsburgh Press*, Oct. 1, 1932; "Pupils in County Schools Will Be Given Free Milk," *Pittsburgh Post-Gazette*, Nov. 14, 1932; "Welfare Fund Plea Made to Wage Earners," *Pittsburgh Post-Gazette*, Nov. 14, 1932.

22. Kaspar Monahan, "Hoover Views Dead Industry," *Pittsburgh Press*, Nov. 16, 1932.

23. "Thousands Greet Hoover Here," *Pittsburgh Press*, Nov. 16, 1932.

24. "Hoover Pledges Needy Aid Amid Turmoil of Campaign," *Pittsburgh Post-Gazette*, Nov. 7, 1932.

25. John B. Townley, "County Drops G.O.P. Meeting," *Pittsburgh Press*, Nov. 6, 1932; Ray Tucker, "Roosevelt Landslide Predicted," *Pittsburgh Press*, Nov. 6, 1932.

26. Weber, 68.

27. "Roosevelt Sweeps County Winning in 41 States," *Pittsburgh Post-Gazette*, Nov. 9, 1932. Cox polled 726 votes in Pennsylvania.

28. "Say Goodbye to Hard Times with Pageant," *Pittsburgh Post-Gazette*, June 1, 1933; "Gigantic Federal Drive Under Way to Deal Death Blow to Depression," *Pittsburgh Post-Gazette*, June 20, 1933.

29. "Government in Washington Scored by Cox," *Pittsburgh Post-Gazette*, Feb. 6, 1932.

30. *Ibid.*

31. "Father Cox Holds to Plans for Capitol March," *Pittsburgh Press*, Dec. 11, 1935.

32. David H. Bennett, "The Year of the Old Folks Revolt," *American Heritage Magazine* 16, no. 1 (December 1964).

33. "Father Cox Holds to Plans for Capitol March."

34. Raymond Z. Henle, "Roosevelt Gives Father Cox Stone from White House for New Church," *Pittsburgh Post-Gazette*, Jan. 14, 1936. A bill similar to the Townsend plan was presented in 1935 to Congress by Roosevelt, who called his plan Social Security. Social Security would pay between $10 and $85 a month to senior citizens based on a two percent tax that would be shared by the worker and his employer on the first $3,000 in income.

Chapter 17

1. "St. Patrick's Destroyed by Fire This Morning," *Pittsburgh Catholic*, March 21, 1935.

2. "St. Patrick's Once a Shrine for Aristocracy," *Pittsburgh Press*, March 21, 1935.

3. *Ibid.*

4. "Celebrate Centenary of Church," *Pittsburgh Post*, April 16, 1911.

5. Barry Paris, "St. Patrick's Church: Year 175," *Pittsburgh Post-Gazette*; Mary Pat Flaherty, "Church Without a Neighborhood," *Pittsburgh Press*, March 13, 1983.

6. "Fire Razes Father Cox's Church," *Pittsburgh Press*, March 21, 1935. One parishioner of Old St. Patrick's was Emil Sitka, who became famous as the "fourth stooge" of Three Stooges fame. Sitka appeared in dozens of short films featuring the Stooges. He played butlers, businessmen and a mad scientist. Always, he was the foil for Moe, Curly and Larry. Sitka was a lanky man with a sharp nose and wide eyes. He was one of five children. When his father died of black lung and his mother was ill, his brothers were placed in foster homes. But Father Cox took in Sitka, who lived in a small room in the rectory and served as an altar boy. When Cox needed the room, Sitka and a brother lived in the shantytown next to the church. He attended Central Catholic High School in Pittsburgh and tried to earn a living as an artist. When the St. Patrick's Day flood of 1936 hit Pittsburgh, Sitka set off for California. Emilsitka.com, "16 and Alone, Studying Art," *Pittsburgh Sun-Telegraph*, July 15, 1931.

7. *Ibid.*

8. "New St. Patrick's Church Progresses," *Pittsburgh Press*, Dec. 12, 1935; "Father Cox Acquires Italian Marble from Natatorium for St. Patrick's," *Pittsburgh Post-Gazette*, Dec. 12, 1935.

9. "The Holy Land Pictures," Cox Papers, Box 1, folder 5, 2.

10. *Ibid.*

11. *Ibid.* During the battle with the Philistines, David said, "Oh, that someone would get me a drink of water from the well near the gate of Bethlehem." Three warriors risked their lives traveling through enemy lines to retrieve the water, but David refused to drink it, instead pouring it out before the Lord. Samuel 23: 25–17.

12. The Via Dolorosa or the "Way of Sorrows" is the path Christ walked carrying his cross to his Cruxifiction. The Valley of Kidron separates the Temple Mount from the Mount of Olives in the Old City of Jerusalem. Judas, according to some biblical scholars, hanged himself from an elder tree, which is the type of wood that Christ was crucified on.

13. "Cox Is Ready to Build New St. Patrick's," *Pittsburgh Post-Gazette*, Aug. 24, 1935.

14. "The Holy Land," 1.

15. "Blarney Stone Gets Place in St. Patrick's," *Pittsburgh Post-Gazette*, Oct. 9, 1935.

16. "Roosevelt Gives Father Cox Stone from White House for New Church," *Pittsburgh Post-Gazette*, Jan. 14, 1936.

17. Scala Sancta (Holy Stairs), *New Advent*

Catholic Encyclopedia, newadvent.org/cath en/135–5a.htm.

18. "10 More Barrels of Lourdes Holy Water Arrive for Use of Faithful," Annals of Our Lady of Lourdes, James R. Cox Papers, Archives Service Center, University of Pittsburgh, Box 1, V.B. Clippings. Lourdes is located at the foothills of the Pyrenees Mountains.

19. "New Arrests Due in Garden Stakes Probe," *Pittsburgh Press*, Jan. 10, 1938.

20. "St. Patrick's Once a Shrine for Aristocracy," *Pittsburgh Press*, March 21, 1935.

21. *Ibid*. The original St. Patrick's was built in 1808 but it was destroyed by fire in 1854. A new church was built, which later was sold to the Pennsylvania Railroad in 1865. The third church was built in the Strip District. The church remains open for daily Mass.

22. "Big Cash Prizes in Cox Contest Given to Relatives of Promoters," *Pittsburgh Press*, Jan. 9, 1938.

23. *Ibid.*

24. *Ibid.*

25. "Here Is Father Cox's Pledge to Contest Entrants," *Pittsburgh Press*, Jan. 10, 1938.

26. "'Stakes' Gave Charity Mite, Jury Charges," *Pittsburgh Press*, April 6, 1938.

27. "Money Located in Cox Inquiry," *Pittsburgh Press*, Jan. 18, 1938.

28. "Cox Case Turns to Six Previous Lotteries," *Pittsburgh Press*, Jan. 12, 1938.

29. "Cox Pool and Club Found to Cost $150,000," *Pittsburgh Press*, Jan. 14, 1938.

30. "Defense Opens in Father Cox Lottery Case," *Pittsburgh Press*, May 9, 1938.

31. "Voting Starts in Ad Club's Search for 10 Outstanding Citizens of Pittsburgh Area," *Pittsburgh Press*, April 14, 1930.

32. Coode and Petrarulo, 232; "Rev. Cox, Others Indicted by U.S.," *Pittsburgh Press*, Feb. 23, 1938.

33. "Prize Charge Surprises Cox," *Pittsburgh Press*, Jan. 10, 1938.

34. "Action Pushed in Cox Lottery Case," *Pittsburgh Post-Gazette*, Jan. 10, 1938.

35. "Father Cox 'Garden Stakes,'" *Pittsburgh Post-Gazette*, Dec. 18, 1937.

36. "U.S. Arrests Father Cox in Lottery Case," *Pittsburgh Press*, Dec. 15, 1937.

37. "Father Cox: Bread Lines & Garden Stakes Makes News," *Bulletin Index*, Dec. 7, 1937.

38. Patricia Matthews, *Gambler in Love* (Philadelphia: SpringStreet Books, 1984).

39. Sylvester Fithian Johnston, *Centennial Volume of the First Presbyterian Church of Pittsburgh Pa., 1784–1884* (Pittsburgh: William G. Johnston, 1884), 39.

40. "Union Canal Lottery," Lebanoncoun tyhistoricalsociety.org/canal-tunnel/union-canal.

41. Mark E. Dixon, "The Better Sort," *Main Line Today*, Sept. 2009.

42. "Ban Figures for Numbers Racket," *Pittsburgh Press*, Dec. 22, 1930.

43. "Police Are Told to Suppress All Forms of Lottery," *Gazette Times*, May 28, 1915.

44. "Lottery or Not Is the Question," *Gazette Times*, July 9, 1912.

45. "Davis Trial Is Adjourned," *Pittsburgh Press*, Sept. 21, 1933.

46. "Davis Ready for New Trial," *Pittsburgh Press*, Feb. 26, 1933.

47. Joe Browne, "Birthplace of Bingo? Right Here in Pittsburgh!" *Pittsburgh Post-Gazette*, Sept. 5, 1980.

48. "Business Body Backs War on Bingo 'Racket,'" *Pittsburgh Press*, Feb. 27, 1938.

49. *Ibid.*

50. "Numbers Players' Hit for $500,000," *Pittsburgh Press*, Aug. 5, 1930.

51. "Lottery Trial Ends in Parole," *Pittsburgh Post-Gazette*, Aug. 17, 1934.

52. "Wins Sweepstakes Prize but Refuses to Believe It," *Pittsburgh Post-Gazette*, March 15, 1932.

53. "Cox Pool and Club Found to Cost $150,000," *Pittsburgh Press*, Jan. 14, 1938.

54. "Cox Case Turns to Six Previous Lotteries," *Pittsburgh Press*, Jan. 12, 1938.

55. "Church Gets Only $4,500; Cox Blames U.S. Meddling," *Pittsburgh Press*, Jan. 6, 1938.

56. "'I'll Tell All,' Harkins Vows," *Pittsburgh Press*, Feb. 1, 1938. Harkins later suffered a stroke and never faced trial.

Chapter 18

1. "Defense Opens in Father Cox Lottery Case," *Pittsburgh Press*, May 9, 1938.

2. *Ibid.*

3. *Ibid*. Eaton was born in 1877 in Brownsville, Pennsylvania, and was in demand as a defense attorney in a variety of cases that had political implications. "Probing Deep into Tax Hike," *Pittsburgh Press*, Dec. 23, 1911; "Deny Wife's Story of Death Inquest," *Pittsburgh Press*, Nov. 18, 1931. He defended Pittsburgh's future mayor and Pennsylvania's future governor, David L. Lawrence, on charges of violating election laws, blackmail and conspiracy for hiring state workers and granting state contracts in exchange for political contributions. Lawrence was acquitted in both cases.

4. *Ibid.*

5. *Ibid.*

6. *Ibid.*

7. *Ibid.*

8. *Ibid.*

9. *Ibid.*

10. *Ibid.*
11. *Ibid.*
12. *Ibid.*
13. *Ibid.*
14. *Ibid.*
15. *Ibid.*
16. *Ibid.*
17. "Father Cox Case Goes to Jury," *Pittsburgh Press*, May 12, 1938.
18. *Ibid.*
19. *Ibid.*
20. *Ibid.*
21. "Jury Reported Split on Cox," *Pittsburgh Press*, May 14, 1938.
22. *Ibid.*
23. *Ibid.*
24. "Cox Jurors Tell of Heated Debate," *Pittsburgh Press*, May 14, 1938.
25. *Ibid.*
26. *Ibid.*
27. *Ibid.*
28. The federal government never retried Cox. Prosecutors said they had no new evidence and didn't think they could get a different verdict if the case was tried a second time. The government had spent $4,000 prosecuting Cox and couldn't justify any more expense with no prospect for success. "U.S. Abandons Case against Father Cox," *Pittsburgh Press*, Nov. 17, 1938.

Chapter 19

1. "'Coxtown' Colony Offered for Sale," *Pittsburgh Post-Gazette*, Feb. 1, 1939.
2. "Coughlin Hit by Father Cox as Hitler Parrot," *Pittsburgh Press*, June 5, 1939.
3. Donald Warren, *Radio Priest: Charles Coughlin, the Father of Hate Radio* (New York: The Free Press, 1996), 155.
4. *Ibid.*, 160.
5. "Hitler's Hatchet Man," address, no date, no publication. James R. Cox Papers, 1923–1950, AIS.1969.05, Archives Service Center, University of Pittsburgh.
6. "Thunder Over St. Patrick's," *Jewish Criterion*, June 9, 1939.
7. Conrad Black, *Franklin Roosevelt: Champion of Freedom* (New York: Public Affairs, 2003), 327.
8. "Father Coughlin Warns of Danger," *Pittsburgh Catholic*, Jan. 18, 1934.
9. James P. Shenton, "The Coughlin Movement and the New Deal," *Political Science Quarterly* 73, no. 3 (September 1958): 353.
10. *Ibid.* Coughlin sent Roosevelt a telegram on April 24, 1939. He sent the missive on behalf of the Hungary Church and Lodges of Flint, Michigan.
11. "Complete Text of Father Coughlin's Speech," *Pittsburgh Press*, Oct. 9, 1936. Coughlin's bishop ordered him off the radio in 1942 and confined him to his parish duties. He retired in 1966 and died in 1979. He was 88.
12. "Coughlin Says Word Was 'Communistic,'" *New York Times*, Oct. 9, 1936.
13. *Ibid.*, 1.
14. Warren, 129–130.
15. "Hitler's Hatchet Man."
16. "Complete Text of Father Coughlin's Speech."
17. "Coughlin Hits Foes, Denies Opposition to Jewish Race," *Pittsburgh Press*, June 5, 1939.
18. *Ibid.*
19. *Ibid.*
20. "Barring Father Coughlin," *Pittsburgh Catholic*, Aug. 20, 1931.
21. *Ibid.*
22. Jenkins, *Hoods and Shirts*, 113.
23. David Goodman, "War, Race, Biography, and History," *Pennsylvania Magazine of History and Biography* 132, no. 4 (October 2008): 350, 352.
24. "Hitler's Hatchet Man."
25. "Oh Lord, How Long," *Pittsburgh Press*, Feb. 12, 1939.
26. "Going to Detroit," *Pittsburgh Press*, May 13, 1933.
27. Warren, 129.
28. *Ibid.*, 135.
29. *Ibid.*, 372.
30. Lynne Olson, *Those Angry Days: Roosevelt, Lindbergh, and America's Fight Over World War II, 1939–1941* (New York: Random House, 2013), 241.
31. Jenkins, *Hoods and Shirts*, 167.
32. The Pennsylvania Ku Klux Klan claimed 90 percent of the immigrants seeking entry into the United States in 1939 were Jews. Jenkins, *Hoods and Shirts*, 115.
33. "Hate by Christians Bars Jews from Accepting Christ, Cox Asserts," *Pittsburgh Post-Gazette*, March 29, 1926.
34. "Carnegie Institute Head Condemns Roumania for Excesses Against Jews," *Jewish Telegraph*, Jan. 13, 1927; "News Brief," *Jewish Telegraph*, Sept. 6, 1929.
35. Marie Christine Athans, "A New Perspective on Father Charles E. Coughlin," *Church History* 56, no. 2 (June 1987): 227.
36. *Ibid.*
37. *Ibid.*
38. *Ibid.*
39. "Hitler's Hatchet Man."
40. "Letters vs. News," *Pittsburgh Press*, June 13, 1939.
41. *Ibid.* Coughlin's criticism of Cox centered on his arrest and near conviction for running an illegal lottery, his Blue Shirt party, and his failed presidential campaign.

42. "Letters vs. News."
43. "More Pro and Con on Father Coughlin," *Pittsburgh Press*, March 4, 1939.
44. *Ibid.*
45. Heineman, 189.
46. Heineman, 188–89.
47. *Ibid.*, 187.
48. "'Social Justice' Not Catholic, Editor Says," *Pittsburgh Post-Gazette*.
49. "Social Justice Magazine Is Not a Catholic Periodical," *Pittsburgh Catholic*, March 19, 1942.
50. John E. Haynes, *Red Scare or Red Menace? American Anticommunism in the Cold War Era* (Chicago: Ivan R. Dee, 1996), 21.
51. Philip Jenkins, "It Can't Happen Here; Fascism and Right-Wing Extremism in Pennsylvania, 1933–1942," *Pennsylvania History* 62, no. 1 (January 1995), 179.
52. "Warnings Against Racial, Religious Hate Issued by Leaders of Three Faiths," *Pittsburgh Catholic*, June 8, 1939.
53. Shenton, 352.
54. Olson, 241.
55. "A Flood of Pictures Included in Latest German Barrage," *Pittsburgh Press*, Nov. 22, 1939.
56. "Father Coughlin: His 'Fact' and Arguments," American Jewish Committee, New York, 1939, 52, ajcarchives.org/AJC-Data/Files?THR41.pdf.
57. "Hitler's Hatchet Man."

Chapter 20

1. Dr. Paul Murray to George E. Brown, Veterans Claims Service, Pittsburgh, Judge Henry Ellenbogen Papers, Box 30, folder 6, H. John Heinz History Center, Pittsburgh, Pennsylvania; Heineman, 196.
2. "Father Cox Ill, Keeps at Work," *Pittsburgh Sun-Telegraph*, Jan. 15, 1933.
3. Cox to Ellenbogen, Sept. 16, 1943. Ellenbogen to Major Gen. Robert D. Richardson Jr., No date. Ellenbogen Papers, Box 30, Folder 6.
4. Vincent Johnson, "Radio to Keep Transcriptions," *Pittsburgh Post-Gazette*, April 21, 1942. There was another song of the same title written in 1944 by Bud Averill and Rome Seemon. There also were several variations published during the war, including "Taps for Japs," "Taps for the Japs and Huns," and "Taps to the Japs."
5. R. LaMont Jones, Jr., "Pittsburghers Contributed Men as Well as Steel to War Effort," *Pittsburgh Post-Gazette*, May 8, 1995; "Solemnity to Mark V-E Day Observance in Pittsburgh Area," *Pittsburgh Post-Gazette*, May 8, 1945.
6. "'Error' Slayer Given Pardon," *Pittsburgh Press*, Dec. 24, 1946.
7. "Roxie Long and Bride Remarried in Church," *Pittsburgh Press*, May 7, 1943.
8. Dr. John A. Nelson, Thomas J. Frailey, and H.M. Seydel, Supplemental Decision, Board of Appeals, Veterans Administration, C-390,653, Judge Henry Ellenbogen Papers, Heinz History Center, Box 30, Folder 6, 2.
9. Transcript, Board of Veterans Appeals, Judge Henry Ellenbogen Papers, Heinz History Center, Pittsburgh, C-390, 653, June 1941, Box 30, Folder 6.
10. *Ibid.*, 2.
11. *Ibid.*
12. Medical Evaluation, Dr. Paul Murray to George E. Brown, Veterans Claims Center, Pittsburgh, Ellenbogen papers, Box 30, folder 6.
13. Cox to Ellenbogen, Nov. 28, 1944, Ellenbogen papers, Box 30, Folder 6.
14. Ellenbogen to Joe McGuffey, March 14, 1946, *Ibid.*
15. Transcript, Board of Veterans Appeals, 2.
16. *Ibid.*
17. Supplemental Decision, Board of Veterans' Appeals, Box 30, Folder 6, Ellenbogen papers, 1.
18. *Ibid.*, 3.
19. Decision, 55.
20. "Dear Friends," no date, Ellenbogen papers.
21. "Palm Sunday Throngs Brave Rainy Weather," *Pittsburgh Post-Gazette*, March 19, 1951. "Heavy Snow Fall Fails to Materialize Here," *Pittsburgh Post-Gazette*, March 20, 1951.
22. "Father Cox Dies Suddenly at 65," *Pittsburgh Sun-Telegraph*, March 20, 1951.
23. *Ibid.*
24. "Father Cox Gives Estate to Kin," *Pittsburgh Post-Gazette*, May 12, 1951.
25. "Father Cox Dies, Aged 65," *Pittsburgh Press*, March 20, 1951.
26. "Father Cox," *Pittsburgh Post-Gazette*, March 21, 1951.
27. *Ibid.*
28. "Father Cox to Be Buried This Morning," *Pittsburgh Post-Gazette*, March 26, 1951.
29. *Ibid.*
30. "High Mass for Father Cox to Be Celebrated Monday," *Pittsburgh Press*, March 21, 1951.
31. "Father Cox Friend of the Poor," undated Cox papers, Box 2, Folder 1.

Bibliography

Newspapers

Berkeley Daily Gazette
Gazette Times (Pittsburgh)
Gettysburg Times
Greensburg (Pennsylvania) Daily-Tribune
Jewish Chronicle
Jewish Criterion
Jewish Telegram
Latrobe Bulletin
Main Line Today (Philadelphia)
New York Times
Out Sunday Visitor
Pittsburgh Catholic
Pittsburgh Courier
Pittsburgh Daily Post
Pittsburgh Post-Gazette
Pittsburgh Press
Pittsburgh Sun-Telegraph
Spokane Daily Chronicle
Standard (Montreal, Canada)
Valley Daily News (Tarentum, Pa.)
Williamsport (Pennsylvania) Gazette and Bulletin

Archives

Billy Adams Papers, 1911–1942, AIS.1977.26, Archives Service Center, University of Pittsburgh.
Charles Owen Rice Papers, 1935–1998, AIS.1976,11, ASC, University of Pittsburgh.
Eddie McCloskey Papers, Johnstown Area Heritage Association.
Elmer Cope Papers, Ohio Historical Society.
James R. Cox Papers, 1923–1956, AIS.1969.05, Archives Service Center University of Pittsburgh.
Dr. and Mrs. Mason, Father James Renshaw Cox Collection, Saint Patrick–Saint Stanislaus Kostka Parish, Pittsburgh, Pa.

National Council of Jewish Women, Pittsburgh Section Records, 1894–2011, AIS.1964.40, Archives Service Center, University of Pittsburgh.

Papers of Henry Ellenbogen, 1918–1985, MSS #305, Historical Society of Western Pennsylvania.

Books

Akerman, James R., ed. *Cartographies of Travel and Navigation.* University of Chicago Press, 2006.

Barber, Lucy G. *Marching on Washington: The Forging of an American Political Tradition.* Berkeley: University of California Press, 2002.

Black, Conrad. *Franklin Roosevelt: Champion of Freedom.* New York: Public Affairs, 2003.

Bodnar, John, Roger Simon, and Michael P. Weber. *Lives of Their Own: Blacks, Italians and Poles in Pittsburgh, 1900–1968.* Urbana: University of Illinois Press, 1982.

Boyle, Charles A. *The Black Hussars.* Bellevue, WA: Mabo Publishing, 1999.

Canadine, Andrew. *Mellon: An American Life.* New York: Random House, 2006.

Catholic Pittsburgh's 100 Years. Catholic Historical Society of Western Pennsylvania. Chicago: Loyola University Press, 1942.

Conner, Lynne. *Pittsburgh in Stages: Two Hundred Years of Theater.* University of Pittsburgh Press, 2007.

Coode, Thomas H., and John F. Baum. *People, Poverty, and Politics: Pennsylvania During the Great Depression.* Lewisburg: Bucknell University Press, 1981.

Dubofsky, Melvin, and Warren Van Tine. *John L. Lewis: A Biography.* Urbana: University of Illinois Press, 1986.

Fried, Albert, ed. *Communism in America: A History in Documents.* New York: Columbia University Press, 1997.

Fullilove, Michael. *Rendezvous with Destiny: How Franklin Roosevelt and Five Extraordinary Men Took America into the War and into the World.* New York: Penguin Press, 2013.

Greenberg, David. *Calvin Coolidge.* New York: Henry Holt, 2006.

Harris, Mary. *Autobiography of Mother Jones.* Chicago: Charles H. Kerr, 1925.

Haynes, John E. *Red Scare or Red Menace? American Anticommunism in the Cold War Era.* Chicago: Ivan R. Dee, 1996.

Hays, Samuel P., ed. *City at the Point.* University of Pittsburgh Press, 1989.

Heineman, Kenneth. *A Catholic New Deal: Religion and Reform in Depression Pittsburgh.* University Park: Pennsylvania State University Press, 1999.

Heisey, Daniel J. *Saint Vincent Seminary from Its Origins to the Present.* Latrobe: Saint Vincent Publications, 2006.

Huber, Raphael, ed. *Our Bishops Speak.* Milwaukee: Bruce Publishing, 1952.

_____, ed. *Statement by the Bishops of the Administrative Committee of the National Catholic Welfare Conference on the Present Crisis.* Milwaukee: Bruce Publishing, 1933.

Jenkins, Philip. *Hoods and Shirts.* Chapel Hill: University of North Carolina Press, 1997.

Johns, Paul. *A History of the American People.* New York: HarperCollins, 1997.

Johnston, Sylvester Fithian. *Centennial Volume of the First Presbyterian Church of Pittsburgh, Pa., 1784–1884.* Pittsburgh: William G. Johnston & Co., 1884.

Kellogg, Paul Underwood. *The Pittsburgh Civic Frontage.* New York: Russell Sage Foundation Publications, 1914.

Kusmer, Kenneth L. *Down and Out, on the Road: The Homeless in American History*. Oxford: Oxford University Press, 2002.

Kyving, David E. *Daily Life in the United States, 1920–1940: How American Lived Through the Roaring Twenties and the Great Depression*. Chicago: Ivan R. Dee, 2004.

Leupp, Francis Ellington. *George Westinghouse: His Life and Achievements*. Boston: Little, Brown, 1918.

Lowitt, Richard, and Maurine Beasley, eds. *One Third of a Nation: Lorena Hickok Reports on the Great Depression*. Urbana: University of Illinois Press, 1981.

Matthews, Patricia. *Gambler in Love*. Philadelphia: SpringStreet Books, 1984.

McCollester, Charles. *City at the Point*. Homestead: Battle of Homestead Foundation, 1924.

_____. *Fighter with a Heart: The Writings of Charles Owen Rice*. University of Pittsburgh Press, 1996.

McGreevy, Patrick J. *Rev. Charles Owen Rice: Apostle of Contradiction*. Pittsburgh: Duquesne University Press, 1989.

Miner, Curtis, *Johnstown and the Great Depression: 1929–1941*. Johnstown: Benshoff Printing, 1993.

O'Connor, Harvey. *Mellon's Millions: The Biography of a Fortune: The Life of Andrew W. Mellon*. New York: John Day Company, 1933.

Olson, Lynne. *Those Angry Days: Roosevelt, Lindbergh, and America's Fight Over World War II, 1939–1941*. New York: Random House, 2013.

Orr, Winnett. *An Orthopedic Surgeon's Story of the Great War*. Norfolk, NE: Huse Publishing, 1921.

Ryan, John A., and Joseph Husslein. *The Church and Labor*. New York: Macmillan, 1920.

Shlaes, Amity, *The Forgotten Man: A New History of the Great Depression*. New York: Harper Perennial, 2008.

Stave, Bruce M. *The New Deal and the Last Hurrah: Pittsburgh Machine Politics*. University of Pittsburgh Press, 2009.

Stone, Kurt F. *The Jews of Capitol Hill: A Compendium of Jewish Congressional Members*. Lanham, MD: Scarecrow Press, 2011.

Tarr, Joel A., ed. *Devastation and Renewal: An Environmental History of the Pittsburgh Area and Its Regions*. University of Pittsburgh Press, 2003.

Warren, Donald. *Radio Priest: Charles Coughlin, the Father of Hate Radio*. New York: The Free Press, 1996.

Watkins, T.H. *The Hungry Years: A Narrative History of the Great Depression in America*. New York: Henry Holt, 1999.

Weber, Michael P. *Don't Call Me Boss: David L. Lawrence, Pittsburgh's Renaissance Mayor*. University of Pittsburgh Press, 1988.

Whisenhunt, Donald W. *Utopian Movements and Ideas of the Great Depression: Dreamers, Believers and Madmen*. Lanham, MD: Lexington Books, 2013.

White, Edward. *Pittsburgh the Powerful: An Interpretation of the Commercial, Financial and Industrial Strength of a Great City*. Pittsburgh: Industry Publishing, 1907.

Whittle, Randy. *Johnstown, Pennsylvania: A History, 1895–1936*. Charleston: History Press, 2005.

Williams, Elizabeth. *Pittsburgh in World War I: Arsenal of Democracy*. Charleston: History Press, 2013.

Zahniser, Keith A. *Steel City Gospel: Protestant Laity and Reform in Progressive Era Pittsburgh*. New York: Routledge, 2005.

Journal Articles

Altenbaugh, Richard J. "The Children of the Instrument of a Militant Labor Progressive: Brookwood Labor College and the American Labor College Movement of the 1920s and 1930s." *History of Education Quarterly* 23, no. 4 (Winter 2000).

"American Government and Political Campaign Funds in a Depression Year." *The American Political Science Review* 27, no. 5 (October 1933). The American Presidency Project, presidency.ucsb.edu/data/financing.php.

Athans, Marie Christine. "A New Perspective on Father Charles E. Coughlin." *Church History* 56, no. 2 (June 1987).

Bennett, David H. "The Year of the Old Folks Revolt." *American Heritage Magazine* 16, no. 1 (December 1964).

Coode, Thomas H., and John D. Petrarulo. "The Odyssey of Pittsburgh's Father James Cox." *Western Pennsylvania Historical Magazine* 55, no. 3 (July 1972).

Cook, Susan L., and Karen Krupar. "Defining the Twentieth Century and Impacting the Twenty-First: Semantic Habits Created Through Radio." *Etc: A Review of General Semantics* (October 2010).

Garland, Robert. "The Scotch-Irish in Western Pennsylvania." *Western Pennsylvania History Magazine* 6, no. 2 (April 1923).

Goldman, M.R. "The Hills as I Knew It." *Western Pennsylvania History Magazine* 51, no. 3 (July 1968).

Goodman, David. "War, Race, Biography, and History." *Pennsylvania Magazine of History and Biography* 132, no. 4 (October 2008).

Heineman, Kenneth J. "A Catholic New Deal: Religion and Labor in 1930s Pittsburgh." *Pennsylvania Magazine of History and Biography* 118, no. 4 (October 1994).

_____. "Iron City Trinity: The Triumphs and Trial of Catholic Social Activism in Pittsburgh." *U.S. Catholic Historian*, no. 22 (Spring 2004).

_____. "A Tale of Two Cites: Pittsburgh, Philadelphia and the Elusive Quest for a New Deal Majority." *Pennsylvania Magazine of History and Biography* 132, no. 4 (October 2008).

Jenkins, Philip. "It Can't Happen Here: Fascism and Right-Wing Extremism in Pennsylvania, 1933–1942." *Pennsylvania History* 62, no. 1 (January 1995).

Kelly, Timothy. "Pittsburgh Catholicism." *U.S. Catholic Historian* 18, no. 4 (Fall 2000).

Knestrick, Ray E. "Hunger March." *The New Republic* 67, no. 868 (July 22, 1931).

Mayfield, Loomis. "Voting Fraud in Early Twentieth-Century Pittsburgh." *The Journal of Interdisciplinary History* 24, no. 1 (Summer 1993).

McDonough, Judith. "Worker Solidarity, Judicial Oppression and Police Repression in the Westmoreland County, Pennsylvania Coal Miners' Strike, 1910–1911." *Pennsylvania History* 64 (1997).

McKeever, Edward M. "Earlier Lawrenceville." *Western Pennsylvania History Magazine*, no. 5 (January 1922).

Olson, James S. "Gifford Pinchot and the Politics of Hunger, 1932–1933." *Pennsylvania Magazine of History and Biography*, no. 4 (October 1972).

O'Neal, James. "Messiah Vs. Messiah Vs. Messiah." The American Mercury (October 1932).

Penna, Anthony. "Changing Images of Twentieth Century Pittsburgh." *Pennsylvania History* 40, no. 1 (January 1976).

Pilgrim, Robert J. "The Strip: A Socio-Economic Survey of a Typical Section of Pittsburgh." *Pittsburgh Christian Social Service Union* (July–September 1915).

Sebak, Rick. "Going Underground in the Strip." *Pittsburgh Magazine* (February 19, 2010).

Shenton, James P. "The Coughlin Movement and the New Deal." *Political Science Quarterly* 73, no. 3 (September 1958).

Smith, Rollin. "Pittsburgh Millionaires and Their Organs." *Annual Organ Atlas*, 2010.

Steffens, Lincoln. "Pittsburg: A City Ashamed–the Story of a Citizens' Party That Broke Through One Ring into Another." *McClure's* (May 1903).

Stocking, Collis A. "A Study of Dance Halls in Pittsburgh." *Pittsburgh Council of Churches*, 1925.

Walsh, Victor A. "Across 'The Big Wather': The Irish-Catholic Community of Mid-Nineteenth Century Pittsburgh and Allegheny City." *Western Pennsylvania History Magazine* 66, no. 1 (January 1983).

Wing, Frank E. "Thirty-Five Years of Typhoid: The Fever's Economic Cost to Pittsburg and the Long Fight for Pure Water." *Charities and Commons* (February 1909).

Websites

The American Presidency Project, Santa Barbara, CA. John T. Woolley and Gerhard Peters. www.presidency.ucsb.edu/ws/?p10=88339.

"A History of Base Hospital No. 27." U.S. Army Office of Medical History, History. amedd.army/mil/booksdoc/html.

Inaugural Address of Herbert Hoover. Avalon Project, Documents in Law, History and Diplomacy, Avalon.law.yale.edu/20th_century/hoover.asp.

1907crisisinhistoricalperspective. Fas.harvard.edu/~histscon/crisis-next/1907.

Perforum.org/2015/01/05history-of-clergy-in-congress.

Quadragesimo Anno. http://w2.vatican.va/content/pius-xi/en/encyclicals/documents/hf_p-xi_enc_19310515_quadragesimo-anno.html.

radiostratosphere.com.

Rerum Novarum. w2.vatican.va/content/leo-xiii/en/encyclicals/documents/hf_l-xiii_enc_15051891_rerum-novarum.html.

Saints in the strip.org/home.html.

"Unemployed Organizing in the 1930s." Mark McColloch, Richard Oestreicher and Joel Sabadasz. Allegheny County Labor Council, aflcio.org.

"Union Canal Lottery." Lebanoncountyhistoricalsociety.org/canal-tunnel/union-canal.

vault.fbi.org.

Theses and Dissertations

Henwood, James, N.J. "Politics and Unemployment Relief, Pennsylvania, 1931–1939." Ph.D. diss., University of Pennsylvania, 1975.

Petrarulo, John D. "A Short Biography of Father James R. Cox of Pittsburgh." Master's thesis, California State College, 1972.

Witt, Sally. "Hell Was Not Made for Us: Father James R. Cox and the Catholic Church of Pittsburgh in the 1940s." Master's thesis, Duquesne University, 1989.

Index